OFF THE BEATEN PATH® SERIES

Alaska

SECOND EDITION

by Melissa DeVaughn

Guilford, Connecticut

The prices and rates listed in this guidebook were confirmed at press time. We recommend, however, that you call establishments before traveling to obtain current information.

Cover and text design by Laura Augustine
Cover photo by PhotoDisc
Maps created by Equator Graphics © The Globe Pequot Press
Illustrations by Carole Drong

Library of Congress Cataloging-in-Publication Data

DeVaughn, Melissa.
      Alaska : off the beaten path / Melissa DeVaughn. —2nd ed.
         p. cm. —(Off the beaten path series)
      Updated ed. of: Alaska / Mike Miller. 1st ed. ©1996.
      Includes index.
      ISBN 0-7627-0261-3
      1. Alaska Guidebooks. I. Miller, Mike. Alaska. II. Title.
   III. Title: Alaska off the beaten path. IV. Series.
   F902.3.D48   1999
   917.9804´51—dc21   99-33144
                                        CIP

Manufactured in the United States of America
Second Edition/First Printing

To Andy and Roan—
my two Alaska boys

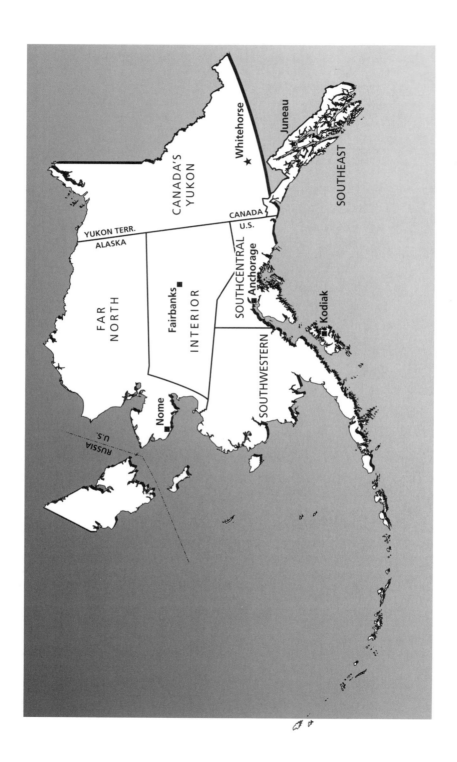

Contents

Introduction vii

Southeast Alaska 1

Canada's Yukon 55

Southcentral Alaska 79

Interior Alaska 129

Alaska's Far North 161

Southwestern Alaska 181

Indexes

    General 200

    Museums 213

    National and State Parks 214

About the Author 214

Help Us Keep This Guide Up to Date

Every effort has been made by the author and editors to make this guide as accurate and useful as possible. However, many things can change after a guide is published—establishments close, phone numbers change, and facilities come under new management.

We would love to hear from you concerning your experiences with this guide and how you feel it could be improved and be kept up to date. While we may not be able to respond to all comments and suggestions, we'll take them to heart and we'll also make certain to share them with the author. Please send your comments and suggestions to the following address:

The Globe Pequot Press
Reader Response/Editorial Department
P.O. Box 480
Guilford, CT 06437

Or you may e-mail us at:
editorial@globe-pequot.com

Thanks for your input, and happy travels!

Introduction

Chances are, if you stay here long enough, someone's going to ask you this: "So, what made you move to Alaska?"

I can't tell you how many times I have been asked that question since I crossed the border into Alaska and settled into my first home here, along the shores of Cook Inlet on the Kenai Peninsula, and now, on a mountainside with a view of the Chugach Range. It seems like people see Alaska as a wonderful place to visit, but to live here—to live way out here—who would do such a thing?

Truth is, living in Alaska is easy. I'll tell you why.

My plan—like many people, I'd venture, who move this far north—was to experience the wilderness and the wonder of Alaska for a year or two, maybe three, then head back east, to the rural Virginia community in which I was raised. My family's there. My friends are there. It was what I knew and what was comfortable to me. Problem is, Alaska grew on me, too, in a comfortable, unexpected way. Before I knew it, I had my own friends and family here (my husband, Andy, was born and raised in Alaska). I see the same faces at the grocery store. I have my own Alaska dentist and doctor, and I've found a mechanic who can't be beat. Now, *I'm* the one who is stopped on the streets and asked for directions.

The landscape, too, has grown on me. The mountains that seemed so impenetrable to me at first now welcome me, much like the Appalachian Mountains welcomed me as a child. The winters—cold and dark and hunkered-down my first winter—are fun now, and getting out means getting on: mushing my dogs, skiing with my husband, tying on snowshoes and exploring a hillside with my son on my back. The cold doesn't hold me back now; rather, it draws me in.

And the summers. The endless sunshine, the liquid blue skies that wrap around the mountains and the abundant wildlife that walks through my yard—right past the front door—well, who *wouldn't* stay?

If you're visiting Alaska for the first time, welcome to my home. If you're returning—because no matter how much you had planned to take a vacation to a place other than Alaska again, you just couldn't stay away—well, welcome back. I don't blame you.

You see, Alaska is an easy place to visit, too. No matter what your interests, you can satisfy them here. And no matter what your interests, it's all pretty much off the beaten path. Think about it. Fewer than 700,000 people occupy this state, the largest in the country, with the most wildlands of just about any place on Earth. When you arrive in Alaska, you're not just off the beaten path—you're frequently not even on a path at all!

Yet Alaska is an accessible place, no matter how you choose to explore it. I've explored this state by plane, train, automobile, boat, bicycle, dogsled, skis, snowshoes, and even, a few times, by snow machine. My preference is on foot or by dogsled. It is conceivable, traveling by my own power or that supplied by my adorable sled dogs, to explore places that perhaps no human has ever seen. Once, sitting atop a ridge in Denali National Park and Preserve, I glanced down and saw a deep grizzly bear paw print mashed into the ground. I wondered, *Are we the only two creatures to have stepped foot here?* Probably not, but it sure feels good to consider such a possibility in this ever-more-crowded world.

With my dogs it is just magical to see winter as they do, full of opportunity, fun—they love to run so—not the cold, bleak place most people think it must be.

But maybe you prefer a less strenuous way to view this beautiful state. Not a problem. Even if you're seated in a luxury motorcoach with plush seats and full meals, just look out the window; wherever you look, the view is bound to be breathtaking. Glaciers are within walking distance, bears and moose will likely amble right across the road, and mountain vistas will fill more than your camera lens can capture. Believe me, you won't be disappointed.

Be careful, though. Like me, you may come seeking adventure and realize you've found home.

A Very Small Sketch of a Very Big State

"All Gaul," declared Julius Caesar in *De Bello Gallico,* "is divided into four parts."

With Alaska it takes five.

All of Alaska, of course, is located north and west of what geographers call "the contiguous states" of the United States. The Canadian Province of British Columbia lies between. The southernmost of Alaska's five regions, and closest to the "Lower 48," as Alaskans call these sister states, is **Southeast Alaska.** It's a place of thousands of forested islands plus a long sliver of mainland abutting northern British Columbia. **Southcentral Alaska** forms an arch around the top of the Gulf of Alaska and extends inland roughly to the Alaska Range of mountains, a towering wall of peaks and masses that separates Southcentral from **Interior Alaska.** Interior, in turn, forms the huge middle of the state, bordering Canada's Yukon Territory on the east. Its westerly border stops just short of the Bering Sea. Farther north, in fact as far north as you can get and still be in North America, lies **Far North Alaska.** Finally, **Southwestern Alaska** takes in the westernmost approaches of the Alaska mainland, the Alaska Peninsula, Kodiak Island, the long, long string of Aleutian Islands, which extends almost to Japan, plus the Pribilof Islands and others of the Bering Sea.

In this book I've added a sixth region, **Canada's Yukon Territory,** because—since it is adjacent both to Southeast and Interior Alaska—you cannot drive from the Alaska panhandle to the main body of Alaska without going through this friendly, fascinating portion of Canada.

Some Notes and Cautions

First, a bit about the Alaska lifestyle and dress. Because we are off the beaten path, things are pretty informal all over the state. Friendly is a way of life up here and you never have to worry about asking an Alaskan for help, or directions, or for the answer to what you think may be a dumb question. "Comfortably casual" is the dress code of the day, every day, even in big city hotels and restaurants. M'lady, if she'd feel more comfortable, can certainly wear a cocktail dress or dressy pantsuit in the evening, and her escort can likewise wear a coat and tie if he'd like, but it really isn't necessary.

For outdoor wear, comfortable walking shoes (or broken-in boots if you're a hiker) are a must. The weather can vary wildly all over the state, so plan to do what Alaskans do: Dress in layers that start with light shirts and/or undershirts then graduate to heavier shirts, sweaters, and even ski-type parkas. The latter are especially useful if you plan glacier cruises, camp outs, or travel in the Arctic. Layering allows you to add protection or to peel off excess clothing as the weather dictates. *Very important:* A lightweight combination windbreaker/raincoat should always be at the top of your pack or suitcase.

Now about money: Truth to tell, the cost of living is higher in Alaska than in most other states, but the differences are narrowing all the time. Depending on where you are (in a large, easily accessible city or a remote bush community), costs for lodging and food could be the same as you're accustomed to paying, or only a few percentage points higher—or they could be a great deal more. I have tried to show prices for most admissions, meals, overnights, and other costs. At the time of this writing all the prices (plus telephone numbers, addresses, e-mails, Web sites, and other such data) were current. But things can change; hotel and meal prices, in particular, may well be higher when you make your trip. When a hotel or B&B price is quoted here, it's usually for a double. Singles may (or may not) be less; extra guests in a room usually cost more. There is no statewide sales tax in Alaska, but most munici-palities impose one on goods, services, and overnight accommoda-tions. Sales taxes are not included in the prices quoted in this book.

Remember that when you travel in the Yukon, distances are measured in metric kilometers, not miles; when speed limits are posted at 90 kilo-meters per hour, that's the same as 55 mph in the U.S. Likewise, our Canadian friends pump gasoline in liters, not gallons.

Friends from Outside often ask "When is the best time to visit Alaska?" The answer is, anytime you want to come. Summer obviously ranks as Alaska's most popular season, but the "shoulder" months of May, September, and early October offer the advantages of fewer crowds, often discounted prices, and an unhurried, more relaxed pace of living.

Winter, perhaps surprisingly, is coming into its own with an active statewide agenda of downhill and cross-country skiing, sled dog mush-ing and racing, winter carnivals, and viewing the eerie and spectacular *aurora borealis,* the northern lights. Obviously you have to dress for the season (snug long johns, heavy sweaters, and extra-warm outerwear for tours and activities out of doors), but if you use common sense and take the advice of the locals you, too, can happily and safely experience Alaska during the time of year many Alaskans enjoy their state the most.

Finally . . . it seems incredible but, more than four decades after becom-ing the forty-ninth state of the United States, Alaskans still get asked if we use U.S. currency and stamps. The answer, of course, is emphatically yes—though if you arrive here with Canadian dimes, quarters, and other small change in your pocket or purse, merchants will accept them at face value. Canadian dollars, on the other hand, will be discounted according to current value on the international money exchanges.

Now, enough of technical stuff. Read on. Come. Visit. Enjoy!

Southeast Alaska

ncredible place, Southeast Alaska (or Southeastern, as Alaskans often call it). It's a place of islands—more than 1,000—and a land of lush forests, snow-capped mountains, cascading waterfalls, steep-walled fjords, and magnificent glaciers. From these latter fall tens of thousands of huge and minuscule icebergs that dot the seascape and glitter within great bays and inlets. It is a region of proud and skillful Tlingit, Haida, and Tsimshian native peoples, whose totems and other works of art are only now beginning to receive the recognition they deserve. It is a land, too, with a colorful, gutsy gold rush past and a place where today huge salmon, monster halibut, and bountiful trout await the angler's lure in salt water, lakes, and streams.

It's an easy place to get to. Literally scores of elegant cruise ships embark each week in summer from West Coast ports en route to the Southeast Alaska panhandle. Stateroom-equipped ferryliners of the Alaska Marine Highway System likewise ply these waters from Belling-ham, Washington, and from Prince Rupert, British Columbia. And of course the jets of Alaska Airlines, plus Delta in the summer, depart daily from Seattle and other cities in the "Lower Forty-eight" states en route to the land that nineteenth-century naturalist John Muir called "one of the most wonderful countries in the world." Here's what Southeast Alaska holds in store for visitors these days.

Southern Southeast

laskans call Ketchikan their First City because it's the first Alaskan port of call for cruise ships, ferries, yachts, and many airlines en route to the forty-ninth state. Spread out along the shores of Revillagigedo Island (the name is Spanish and almost unpronounce-able; locals just say Revilla), the town is just a few blocks wide, but it's miles long. The hustling, bustling city's economy lies in commercial fishing and tourism. Timber, once a thriving business, has all but halted in Southeast, but a few persons still make their living with small log-ging projects. Sportfishing for salmon, halibut, and freshwater species

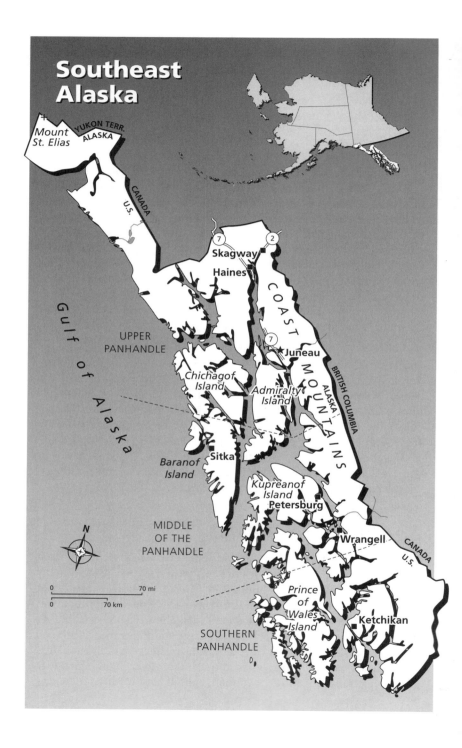

Southeast Alaska

Mount St. Elias

YUKON TERR.
ALASKA

CANADA
U.S.

Gulf of Alaska

UPPER PANHANDLE

Skagway

Haines

COAST MOUNTAINS

Juneau

BRITISH COLUMBIA
ALASKA

Chichagof Island

Admiralty Island

Baranof Island

Sitka

MIDDLE OF THE PANHANDLE

Kupreanof Island

Petersburg

Wrangell

CANADA
U.S.

N

0   70 mi
0   70 km

Prince of Wales Island

Ketchikan

SOUTHERN PANHANDLE

Top 10 Places in Southeast Alaska

Dyea Campground

Blueberry Hill Bed
and Breakfast

Skagway Brewing
Company

Fiddlehead Restaurant
and Bakery

Waterfall Resort

Seawolf Wilderness
Adventures

Chilkoot Trail

Alaska Llama Guides

Sitka Wildlife Quest

GreatLand Guides
of Alaska

can be superb. So is the sight-seeing at local totem parks and from the decks of small cruisers that explore nearby islands and waters.

For travelers who seek a cruiselike experience, the small ships of half a dozen companies offer comfortable vessels with staterooms, dining rooms, ample decks, observation lounges, and bars—but not the Vegas-like theaters, ballrooms, casinos, boutiques, and crowds of the big liners. It's great the way a number of these boats can nose into small bays and inlets for close-up looks at bears, deer, and other wildlife. Also pleasureable are the whales. When they are in the vicinity, the skipper can cut the engine and drift for a half hour or more to watch the water acrobatics of the great beasts. *Alaska Sightseeing/Cruise West* (800–888–9378) operates two such ships on weekly cruises from Seattle: the deluxe *Spirit of Endeavour* and Victorian era–designed *Spirit of '98*. Each carries up to one hundred guests and offers up-close wildlife viewing from forward viewing lounges and generous deck areas. For an in-state cruise focusing on wildlife and local villages, try one of three *All-Alaska Adventure* cruises aboard the *Spirit of Endeavour, Spirit of Discovery,* or *Spirit of Columbia*. These small ships sail between Ketchikan and Juneau, passing the area's most impressive glaciers, crossing the whale feeding grounds of Frederick Sound, and making stops at any number of communities along the way.

Don't want to spend an entire week on a cruise ship but are intrigued by the idea of sailing? A new twist Cruise West offers includes a four-day exploration of *Alaska's Inside Passage* coastline aboard the *Sheltered Seas* motoryacht, where you'll see the sights by day but stop in communities along the way to sleep at night. This mix of daylight-only cruising with overnight stops at ports of call provides an intimate view of both Alaska's wilderness *and* its communities and the people who live there. *Glacier Bay Tours and Cruises,* owned by a local Native corporation, offers trips on the speedy forty-nine-passenger catamaran *Executive Explorer,* which sails between Ketchikan, Juneau, and Glacier Bay. Call (800) 451–5952 for more information.

You'll discover more authentic Native-carved totem poles around Ketchikan than any place else in the world. One of the outstanding collections stands at *Saxman Native Village,* 2½ miles south of Ketchikan on South Tongass Highway. Deeply carved figures represent eagles and ravens, bears and killer whales, and even the figure of a hapless, drowning Indian youth caught in the bite of a giant rock oyster as the tide comes in. Elsewhere in the park you'll find a traditional Beaver Clan community house, an on-site carving center. Two two-hour motor coach tours by *Cape Fox Tours* (907–225–4846 or 907–225–5930) include a visit to Saxman Village and a tour of historic Ketchikan.

The *Tongass Heritage Center,* located at the edge of Ketchikan's city park, a half mile or so from downtown, houses priceless nineteenth-century totems rescued from decay at abandoned Native villages and sites. They are absolutely majestic, with their deeply carved crests and legends from the cultures of Tlingit and Haida peoples. The *Tongass Historical Museum,* downtown at 629 Dock Street, contains exhibits and artifacts from Ketchikan's Native past and its fishing-mining-timbering heritage. Admission to the center is $4.00; admission to the museum is $3.00. Call (907) 225–5600 for more information.

If you're a hiker, you'll find Ketchikan a great place to roam from, with lots of ocean, forest, lake, and mountain trails. The 3½-mile *Deer Mountain Trail,* which begins practically downtown and runs to the 3,000-foot summit, provides a particularly grand vista of the city below and nearby islands and ocean waters. Ask for directions to the trailhead at the *Visitor Information Center,* downtown on the Front Street cruise ship dock. Call the visitor center at (907) 225–6166 for more information, or visit the Web site at www.visit-ketchikan.com. E-mail is kvb@ktn.net.

Earlier we mentioned the opportunity to explore waters around Ketchikan by small sightseeing cruiser. Dale Pihlman's *Alaska Cruises* (220 Front Street; 907–225–6044) offers a six-hour excursion from downtown Ketchikan to *Misty Fjords National Monument,* a wondrous nearby wilderness area of steep-walled fjords, sheltered bays, tiny inlets, islands, isles, mountain trails, lakes, and green, green forests— not to mention whales, seals, bears, and mountain goats. The cost, including a light meal and beverages, is $145 for adults. If time is limited (or even if it isn't), you may opt for a $198 four-hour fly/cruise version of the trip, which offers a breathtaking aerial perspective.

If you want professionals to organize, equip, and guide you on a Misty Fjord kayaking trip, Betsey Burdett and Geoff Gross offer four-, six-, and eight-day excursions within the monument as well as among the Barrier Islands in the South Prince of Wales Island Wilderness area. Their company, *Southeast Exposure* (507 Steadman Street; 907–225–8829), also offers day trips along the Ketchikan waterfront and into semiwilderness waters nearby. Single fiberglass kayaks rent for $40 per day. Guided three-hour tours start at $50.

Speaking of camping, this might be a good place to mention an unusual opportunity that many consider the greatest travel bargain in America: a network of **U.S. Forest Service cabins** in the Alaska wilderness. The USFS maintains more than 150 warm and weather-tight cabins beside remote mountain lakes and isolated ocean shores throughout the **Tongass National Forest** that comprises most of Southeast Alaska. An additional forty such units exist in the Chugach National Forest in Alaska's Southcentral region. You can reserve units for up to a week at a time—at a modest daily rate starting at $25 *per group.*

Most units have bunks to accommodate up to six and contain either wood- or oil-burning stoves. Don't, however, expect a "Hilton in the wilderness." You bring your own food, sleeping bags, and other supplies. Privies are "down the path." Mostly these are fly-in units, though you can reach a few by boat or hiking trail. For bear protection Alaskans and visitors often carry 30-06 or larger rifles. No permit is required. It's seldom, however, that someone has to use one. Virtually every town in both regions has charter air services that specialize in serving fly-in campers. Rates vary with the distance you need to fly.

Little Norway Festival in Petersburg; held each May to celebrate Norwegian Independence Day. For information call (907) 772–4636.

Juneau Jazz and Classics, a weeklong celebration in May of some of the best jazz around. For further information call the Juneau Convention and Visitors Bureau at (888) 581–2201.

Southeast Alaska State Fair, held each year in Haines. Five fun-filled days every August, with parade, entertainment each night, and more. For information, call (907) 766–2476.

Klondike Road Relay, held each September; a running road relay from Skagway, Alaska, to Whitehorse, Yukon Territory. For information call the Skagway Convention and Visitors Bureau at (907) 983–2854.

For information about Tongass cabins, call (907) 228–6214. For similar information concerning the Chugach, contact the Alaska Public Lands Information Center in Anchorage at (907) 271–2737. To reserve a Forest Service cabin, call (877) 444–6777 or access www.reserveusa.com on the Web.

From Ketchikan a popular fly-in choice is **Patching Lake Cabin,** a wood stove–equipped mountain lake unit with a skiff on-site. You'll find trout in the water for fishing plus the possibility of deer and black bear in the woods for viewing. (Don't, however, even think of feeding these critters or observing them too closely.) The local USFS number for information is (907) 225–2148. A fly-in charter to Patching Lake would be in the neighborhood of $350 for a party of two.

While in Ketchikan, don't pass up two boating opportunities offered by *Alaska Travel Adventures.* Try paddling a 37-foot Native-style canoe on a pristine mountain lake, or squeeze yourself into a sturdy kayak and explore Pennock Island and Whiskey Cove. After a short kayaking lesson along the waterfront, glide your kayak to the hiding places of the rumrunners of the Prohibition days. Or wander up Ketchikan Creek. It'll be the best $75 you ever spent, unless, of course, the Native canoe tickles your fancy. For $73 and two hours of your time, you'll glide across a quiet lake surrounded by forest and mountains. Look closely for bald eagles. A guide will help maneuver the boat while also teaching about the surrounding Tongass rain forest and the plants and animals that flourish there. For further information call (800) 478–0052 in Alaska or (800) 791–2673 outside Alaska. The company's e-mail is ataalaska@aol.com. The Web site is www.alaskaadventures.com.

Ketchikan-based *Taquan Air* (907–225–8800 or 800–770–8800) has been flying visitors and locals alike on air excursions since 1977, and the company boasts that it's the largest floatplane service in the state. Taquan offers wildlife-watching on *Eagle Island* and *Smuggler's Cove,* as well as flight-seeing over *Misty Fjords National Monument.* Overnight fishing and kayaking trips on Prince of Wales Island are a fine choice, but if you're looking for something a little shorter, there are five-hour kayak expeditions from *El Capitan Lodge* on Prince of Wales Island. Taquan makes regular "Canadian Discoverer" flights to *Prince Rupert* in northern British Columbia, three-hour trips to the more northerly *Anan Creek Bear Observatory,* and daily flights to *Metlakatla,* a close-by Tsimshian Native village on Annette Island. Among sites to see and explore in Metlakatla is the village founder *Father Duncan's Cottage,* now a fascinating museum that chronicles the history of Annette Island's formerly Canadian Indian peoples and the lay Anglican priest who brought them to Alaska. The museum is open from 1:00 to 4:00 P.M. Monday through Friday and by appointment on Saturday. One of Taquan's most popular tours is a Sunday-only four-hour flight and ground experience that includes a two-hour tour escorted by U.S. Forest Service naturalists through *El Capitan Cave* on Prince of Wales Island. The flight departs Ketchikan at 7:00 A.M.

If landing on the water makes you a little weak in the knees, don't fear. Taquan's newest venture is *AirOne,* an all-weather commuter airline offering regular flights to and from locations throughout Southeast, using wheeled airplanes. For further information on Taquan's offerings, check out their Web site at www.taquanair.com, or e-mail taquan@ptialaska.net.

It's not located off the beaten path, but the smallish, moderately priced *Gilmore Hotel,* at 326 Front Street (907–225–9423), is often overlooked. The hotel offers a commanding view of Ketchikan's frantic waterfront, taking in fishermen preparing their nets, luxury cruise liners in port, freighters heaped with cargo, and a constant stream of floatplanes landing, taking off, or flying down the channel. Built in 1927 of solid concrete, the hotel's forty rooms are modern, clean and have full baths and color TVs. Summer rates begin at $68 for a double. It's on the National Historic Register. *Annabelle's Famous Keg and Chowder House* off the hotel lobby offers room service or restaurant dining on the premises. The gorgeous 20-foot mahogany bar at Annabelle's is well worth a look-see, as are the murals that depict Ketchikan's notorious old Creek Street red-light district, where Annabelle entertained as a favorite "lady of the night" in the 1920s.

Speaking of *Creek Street* and its entrepreneurs, do give the lane a stroll, off Stedman Street opposite the big harbor downtown called Thomas Basin. A former brothel called *Dolly's House* (open daily in the summer) has been restored as a museum there, as have numerous other "houses," which now contain boutiques, gift shops, and galleries.

Fourteen miles north of Ketchikan the nicely named *Eagle's Roost Bed and Breakfast* (907–247–9187; 410 Knudson Cove Road; eaglesroostbb@att.net; www.cruising-america.com/eagles.html) perches just above Knudson Cove harbor and marina. A large covered deck allows for taking in the surrounding rain forest, even if it's sprinkling. Rates are $75 to $90 for two.

Al and Carol Johnson's *Great Alaska Cedar Works Bed and Breakfast,* 11 miles north of Ketchikan at 1527 Pond Reef Road, comprises two cottages—one on the beach, complete with views of passing cruise ships, fishing vessels, eagles, and sea birds. Both have private baths, feather beds, and continental breakfasts featuring home-baked goodies from Carol Johnson's oven. For reservations and information, call (907) 247–8287. Rates start at $75, single or double, nonsmokers only.

She will never serve the masses, but for a select few visitors who want really personalized tour attention, former schoolmarm Lois Munch will introduce you to Ketchikan's Native history, take you to totem parks, tell you about the critters in a saltwater tide pool, explain the flora and fauna of the area, and even show you an occupied eagle's nest. She calls her operation *Classic Tours.* You can't miss her restored, blazing-red '55 Chevy, which she'll use to take you touring. Two-hour tours are $43 per person, and three-hour tours run $57 per person. But call Lois if you're looking for something even more personalized. For $60 per hour for one to two people, she'll create a tour to match your interests to a T. She can be reached by phone at (907) 225–3091 or e-mail at classic@ ptialaska.net. Or visit her Web site at www.classictours.com.

For an oasis in the middle of town, make reservations at **Blueberry Hill Bed and Breakfast,** an artistic getaway owned by Elsan Zimmerly and her husband, Hank Newhouse. They have turned their historic home, located at 500 Front Street, into a serene bed-and-breakfast. Elsan, a photographer for more than fifteen years, makes delicious homemade meals, and you can spend hours relaxing in the spacious house's many rooms. There are four rooms available, all with private baths, ranging from $85 to $105. For reservations call (907) 247–2583, e-mail blu-brry@ptialaska.net, or visit www.ptialaska.net/~blubrry.

Southeast Alaska Facts

More than a thousand islands make up the 500-mile-long Alexander Archipelago, which extends from Icy Bay, north of Yakutat, to the border between the United States and Canada at the south end of Prince of Wales Island.

It's not quite the biggest island under the American flag (the Big Island of Hawaii and Kodiak Island in Southwest Alaska rank first and second in that category) but **Prince of Wales Island** (POW) is huge, nonetheless: 2,231 square miles of forested mountains, deep U-shaped valleys, lakes, streams, and 900 miles of coastal shores, bays, and inlets. You get to Prince of Wales by state ferry from Ketchikan or by plane. POW is not without controversy: Environmentalists say the island has been overlogged; the timber industry says reforestation is coming along very nicely. You decide for yourself. One thing logging has done is create lots of roads (some gravel, others asphalt) that you can use for exploring and camping. Kayaking or canoeing is superb at lots of freshwater and saltwater access points.

It's definitely remote and accessible only by air, but any reference to roughing it on the island at **Waterfall Resort** would be outrageous. The made-over former fish cannery gives the word "resort" a whole new meaning. Take fishing. You don't just check out a skiff and head for the fishing grounds. Instead you're assigned a spiffy cabin cruiser and a personal fishing guide for the length of your stay. The angling is world class for king and silver salmon, halibut, lingcod, and red snapper. Accommodations in rooms, condos, and cottages are "plush rustic" and leave nothing to be wished for. Meals feature a generous choice of fish or other entrees. It's pretty expensive (prices start at $2,860 per person for four days, three nights), but if you can afford the tariff, it's worth every penny. Or try traveling during the shoulder seaon of May, June, or September when the rates go down to $1,795. Call (907) 225–9461 in state or (800) 544–5125 out of state, or visit www.waterfallresort.com. E-mail is water-fall@ktn.net.

Another fishing lodge in the luxury category is the **Whales Resort** on the northern shores of the island. Here, too, the emphasis is on quality, with guided fishing, deluxe cabin cruisers, and gourmet dining cuisine. For information call (800) 531–9643, e-mail wresort@aol.com, or visit the Web site at www.whalesresort.com.

For do-it-yourselfers the **U.S. Forest Service** has two campgrounds and more than twenty $25 to $40 rental cabins on lakes and inlets through-out the island. Call (907) 826–1604 in Craig; (907) 828–1604 at Thorne Bay. For reservations call (877) 444–6777. The **Log Cabin RV Park and Resort** (800–544–2205) offers cabins at $50 per night plus camper facilities and fishing out of Klawock. Beachfront condo units or a log house are $120 a night for two, or $800 for the week. The **Fireweed Lodge** (907–755–2930; fireweedlo@ aol.com), also in Klawock, offers twenty rooms at $75 for doubles plus meals, rental cars, fishing char-ters, and access to excellent hiking and canoeing. **McFarland's Floatel** (888–828–3335) provides beachfront log cabins at Thorne Bay. The $200-per-night units are suited for up to four guests, but six can fit comfortably for an extra $40 per additional person. Owners Jim and Jeannie McFarland also offer guided and nonguided fishing trips around Thorne Bay. Charter the 32-foot *Jeannie M* for an all-day guided charter ($200 per person), or rent a 15-foot aluminum skiff for $65 and hit the water on your own.

It would be easy to miss **Hyder,** in southernmost Southeastern. In fact, sadly, most travelers do. If you're Alaska-bound, however, and traveling along British Columbia's Yellowhead Highway between Prince George and Prince Rupert, take the 140-mile paved Cassiar Highway north from its junction with the Yellowhead Highway (about 150 miles before Prince Rupert). Then take the access road off the Cassiar to Hyder. This road also leads to Hyder's very close neighbor, **Stewart.** Stewart (population 400 or so) sits in British Columbia, Canada, and Hyder (population 90) lies in Alaska. They're separated by 2³⁄₁₀ miles and the U.S.–Canada border. After your visit, if you don't want to retrace your path down the Cassiar, you can board the small Alaska ferry *Aurora* once a week for a direct con-nection to Ketchikan. Similarly, of course, if you're heading south from Ketchikan, you can take the *Aurora* to Hyder instead of Prince Rupert.

What's to see in and around Hyder? For one thing, you'll find spectacular glaciers to view, including **Salmon Glacier,** the world's fifth largest, only

20 miles north of town. You'll also find abandoned mine sites, late nine-teenth–century buildings to photograph, superb fishing, hiking trails, and—3 miles north of town—a salmon stream and bear observatory where you can see black bears or brownies. Your first stop in this part of Alaska should be at the **Hyder Community Association** building in town. There you can get information on the area as well as check out a small collection of museum items that tell the story of Hyder. In Stewart, the **Stewart Historical Society Museum** displays wildlife in the Fire Hall as well as bits and pieces of local history.

The **Grand View Inn,** located ¾ mile from the border on Hyder's main road, has ten clean, private rooms, four with kitchenettes, in quiet, woodsy surroundings. The rate is $55 per night, U.S. funds. Call (250) 636–9174, or e-mail grandview@myhome.net.

The Middle of the Panhandle

W **rangell** is a natural for the visitor who wants an out-of-the-way travel experience in a locale that's still a little rough around the edges. It's clean, neat, and easy to get around, but everything isn't laid out for you. You get there either by a daily Alaska Airlines jet from Juneau, Ketchikan, or Seattle or by the ferries of the Alaska Marine Highway System. The tour company movers of masses have seemingly passed Wrangell by, at least for now. The mega–cruise ships rarely call, and even medium or small vessels stop much less frequently than in Ketchikan, Sitka, and Juneau. The result is that it's a made-to-order destination for travelers who enjoy ferreting out backcountry or backyard jewels in the rough (literally and figuratively)—from semiprecious garnets you can literally collect yourself on a nearby ledge to some of the best and most photogenic totem poles in Alaska. Now for a little background.

Wrangell history goes back possibly 8,000 years, when someone (no one knows who) was here and carved mysterious stick-figure petro-glyph etchings in stone along the seashore. More recently, according to Tlingit oral history, the present Native peoples settled the area more than 2,000 years ago, arriving via the Stikine River. Sometime in the 1700s a Tlingit chief named Shakes (the first of several to claim that name) selected the present site of Wrangell as home for his people.

In the early 1800s English, American, and Russian ships came explor-ing. The Russians established Redoubt St. Dionysius in 1834. The Eng-lish obtained a lease and occupied the same site, calling it Fort Stikine, in 1840. With the sale of Alaska to the United States in 1867, the community came under American jurisdiction and was called Fort Wrangell. Gold mining, fur trading, fisheries, and commerce have been Wrangell's economic staples since.

Recent years have seen the modest beginnings of tourism, and it's true, there's a lot in and around the community for visitors to experience. A good place to visit early, in order to get oriented, is the **Chamber of Commerce Visitor Information Center** at 107 Stikine Avenue, near the city dock (800–367–9745; e-mail: wrangell@wrangell.com). Another is the **City of Wrangell Museum,** in the basement of the city Community Center between the Presbyterian Church and the high school on Church Street. A combination visitor center/museum is in the works for the year 2000. The collection is well worth a visit. It includes masterfully carved totemic house posts, dating to 1770–1790, from the Bear Tribal House on Chief Shakes Island. Also on display: artifacts from the Russian and British occupations and from the gold rush era, petroglyphs, bird and natural history exhibits, minerals, and various other items. Hours are 10:00 A.M. to 5:00 P.M. Monday through Friday and 1:00 to 5:00 P.M. Saturday if staffing is available. The museum is closed on Sunday.

Southeast Alaska Facts
The city of Wrangell on Wrangell Island in Southeast Alaska has been ruled by three nations since its founding by fur traders in 1811: Russia, Great Britain, and the United States.

The most notable cultural site in the community is **Chief Shakes Island,** connected to Wrangell by a walking bridge and located in the middle of Wrangell Harbor. The tribal house and totems there are among the best carved and most colorful in Alaska.

You can see some **petroglyphs** on display at the city museum and library, but most must be sought out at low tide on Wrangell Island's mysterious **Petroglyph Beach** north of town. The etched figures on the rocks, three dozen or more, seem to depict spirit faces, fish, owls, spirals, and other designs, although no one knows what the figures really mean or who created them. To reach them, turn left on Evergreen Avenue from the ferry terminal. Walk north on Evergreen about ¾ mile to a boardwalk leading to the beach. Walk down the boardwalk and head right toward the big rock outcropping on the northern high-tide limit of the beach. Don't, under any circumstances, attempt to move these rocks. You may, of course, photograph them.

A moderately difficult hike (due to a rapid ascent) over the **Rainbow Falls Trail** can be short or long, depending on whether you extend the distance by also hiking the high country ridges along the 2⁷/₁₀-mile

Institute Creek Trail that junctions along the way with the Rainbow Falls Trail. The basic route takes you about ¾ mile from its start at mile 4.6 on the Zimovia Highway to an observation platform and a great view of picturesque Rainbow Falls, then later to a sweeping view of Chichagof Pass. Another popular hiking choice in town is *Mt. Dewey,* also called Muir Mountain since John Muir climbed it in 1879 and caused a considerable stir among the locals when he lit a huge bonfire at the top. The trail is primitive in places, but the view from the top is considered well worth the effort.

If that's not enough outdoor recreation for you, try *Rainwalker Expeditions* for bike and walking tours or *Alaska Vistas* for canoe and kayak trips. Rainwalker Tours, operated by Marie Oboczky (907–874–2549), features bike rentals and guided walking tours of the area. Alaska Vistas (907–874–3006) offers adventures on the Stikine River and in the surrounding Tongass National Forest.

Totem pole on Chief Shakes Island

There are two ways to get one or more of Wrangell's well-known garnets. The easiest is simply to buy one from youngsters you'll find selling them at the docks to cruise ship and ferry passengers. Local kids sell the garnets for $1.00 to $50.00, depending on size. Or you can purchase a $10 daily permit at the Wrangell Museum and chip your own garnets from *Wrangell Garnet Ledge,* located on the mainland near the mouth of the Stikine River, about 7 miles northeast of Wrangell Island. Waterborne sight-seeing tours often stop at the site.

And then there's *Our Collections.* Most visitors overlook it, but shouldn't. Some call it a museum. Others see it and claim it's more of a garage sale that's never happened. What it is, is an incredible display of collectibles that Elva Bigelow and her late husband, Bolly, saved and lovingly preserved over six decades of living in Wrangell. You'll find gold rush paraphernalia from mining days up the Stikine River, old-time logging tools, early day fishing gear, trapping supplies, even hand-crank sewing machines, and clocks, waffle irons, and copper wash kettles. It's the kind of place you can happily rummage around in, wondering why you're doing it, but having the time of your life. You locate Our Collections by walking up the road from the ferry terminal and turning left on Stikine-Evergreen Avenue. It's the same route you take to Petroglyph Beach. Along the way, take the time in June and July to sample tasty salmonberries and thimbleberries growing alongside the road. Before you get to the beach, you'll come to the Bigelows' big metal building on the seaward side of the avenue. Our Collections is open when cruise ships or ferries are in port, or by appointment by calling (907) 874–3646. No admission, but donations are gratefully accepted.

For close-to-town overnight accommodations call Gertrude Rooney to reserve a room with private or shared bath at ***Rooney's Roost Bed and Breakfast*** (907–874–2026), located at 206 McKinnon Street just a block from downtown. Prices start at $55 for units with private baths. Also in town is Wrangell's largest (yet with thirty-three rooms, minute in comparison to large city hotels) hotel, the ***Stikine Inn,*** complete with restaurant and meeting rooms. Prices vary, depending upon the room, and reservations can be made by calling (888) 874–3388 (e-mail: inn@stikine. com; Web site: www.stikine.com). Another option, this one close to Chief Shakes Island, is the ***Hungry Beaver*** (907–874–3005) just behind the restaurant and lounge of the same name at 274 Shakes Street. Four comfortable rooms with kitchenettes run $65 for singles. For at least one meal partake of the restaurant's locally famous pizza fare. For the economy minded, the ***Wrangell Hostel,*** operated by the First Presbyterian Church at 220 Church Street, opens mid-May through Labor Day and charges $10 per person per night. Phone (907) 874–3534.

Bruce Harding's ***Old Sourdough Lodge,*** 1104 Peninsula Avenue, started life some years back as a small bunkhouse for loggers. Today the rustic log lodge offers a wide selection of comfortable accommodations, including the Jacuzzi-equipped Harding River suite that sleeps six, as well as standard rooms with bath. Also on-site: a sauna and steam bath, plus the Sourdough Room cocktail lounge. Standard room rates start at $75 for singles; bed-and-breakfast accommodations start at $85 for singles. Meals cost $10 for breakfast or lunch; dinners start at $16. Call (800) 874–3613 for information, or visit the lodge's Web site at www.akgetaway.com.

Todd Harding operates **Stikeen Wilderness Adventures,** offering one-day trips through forested wilderness up the Stikine River aboard the eighteen-passenger *Iskut Express* and *The Wild Side.* The latter vessel carries five passengers and offers adrenaline-seekers a "Ride on the Wild Side." Both vessels were specifically designed and built to navigate the Stikine, the fastest flowing navigable river in North America. The company also offers trips south of Wrangell to **Anan Creek Bear Observatory,** the only black bear observatory in Southeast Alaska. The Stikine River and Anan trips cost $155. For information call (800) 874–2085; e-mail wildside@akgetaway.com, or visit www.akgetaway.com.

Southeast Alaska Facts

The name Ketchikan is derived from the Tlingit word Kitschk-Hin, *meaning "the creek of the thundering wings of an eagle."*

For another option try Eric Yancey's **Breakaway Adventures,** a jet boat tour operation that's been on the Stikine River for ten years. Yancey's tours, priced at $135 per person with discounts for groups, seniors, and children, take passengers up the Stikine River and to **LeConte Glacier,** whose claim to fame is that it is the southernmost salt-water glacier in North America. The 22-foot inboard jet boats also travel to the Anan Creek Bear Observatory. Passengers will receive an area map and historical tour along the way. For more information call Yancey at (907) 874–2488 or (888) 385–2488, or visit www.breakawayadventures.com on the Internet. Yancey's e-mail is Eric@BreakawayAdventures.com.

Harbor House Lodge adjoins Wrangell's main harbor just a three-minute walk from the charter boat fleet. The lodge features two suites with full kitchens, balconies, and harbor views. Rooms with access to laundry and limited cooking are also available. Chief Shakes Island is just across the street, and restaurants and town stores are all within a 2-block walk. Suites are $110 a day for two persons and $15 for each additional adult. Rooms with a shared bath are $55 for singles and $65 for couples. Owners Ken and Toni Wyrick can be reached at (970) 626–5417 in Colorado. Or e-mail ken@kenwyrick.com. The Web addresses are www.kenwyrick.com/alaska and www.kenwyrick.com/harborhouse.

Remember those bargain-priced ($25 to $40 per night) fly-in **U.S. Forest Service cabins** in the wilderness? Twenty-two of them are located in the Wrangell Ranger District, including one near the Anan Creek Bear Observatory. Call (907) 874–2323 for information. For reservations call the Park Net reservation system at (877) 444–6777 or visit www.reserveusa.com. If you're a hot-tub buff, ask for information about the **Chief Shakes Hot Springs** tubs (one sheltered, one not) that the USFS has placed along the Stikine River about 22 miles from Wrangell. Ask, too, about summertime ranger-led walks along trails and beaches.

High above the surface, **Sunrise Aviation** (907–874–2319; bconine@ ibm.net) will take you flight-seeing over the Stikine River and several glaciers, ice-clogged LeConte Bay, and various high-country lakes, for $95. You even get a souvenir T-shirt or cap. On the ground, Mark Galla's **Alaska Peak and Seas** (907–874–2454) will take you into the backcountry for just about any trip you can imagine. Guided **hunting trips** for brown bear, black bear, Sitka blacktail deer, and mountain goat run $500 to $900 per person per day, depending on what you're hunting. Charter fishing packages aboard the 38-foot yacht *Excaliber* can be arranged for half a day to multiple days and range from $125 to $300 per person. And if a jet boat is your idea of fun, Galla has that, too. His jet boat excursions will take you through the Stikine-LeConte Wilderness in the 24-foot, heated and enclosed *Stikine Spirit*.

Back in 1897, when the rest of the world went crazy over gold in the Klondike, Norwegian-born Peter Buschmann came north, too, but only as far as Mitkof Island in Southeast Alaska. He settled there to fish and eventually build a salmon cannery and sawmill. Other Norwegians, noting the great fisheries of the region, the abundant ice from nearby LeConte Glacier, and the majestic surroundings, joined Buschmann and his family and named their community **Petersburg.**

Today, Peter's *burg* thrives as one of the most active fishing ports in the United States. Fishermen seine, troll, and gillnet for salmon in the summer, seek halibut into the fall, fish for herring in the spring, go after crab in the winter, and harvest shrimp year-round. Sport fishing for salmon and halibut is especially rewarding.

About 3,700 Alaskans call Petersburg home. Most of them fish or work in the fisheries industry or in businesses that service the fishermen. In the summer one of the most pleasant no-cost "tours" you can take is simply to wander in Petersburg's three **public harbors** along 2½ miles of floats, taking in the 1,200 or so commercial fishing vessels that may be in port at any one time. Tourism is a rapidly growing but not yet dominant industry in Petersburg, and therein—as in Wrangell—lies much of the community's charm. The town is "real." And it's clean, neat, well laid out, and noticeably Norwegian, with its Scandinavian rosemaling floral designs on buildings and homes, its huge, white 1912 **Sons of Norway Hall** downtown (complete with a **Viking sailing vessel** ready to put to sea). If you're lucky you'll find Norwegian seafood specialties on menus at local restaurants. (Beer-batter halibut is a particular pleaser. So is the tiny, succulent, popcorn-sized shrimp for which the community is known.) The town, no surprise, is nicknamed Little Norway, and its biggest celebration is the **Little Norway Festival,** timed each May to celebrate Norwegian Independence Day.

A good place to start your visit to Petersburg is the **Visitor Information Center** at First and Fram Streets. Office hours are 9:00 A.M. to 5:00 P.M. Monday through Saturday and noon to 4:00 P.M. Sunday in the summer (www.petersburg.org). Phone (907) 772–4636 for information.

The community's biggest visitor attraction is nearby **LeConte Glacier,** one of the most active in North America, with a constant succession of icebergs calving and crashing explosively from its wide face into the frigid waters of **LeConte Bay.** Many days the big and little bergs literally carpet bay waters from shore to shore, and sight-seeing boats must gently push the ice aside as they cruise in front of the glacier.

The waters of North Frederick Sound, also near Petersburg, provide superb viewing of another major visitor attraction: great **humpback whales.** Large numbers of these gentle giants feed here in the summer months, to the considerable delight of visitors as well as locals. Several charter operators offer LeConte glacier and whale-watching excursions that you can arrange through **Viking Travel** (800–327–2571). Among those trips is the **Kaleidoscope Cruises** tour, with retired marine biologist and naturalist Barry Bracken as your captain. With more than thirty years' experience, Bracken is well versed in glacier ecology as well as marine wildlife. He'll take you aboard his 20-foot

Stories in Wood

*T*otem poles were erected as "story poles" by Tlingit and Haida people who live in Southeastern Alaska, as well as the northwest coast of the United States and Canada, and are unique to these regions. They are usually carved from yellow or red cedar and stand for fifty or sixty years. Totem poles can be seen today at several locations, including the Totem Bight Park, Saxman Totem Park, and the Totem Heritage Cultural Center near Ketchikan; Klawock Totem Park on Prince of Wales Island; and the Sitka National Historical Park.

Island Dream in search of whales, other marine wildlife, and calving glaciers. Tours are anywhere from four and one-half to eight hours long, and prices range from $90 to $150 per person, with a minimum of two and maximum of six people per tour.

Viking Travel, incidentally, provides handy one-stop shopping for several tours, including guided land excursions around Mitkof Island by *See Alaska* for $20 or $35, depending on length, and four-hour sea kayaking trips with *Tongass Kayak* for $60. For the really adventurous, Tongass also offers guided three- to eight-day kayak tours for $675 to $1,680. Viking will also arrange independent travel throughout Alaska.

For a bird's-eye view of LeConte Glacier, you can book a flight-seeing excursion with *Pacific Wing* (907–772–4258 or pacwing@alaska.net). A forty-five-minute flight costs $210 for up to three passengers.

For the visitor who enjoys walking tours, the tabloid-sized *Viking Visitor Guide,* available at the Visitor Information Center, provides an easy-to-follow walking tour map covering more than thirty points of interest, from major fish processing plants along the waterfront to *Eagle's Roost Park* off Nordic Drive just a few minutes walk from downtown. One or two eagles are almost always in residence to pose for pictures on their craggy perches.

You'll know you've arrived at the *Clausen Memorial Museum,* located at Second and Fram Streets, when you see the large bronze sculpture called *Fisk* (Norwegian for "fish"), which displays the many species of fish to be found in these waters. Inside, exhibits vary from an old-time fish-gutting machine (called an iron chink) to the re-created office of a pioneer cannery owner. There are also fur farming exhibits, Native artifacts, including an old Indian canoe, and early-day community photographs. Don't miss the two huge wall-mounted salmon, one of them the largest king ever caught (126$\frac{1}{2}$ pounds) and the other, the world's largest chum (a 36 pounder). The museum's phone number is (907) 772–3598.

For a real treat sign up for the "Patti Wagon Tour," run by Patti Norheim. Her business, *Tongass Traveler,* carries customers on a three-hour tour in a fifteen-passenger van that takes in a seafood cannery and other sights. Afterward, visitors will retire to Norheim's Wrangell Narrows home and enjoy shrimp cocktail and beverages on her 72-foot deck. The cost is $30. Call (907) 772–4837.

The U.S. Forest Service rents numerous cabins in the National Forest around Petersburg, including *Ravens Roost,* one of the relatively few USFS shelters you can hike to. It's located on the mountain behind Petersburg Airport, nearly 4 miles by trail or 3 by helicopter. The Raven Trail begins near the orange-and-white tank south of the airport with 1 mile of boardwalk through muskeg (spongy bog) before the trail's ascent begins. The middle section is relatively steep, then flattens along the ridge top. The easy way to enjoy the experience is to fly in by helicopter, then hike out downhill. The cabin rents for $35 per night per party. For details from the USFS Petersburg Ranger District; call (907) 772–3871. Temsco Helicopters will drop you off at the cabin for $333.75, which is its minimum charge for a half-hour flight. Call (907) 772–4780 for more information.

When Petersburg folk talk of driving "out the road," they're referring to the 34-mile *Mitkof Highway,* along which you can visit the *Falls Creek Fish Ladder* near mile 11, and the *Crystal Lake Fish Hatchery* and *Blind Slough recreation area* at mile 17.5. Birders visiting in the wintertime will especially enjoy the **Trumpeter Swan Observatory** at mile 16.

One of Alaska's rarer boating experiences is a three-hour outing aboard a genuine workboat, *Syd Wright's* **Chan IV.** Wright, a retired educator, is a walking, talking, entertaining encyclopedia of things Alaskan. One of the highlights of the trip will be a sampling of crab, shrimp, or other seafood delicacies. The fee is $85; call (907) 772–4859 for more information. For the fisherman, *LeConte Outfitters* offers quality fishing and sight-seeing trips through the island-studded waters of the area. The cost is $200 per day per person, multiple-day trips only. For more information call (907) 772–4790.

If you're looking for a downtown lodging location call the *Tides Inn* (907–772–4288; First and Dolphin Streets; tidesinn@alaska.net). Ask for a room overlooking the harbor. Owner Gloria Ohmer was born and raised in Petersburg, and she's an absolute fount of knowledge about things to see and do. Rates start at $65 in the winter and $70 in the summer, including complimentary continental breakfast. Nonsmoking rooms are available. *Nordic House Bed and Breakfast,* 3 blocks north of the ferry terminal (806 South Nordic Drive; 907–772–3620; nordicbb@alaska.net), offers a view of Wrangell Narrows, boats, planes, sometimes even wildlife. Rates are $75 for a double with shared bath and $65 for a single with shared bath. A private room with bath and kitchentte is $85 for double. The *Rocky Point Resort,* 11 miles south of town on Wrangell Narrows, offers saltwater fishing for salmon, halibut, trout, crab, and shrimp in protected waters. The $265 rate per person per night includes a cabin, a skiff with motor, meals, fishing gear, and freezing facilities so that you can take your catch home. Call (907) 772–4420 for reservations and information.

For one of life's memorable seafood dining experiences, plan at least one dinner at the **Viking Room** of the **Beachcomber Inn** (907–772–3888), located about mile 4 on the Mitkof Highway. Steaks are available as well. You can enjoy cocktails in the Cannery Lounge. The inn is actually a converted cannery offering quiet, cozy accommodations.

Many Alaskans and most visitors rank Sitka the most visually beautiful community in the state. Perched at the base of majestic mountains on Baranof Island, the community looks westerly toward Pacific Ocean waters upon hundreds of big and little, near and distant isles, mountains, and a massive volcano. Native Alaskan and Russian history abounds in this community. It was the hub and headquarters of Russian America and the czars' vast fur seal gathering and trading empire until the United States purchased Alaska in 1867. Sitka served as the territory of Alaska's capital until the early years of the twentieth century. It is, today, a forestry, fishing, travel, and education center.

If one of your goals is to save money, consider overnighting in the student apartments at **Sheldon Jackson College** on Lincoln Street between

Castle Hill: A Palace Fit for a King—or at Least a Governor

*O*nce a rocky fortress, surrounded on three sides by water, Castle Hill still is the high point between downtown Sitka and the bridge to Japonski Island. Here the Russian governors, beginning with Alexander Baranov, presided over Russian America. Two buildings occupied the site before the "castle" was built. The first was destroyed by fire, the second by earthquake. The "castle," or "Baranov's Castle," was built in 1830 and was renowned for its opulence in what was then a remote and wild country.

A light placed at the top of the castle to guide mariners made the building the first lighthouse in Alaska.

After the U.S. purchase of Russian America in 1867, Baranov's Castle fell into disrepair; in 1894 it burned to the ground.

Today it is a historic monument where Russian cannons bristle from the hill's crest and a commanding view of Sitka and the surrounding islands can still be had. Ramps are being constructed to make the one-time fortress handicap accessible.

Jeff Davis Street and College Drive. The rooms are spartan, and showers and toilets are down the hall (so is a lounge with TV), but you'll find everything clean and everybody friendly. The price is right: $50 for two to a room and $40 for singles. (Incidentally, first priority for rooms goes to visitors attending college conferences.) The surrounding campus is woodsy, tranquil, and historic and allows a spectacular view of the sea. Downtown Sitka lies only a seven-minute stroll away. For reservations or information call (907) 747–2540. You can take cafeteria meals on campus as well: $5.00 for breakfast, $5.00 for lunch, and $10.00 for dinner.

Whether or not you opt to house on campus, don't fail to visit the **Sheldon Jackson Museum,** at 104 College Drive on the campus. Actually, the octagonal-shaped building itself ranks as something of an artifact, having been constructed in 1895 as the first concrete structure in Alaska. It's named for the nineteenth-century Presbyterian missionary and educator who supplied a large portion of the collection. The museum is small and sometimes overlooked, but most visitors find it well worthwhile. The well-presented collection emphasizes the Native peoples of Alaska—Tlingit and Haida Indians of the Southeast, Athabascan Indians of the interior, Aleuts from the Southwest, and Eskimos of the far north. You'll never get a better, closer look at a Tlingit dugout canoe, an Athabascan birch-bark canoe, an ancient two-passenger Aleut baidarka (kayak), and two Eskimo kayaks. You'll see Indian battle armor as well as exquisite Eskimo fur parkas. Also on display: three "mystery balls"—big perfectly round balls of stone, two of them around 10 inches in diameter and one perhaps 16 inches. A museum sign asks, presumably with tongue in cheek, could they be "whale kidney stones, petrified pterodactyl eggs, or giant cannon balls"? The museum operates 9:00 A.M. to 5:00 P.M. daily in summer; 10:00 A.M. to 4:00 P.M. Tuesday through Saturday in winter. Admission is $3.00. For information visit the Web site at www.educ. state.ak.us/lam/museum/home.html, or call (907) 747–8981.

For visitors with RVs or tents, the campgrounds of choice in Sitka are clearly the two **U.S. Forest Service campgrounds at Starrigavan Bay,** close to 8 miles north of town on Halibut Point Road. Both feature separated, private campsites surrounded by thick, towering trees. Near the entrance to the upper campground you'll also find one of Alaska's easiest walking trails. The **Starrigavan Estuary** wheelchair accessible trail, a 1/2-mile elevated boardwalk, takes you beside open wetlands and into deep and dark woods of spruce, hemlock, and alder trees.

Another short and gentle hike, this one at the south end of Lincoln Street on the shores of Sitka Sound, lies within **Sitka National Historical**

Park. Actually you can enjoy two trails there—one a 1½-mile stroll back into Alaska history on the site of the bloodiest battle fought between Tlingit Indians and nineteenth-century Russians, the other (less frequented by visitors) a ¾-mile jogging course.

If your tastes run far off the beaten path, you may consider chartering a boat for a drop-off at the sea-level trailhead of the **Mt. Edgecumbe National Recreation Trail** on Kruzof Island, about 10 miles west of Sitka. The 6⁷⁄₁₀-mile trail up the side of this volcanic crater (a look-alike for Japan's Mt. Fuji) is steep and usually takes about eight hours. The view from the summit of ocean waters and myriad islands is a mind-boggler.

If you've never experienced the fun of a kayak ride, here's a good place to start. **Alaska Travel Adventures** offers a three-hour **Sitka Sea**

A Place of Honor

*I*f you happen to wander through Sitka National Historical Park's visitor center, and you marvel at the beautiful Tlingit totem poles there with their twin wolf design and intricate carvings, you can thank the Indians of the Tlingit Eagle clan for making them, and you can thank my father-in-law, whose Tlingit name is Shuk Shah Ni Ish, for putting them there.

The year was 1962 and my father-in-law, park historian George Hall, had learned that several totem poles and a house front—made up of nine wooden planks incised with an elaborate Tlingit bear design—were in the dilapidated, roofless remains of an old house. As soon as he saw the ornate poles, he knew they had to be protected.

Tlingit Alex Andrews, a friend of my father-in-law and "a man of admirable character," helped form a group that went to the old house, removed the poles and planks, and moved them to another house to protect them from the elements. Tlingit Patrick Paul was the clan custodian, and he also helped.

At this new location, a party was about to get under way to celebrate saving the poles. The Tlingit women were cooking, the men were preparing for song. And my father-in-law, little did he know, was about to be given the honor of a lifetime.

Midway through the celebration, Alex called George forward. His actions—helping save the precious Eagle-clan poles from a sure demise—reminded the Tlingits of something one of their own people would do. In fact, it reminded them of someone they admired, a Tlingit long dead, but now thought to be reborn—in my father-in-law. For that, they gave him the name, Shuk Shah Ni Ish, "mountain," "bird," "person." And they later "gave" Shuk Shah Ni Ish the poles and the house front to place them where he thought was best. His choice: the visitor center, where they will be preserved for everyone.

Kayaking Adventure, led by experienced guides through protected island waterways. The $75 tour often includes views of deer, brown bears, seals, and (always) eagles. For advance reservations or more information call (800) 478–0052 in Alaska or (800) 791–2673 outside Alaska (e-mail: atabob@ptialaska.net; Web site: www.alaskaadventures.com). *Bidarka Boats* (907–747–8996; execpc.com/;bboats) will likewise outfit you with single- or double-seat kayaks for half-day ($25 and $30, respectively), full-day ($35 and $50), or longer trips in Sitka Sound and environs.

Sitkan Jane Eidler and her business partner, Lisa Busch, arrange fascinating ninety-minute historic *walking tours* of downtown Sitka taking in a lofty view of ocean and islands from *Castle Hill* (where "Russian America" officially became "Alaska, U.S.A." in 1867), a re-created *Russian blockhouse,* the old Russian cemetery, the Lutheran Cemetery where, interestingly, Russian Princess Maksoutoff lies buried, historic houses, the *Saint Michael's Russian Orthodox Cathedral,* the *Russian Bishop's House* (part of Sitka National Historical Park), and more. Primarily these are group tours, but you can call (907) 747–5354 or (907) 747–5353 to see if there's a group scheduled with which you can tag along. The Park Service also offers walking tours. For further information call (907) 747–6281.

On days when cruise ships are in port—which is almost every day in the summer—the *Sitka Tribe of Alaska's Tribal Tours Historical and Cultural Sight-seeing Tours* offers a tour from the perspective of the Indian people who lived here before, during, and after the Russians. The narrated two-and-a-half-hour excursion, priced at $26, takes in *Sitka National Historical Park, Sheldon Jackson Museum,* a narrative drive through *Sitka's native village,* and a Native dance performance. For details call (907) 747–7290 or visit www.sitkatribe.com.

The USFS lists twenty-four fly-in or boat-in cabins accessible from Sitka. Probably the most exotic in all of Alaska is the *White Sulphur Springs cabin,* on nearby Chichagof Island. It features a weather-tight log cabin

Second to One

*W*hen you visit Sitka you visit the largest city, in area, in the Western Hemisphere. It's the second largest in the world. There are 4,710 square miles within the unified city and borough municipal borders. (Juneau, at 3,108 square miles, comes in third; Kiruna, Sweden, with 5,458 square miles, ranks as the world's largest city.

with large windows facing out from a picturesque rocky beach onto the broad Pacific—plus an adjacent structure containing an oversize hot springs bath (almost a pool) with the same awesome ocean view. (*Note:* Rental of cabin does not include exclusive use of the hot springs. Locals, fishermen, and visitors can and do frequent this spot.) Getting to this cabin is costlier than most because you have to helicopter in, but if you can afford the tariff, the trip itself will rank as one of your vacation highlights of a lifetime. The local USFS number in Sitka is (907) 747–6671. For reservations call (877) 444–6777, or access www.reserveusa. com on the Web.

For a wildlife-viewing excursion without the hordes of cruise-ship passengers, check out the **Sitka Wildlife Quest,** a two-hour cruise through some of the great bays and narrow passages in and around Sitka. The tour only runs on days when cruise ships are not in town, so you're guaranteed some personal attention. While on the water, look for sea otters, three species of whales (humpbacks, killer, and minke), brown bears, sea lions, black-tailed deer, seals, and eagles. The tour runs $49, not including city tax. For more information call (907) 747–8100.

Here's another quality wildlife viewing excursion by water: *Sitka's Secrets* (907–747–5089) offers four-hour trips for $85 on the 27-foot vessel *Sitka Secret* to **St. Lazaria National Wildlife Refuge** for a view that sets birders cackling. St. Lazaria, a sixty-five-acre island some 15 miles west of Sitka, contains the nests of an estimated 2,000 rhinoceros auklets, 5,000 common and thick-billed murres, 2,000 tufted puffins (comical little creatures sometimes called sea parrots or flying footballs), 450,000 fork-tailed and Leache's storm petrels, plus eagles and other winged species. En route there's a good possibility you'll view whales, seals, sea lions, and sea otters.

John Yerkes' **Sitka Sportfishing** (907–747–5660; sitka.sportfishing@ worldnet.att.net) provides more than the name implies. From his 38-foot modern motor yacht, *Rubato,* Yerkes arranges outer coast hikes, beachcombing, kayaking, hot tubbing, whale watching, and exploring. Half-day sight-seeing trips start at $100, three-guest minimum. Yerkes also offers three-day overnight charters that run about $250 per person for up to five people.

The primary goal of the **Alaska Raptor Rehabilitation Center,** at 1101 Sawmill Creek Road (arrc@ptialaska.net), is healing injured birds of prey, especially eagles, but the center has a worthy program for two-legged human types as well. Guided and unguided tours take place on the center's seventeen-acre campus, which is home to more than twenty recovering birds, including peregrine falcons, bald eagles, golden eagles, and countless owls. A ¼-mile nature trail offers visitors a chance to see bald eagles close-up, in an uncaged natural habitat. And if you've got extra time, try something really different and volunteer at the center. A training program offers volunteers a minilesson in raptor rehabilitation. Call (907) 747–8662 for daily tour schedules.

Southeast Alaska Facts

The Tongass National Forest, in Southeast Alaska, is the largest U.S. forest, with sixteen million acres.

If you're into two-wheel tripping, Al Segovia's *Southeast Diving and Sports* (907–747–8279; 329 Harbor Drive) downtown, will rent bikes by the hour or day. Segovia also offers personalized dive tours, with all gear supplied.

Sitka contains a bevy of B&Bs, virtually every one of them more than adequate; several are outstanding. Among the latter: *Alaska Ocean View Bed and Breakfast* (aovbb@ptialaska.net), run by Carole Denkinger, provides gourmet breakfasts at times convenient to her guests plus snacks in the afternoon. These latter munchies are best enjoyed while basking in an outdoor spa on her red cedar executive-home patio. As the name implies, the view takes in ocean, islands, and mountains, yet it's close by harbors, shopping, and restaurants. Rates for singles range from $69 to $109 for a suite. For information call (907) 747–8310 or visit Denkinger's Web site at www.wetpage.com/oceanview.

Burgess Bauder's Lighthouse is, well, different. It's not exactly a B&B, since the host doesn't reside in or near the premises. But it certainly isn't your usual lodge or inn, either. What it is, is a real lighthouse that Bauder constructed and located on an island a few minutes by boat from downtown Sitka. Bauder provides you with a skiff for comings and goings, though you may not wish to stray far from the tranquil surroundings. Small wooden hot tubs offer relaxing moments in the evening. The Lighthouse will sleep eight. The two bedrooms located in the tower offer particularly commanding views. You do your own cooking. Rates start at $125. Call (907) 747–3056.

For not-so-fancy but organized and clean lodging, look up American Youth Hostel's *Hosteling International-Sitka,* with dorm-style rooms in the basement of the United Methodist Church, at 303 Kimshan Street. The atmosphere is friendly and guests are responsible for their own food and cleaning. The cost is $10 for AYH members or $13 for nonmembers. For further information call (907) 747–8661.

Port Alexander is one of those small, isolated communities that infrequent visitors end up raving about. Located at the southern tip of

Baranof Island, the town once boasted 2,000 residents. Today there are about 125, among them Peter Mooney, who with his wife, Susan Taylor, operates *Laughing Raven Lodge,* a secluded getaway offering wildlife viewing, hiking, kayaking, and fishing. Rooms are located right by the water, so don't be surprised if you're awakened during the night by whales spouting. Three rooms are available, each with its own bath, and skiffs and kayaks can be rented for exploring the water. Rates run about $300 a day for room, board, fish processing, and packaging. Call (907) 568–2266, or visit www.portalexander.com on the Internet. Air access (for about $90 one way) is via Sitka, 65 miles north. Call Taquan Air at (888) 474–0088 for reservations.

The Upper Panhandle

J uneau, Alaska's state capital, is arguably the most scenic capital city in the nation. The most populated portion of town sits on the shores of Gastineau Channel, backed up by awesomely steep Mt. Juneau, Mt. Roberts, and various other peaks in the 3,000-foot-and-higher class. Within Juneau's 3,108 square miles you'll find big bays, tiny inlets, thickly vegetated islands, and numerous glaciers (including *Mendenhall Glacier,* the second most visited river of ice in Alaska). The town also contains large portions of the Juneau Ice-field—a 1,500-square-mile, high-altitude desert of hard-packed ice and snow that extends from behind the city to beyond the Canadian border. It's from the overflow of this ice field that Mendenhall, Taku, and other great glaciers descend. Juneau had its start in 1880 as a miners' camp after a local Indian chief, Kowee, led prospectors Joe Juneau and Dick Harris over Snowslide Gulch into Silver Bow Basin. They found, according to Harris's account, gold "in streaks running through the rock and little lumps as large as peas or beans."

You can see exhibits of the community's gold mining history in the small, often overlooked *Juneau–Douglas City Museum* at Fourth and Main Streets, open 9:00 A.M. until 5:00 P.M. weekdays; 10:00 A.M. to 5:00 P.M. weekends. Admission is $1.00. For more information check out www.juneau.lib.ak.us.parksrec/ on the Web, or call (907) 586–3572. You can view more history (including native Eskimo, Indian, and Aleut displays) and wild animal dioramas (including a spectacular multistoried eagle's nest tree) in the *Alaska State Museum,* 395 Whittier Street, a couple of blocks from downtown. If you're traveling with young children, don't miss the Discovery Room on the second floor where kids can climb aboard a playlike copy of Captain James Cook's eighteenth century vessel *Discovery,* stroke wild animal pelts, and dress in period costumes. Museum admission is $4.00. Hours are 9:00 A.M. to 6:00 P.M. weekdays; 10:00 A.M. to 6:00 P.M. weekends. For information call (907) 465–2901, or visit www.educ.state.ak.us/lam/museum/home.html.

Southeast Alaska Facts

The Stikine River is the fastest free-flowing river in North America.

Also often passed by—but for history buffs well worth the effort of a few blocks' climb to Chicken Ridge from downtown—is **Wickersham House,** the restored Victorian home of Judge James Wickersham, a pioneer jurist and Alaska territorial (nonvoting) delegate to Congress. You can see the judge's artifact collection and period furniture as well as interpretive displays and a grand hilltop view of the city's business district. Here you can enjoy a **Tea Social With the Judge,** offered five times a day, with seating limited to eight people per meeting. During this living history tour, the judge will show you his artifacts, even passing them around to each guest, all while enjoying tea and sourdough cakes on the patio. Admission is $12.50 per person. Call ahead (907–586–9001) for reservations. If you don't want to climb the steep streets and walkways to this state historic site, take a cab to 213 Seventh Street. Hours are 10:00 A.M. to 4:00 P.M. Thursday through Sunday; 10:00 A.M. to 6:00 P.M. Monday.

Juneau is blessed with an incredible number of hiking trails, many of them remnants of old mining roads dating back to the 1920s and even earlier. If you lack wheels, you can easily reach several from downtown Juneau, including the **Mt. Roberts Trail** ($2^7/_{10}$ miles one way), which begins at the end of Sixth Street; **Perseverance Trail** ($3^1/_2$ miles one way), which you access by walking up Gold Street to Basin Road; and the **Mt. Juneau Trail** (2 steep miles one way), which begins as a side trail about $^1/_2$ mile along the Perseverance Trail. The Mt. Roberts and Mt. Juneau treks meander through thick forests until they break out, finally, above timberline for awesome aerial views of green forests, Gastineau Channel, and Douglas Island, across the water.

Near **Mendenhall Glacier,** 13 miles north of downtown, the **West Glacier Trail** ($3^1/_2$ miles one way) takes you from the parking lot on the west side of Mendenhall Lake through alder and willow forests for a mostly gradual climb up the side of Mt. McGinnis. Your destination is a 1,300-foot vantage point, where you can look down on the rolling white expanse of the glacier. If you want knowledgeable local expertise while you're trekking in the area, **Gastineau Guiding** (907–586–2666; hikeak@ptialaska.net; www.ptialaska.net/~hikeak) offers daily three- and four-hour escorted hikes along forest trails to saltwater shores and

alongside historic remains and relics of the community's gold producing heyday. Prices range from $40 to $75. The *City and Borough of
Juneau* offer free guided hikes on Wednesdays and Saturdays during
the summer. Call (907) 586–5226 for details.

Beer aficionados take note: *Alaskan Brewing Company*'s amber beer
and pale ale brews have taken gold medals and blue ribbons in tasting
competitions across the country. You can tour Alaska's pioneer micro-
brewery on Shaune Drive off Old Glacier Highway, about 4 miles from
downtown. The company offers free tours and tastings 11:00 A.M. to
4:30 P.M. Tuesday through Saturday in the summer, but it's the most
fun on bottling days. Call (907) 780–5866 for bottling days and times.
Speaking of tasting brews, Alaska's best-known saloon, the *Red Dog,*
is located downtown at 278 South Franklin Street, but don't overlook
the saloon in the *Alaskan Hotel and Bar,* at 167 South Franklin. The
big, ornate back bar there is worth a look-see, whether or not you
imbibe. The hotel, incidentally, was built in 1913 and offers refurbished rooms with private and shared baths. The rates are $55 with
shared bath, $70 with private bath, and $90 for a studio suite. Phone
(800) 327–9347.

About dining in Juneau: The opportunities are mouthwateringly
wide, from Mexican and Tex-Mex cuisine downtown at *El Sombrero*
(157 South Franklin; 907–586–6770) and the *Armadillo Cafe* (431
South Franklin; 907–586–1880) to arguably Alaska's best Friday clam
chowder at the old-fashioned *Douglas Cafe* (907–364–3307) across
the bridge at 918 Third Street, in the community of Douglas. The cafe
is perhaps the only restaurant in Juneau that features the tasty amber
clams and amber mussels. Virtually unknown to the tourist trade is
the tiny *Hot Bite,* open summers only on the dock at Auke Bay, 13
miles north of downtown. There the proprietors have raised the cre-
ation of hamburgers to an art form. Off the usual tourist track but
probably Juneau's favorite restaurant, for good reason, is the *Fiddlehead
Restaurant and Bakery* (429 West Willoughby; 907–586–3150), a

True and Unexpected

*J*ustice Creek in Glacier Bay National
Park and Preserve was named by the
National Park Service after a story by
Jack London titled "The Unexpected,"
in which justice was provided by two
prospectors who, in the absence of a
court, tried and executed a third person for a double murder. The story was
based on actual events that happened
in the vicinity of the creek.

short drive or a longish walk from city center. The menu varies from the likes of a modestly priced meal of black beans and rice to more expensive full-dinner offerings of fresh-caught salmon, halibut, or beef. If you can, time your luncheon visit to avoid the noon-hour crowd of state workers.

Gourmet diners and history buffs will enjoy the atmosphere and the food at the historic **Summit** restaurant in the **Inn at the Waterfront** (455 South Franklin; 907–586–2050) or the equally long-lived **Silverbow Inn** (120 Second Street; 907–586–4146). Both enterprises also offer a small number of hotel accommodations, and both structures, although thoroughly modern, date back to the late nineteenth century.

If you're a Friday visitor, plan to pick up a sack lunch at any of several downtown sidewalk vendors and head for the State Office Building—**the S.O.B.,** in local parlance. There in the structure's great atrium, local and visiting organists perform each week on a grand and lusty old Kimball theater pipe organ, to the considerable delight of scores of brown-bag lunch consumers perched on benches and ledges.

One of the best ways to really appreciate Juneau is by staying in one of those nifty **U.S. Forest Service cabins** scattered throughout the area. There are five cabins you can hike to straight from Juneau and dozens that are accessible by air or boat. Two of the closer (and therefore less costly to reach by plane) lakeside cabins are the **East Turner Lake** and **West Turner Lake** units up Taku Inlet, south of the city. Trout and char fishing can be productive from either end of the lake, and wildlife watching can include brown bears (from a distance, please!), deer, mountain goats, and waterfowl. The cabins rent for $25 to $45 a night. For more information visit the U.S. Forest Service Information Center in the Centennial Building, downtown at 101 Egan Drive, phone (907) 586–8751. Reservations may be made by calling (877) 444–6777 or signing up on the Web at www.reserveusa.com.

Silver Bow and Gold

*A*n Auk Tlingit Indian named Chief Kowee is the true discoverer of gold in the Juneau area, not Joe Juneau and Dick Harris, the two prospectors often credited. It was Kowee who brought ore samples to entrepreneur Richard Pilz, hoping to bring prosperity to his people. Pilz then outfitted Harris and Juneau and sent them to find the source. When they returned empty-handed Kowee led them to the source at Gold Creek in Silver Bow Basin in 1880.

Don't overlook the *Alaska State Parks cabins,* as well. They are equally nice, and several are accessible by trail. The *Juneau Convention and Visitors Bureau* can give you more information by phone at (888) 581–2201 or on the Web at www.juneau.com.

Alaska Discovery (800–586–1911; akdisco@alaska.net; www.akdiscovery.com) is one of the state's longtime and very special practitioners of the outdoor guiding art. Whether you're shopping for a day's sea kayaking adventure in protected waters north of Juneau or a week's canoe or float trip in the Arctic wilderness, Alaska Discovery has a trip tailored to your skills, budget, and inclinations. From Juneau, two one-day options are outstanding: Their *Juneau Sea Kayaking* excursion includes instruction for the uninitiated, five hours of paddling along forested beaches and coastal islands, plus lunch and beverage. Wildlife commonly seen includes seals, sea lions (possibly hundreds ashore on an island rookery), bald eagles, and—if you're really lucky—humpback or orca (killer) whales. Alaska Discovery offers similar excursions in Glacier Bay. The trip is priced at $95.

Their *Admiralty Island Kayaking* trip takes you by air to the nearby island that Tlingit Indians called *Kootz-na-hoo,* or "Fortress of the Bears." This trip offers an almost unparalleled opportunity to view brown (grizzly) bears in their natural forest habitat at and near *Pack Creek,* where the U.S. Forest Service has constructed an elevated observation platform. The 7:00 A.M. to 5:30 P.M. trip is fully guided. It includes float plane transportation from Juneau, a ¼-mile kayak paddle in protected waters, ample time ashore for hiking and bear viewing, rubber boots and gear, plus lunch and beverages. Participants must be 14 years or older. The cost is $450.

For one-day and multiday wildlife viewing, boating, or camping expeditions, call *Wilderness Swift Charters* at (907) 463–4942 (Web: www.alaska.net/~tongass; e-mail: tongass@alaska.net). Wilderness Swift claims to be Juneau's only active boat charter service holding permits to Pack Creek's brown bear sanctuary. They'll drop campers and kayakers off at any number of destinations as far away as Glacier Bay. Trips start at $385, with a four-person minimum and six-person maximum.

Here's another Pack Creek option: Among a variety of fishing and wildlife viewing excursions packaged by *Alaska Fly 'n' Fish Charters* (907–790–2120; akbyair@ptialaska.net; www.alaskabyair.com) is a one-day guided floatplane visit to the bear sanctuary. Like Alaska Discovery, the company is one of several allowed to guide a limited number of visitors at this truly world-class viewing site, but in addition to the guided visit, the firm offers drop-off and pickup flights for persons who

Southeast Alaska Trivia

have obtained their own $50 permits for unguided visits. An Alaska Fly 'n' Fish guided trip to Pack Creek runs $400 per person and from $140 to $200 for air only, depending on the number of passengers. For more information from the USFS, including a list of approved guiding companies and procedures for getting an unguided visit permit, call (907) 586–8751. You can get this information in person at Centennial Hall in downtown Juneau, but travelers who wait until they get here usually find the limited number of permits are long gone.

In Juneau, *Alaska Travel Adventures* offers two splashy *Mendenhall Glacier Float Trips* down almost whitewater on the Mendenhall River for $89, a *Gold Panning and Gold History Tour* in the shadow of the old AJ mine for $32, *Auke Bay Kayaking* through protected waters north of town, priced at $69, and the outdoor *Gold Creek Salmon Bake,* now located on Salmon Creek near the hospital, for $22. This, incidentally, is Alaska's longest-running salmon bake and many, including my Juneau friend Pete, say it's the best in the state. The menu includes not only fresh king salmon steaks (grilled on an open pit over alder coals and glazed with a brown sugar and butter sauce) but barbecued ribs, baked beans, lots of other trimmings, plus your choice of complimentary wine, beer, coffee, or soft drink. All this in sheltered surroundings alongside a sparkling stream and waterfall at the site of old mine diggings. And don't forget the live folk music to enhance the entire scene. To avoid a cast of thousands, call ahead (800–478–0052 in Alaska or 907–789–0052 locally), ask when the busloads of cruise ship passengers are expected, then plan your own arrival earlier or later. To visit Alaska Travel Adventures on-line, go to www.alaskaadventures.com, or send an e-mail to atabob@ptialaska.net. Also on-site: the *Juneau Raptor Center,* where you'll find live eagles and other birds of prey plus exhibits you can enjoy and learn from. There's no charge for viewing the birds. Call (907) 586–2722.

Still another sea kayak rental firm, *Adventure Sports,* offers rentals, guided tours, and free advice. The owners will help plan independent day trips, overnight trips, three-day trips, or even longer. If after all your planning you want a guide, they can provide that, too. For more information call (907) 789–5696; e-mail gunnar@alaska.net, or visit www. adventuresports.com/asap/kayak/seakayak/.

If a really serious kayak trip is more to your liking, **GreatLand Guides of Alaska** has the perfect trip for you. The company offers a variety of guided kayaking adventures, but their favorite is **The Ultimate Expedition,** a six-night, seven-day kayak trip that retraces naturalist John Muir's 1879 canoe trek. During the trip, you'll paddle most of the length of Lynn Canal Fjord, described by Muir as "the most beautiful and spacious of all the mountain-walled channels that we have yet seen." The 75-mile paddle, which passes by old lighthouses and calving glaciers, is labeled "very challenging." It's a wonderful trip, and at $1,275 (including return ferry from Haines), it's worth every penny. For more information call (907) 463–4397, e-mail greatland@empnet.com, or visit www.empnet.com/greatland.

If skiing's your thing and you're in Juneau during the winter months, **Eaglecrest Ski Area,** about twenty minutes from downtown off North Douglas Highway, offers slopes (and two double chairlifts) for everyone from beginner to expert. For information in season call (907) 586–5330 for recorded snow conditions.

You'll find numerous ways to see glaciers around Juneau—on motor-coach tours, from boats, during hikes, and looking down from airplanes. Perhaps the most exciting way to see glaciers (short of actually hiking there on your own) is by helicopter. Several companies have filled that niche, including **Era Helicopters** (800–843–1947; fltsg@era-aviation.com; www.era-aviation.com) and **Coastal Helicopters Inc.** (907–789–7076; coastal@ptialaska.net; www.alaskaone.com/coastal), and **Temsco Helicopters** (907–789–9501; temscoj@ptialaska. net; and www.temscoair.com). During these flights you not only fly over one or more rivers of ice, you also touch down and disembark from your chopper for twenty minutes or so of frolicking on the hard-packed ice. Fares are in the $150 to $200 range.

The longest-running operator of day cruises from downtown docks to spectacular **Tracy Arm Fjord** and twin Sawyer glaciers, **Glacier Bay Tours and Cruises** offers all-day options for $131.60 aboard the *Glacier Spirit* as well as half-day cruise/fly excursions priced at $210.13. Tracy Arm is a long, deep, meandering fjord whose steep walls rise dramatically for thousands of feet. Whales, seals, mountain goats, deer, and bears are among the wildlife viewing possibilities. Call (907) 463–5510 for information.

The Alaska traveler seeking a *really* offbeat challenge should contact Bruce Grigg's **Out of Bounds Adventures.** This Juneau-based outfit packages not-so-soft adventure as diverse as heliskiing or snowboarding in the snow-capped Chilkat Mountain Range, glacier hikes and climbs on Mendenhall Glacier, paragliding off Thunder Mountain in Juneau's Mendenhall Valley, mountain biking for 1,000 miles beside the Alaska Pipeline from Valdez to Prudhoe Bay, surfing remote beaches below 18,000-foot Mt. Saint Elias near Yakutat, plus (somewhat tamer) shore fishing, charter fishing, and sea kayak trips. For details call (907) 789–7008 or visit www.ptialaska.net/~akskiing on the Internet. E-mail is akskiing@ ptialaska.net.

You can charter Andrew Spear's thirty-ton, 50-foot, three-stateroom Down East sailing cutter **Adventuress** under three options: full service (Andy provides everything, including wine with gourmet meals), crew assisted (well, you have to make your own bed, buy your own food, and do the cooking), or bare boat (for completely knowledgeable sailors). Call (907) 789–0919 for brochures and information.

Francis and Linda Kadrlik's *Adventures Afloat* (800–3AFLOAT; e-mail: valkyrie@ptialaska.net) will likewise introduce you to the wilderness of Southeast Alaska with a flight-seeing arrival at their base of operations. In this case the base is the elegant 106-foot classic yacht M.V. *Valkyrie,* your floating home for two-, three-, or six-day ecotours that include wildlife watching, exploring, and fishing from the smaller (32-foot) *High Roller.* Prices start at $390 per person a day, with discounts for groups.

You'll find a number of good value B&B accommodations in and around

A small cruise vessel in Tracy Arm Fjord

Juneau. Here are two B&Bs about 11 miles from downtown and close to Juneau's number one visitor attraction, Mendenhall Glacier. Guests at **Pearson's Pond Luxury Inn** enjoy private or shared baths, queen beds, private entries and decks, robes, slippers, and self-serve continental breakfasts plus the use of the spa, kitchens, barbecue, rowboat, and bikes. Rates are $129 and $149 for double rooms with private baths. For details, call (907) 789–3772. **Sepal Hollow Bed and Breakfast,** 10901 Mendenhall Loop Road, offers a home of completely remodeled California contemporary design adapted to a vintage Alaskan backwoodsy setting. The B&B offers queen-sized beds, hearty breakfasts, an enormous deck (from which to observe eagles, porcupines, and squirrels), an expansive fireplace, and Georgia Sepal's enthusiastic hospitality and local knowledge. Rates are $75 per night, with senior citizen discounts making it even less, for two. For more details call (907) 789–5220.

If you've got the time, it's well worth your effort to call **Alaska Rainforest Tours** and get their free seventy-two-page catalog that outlines trips across the state, with an emphasis on Southeast. The catalog contains package tours, day trips, bed-and-breakfast accommodations, and just about any trip your imagination can come up with. If you're into sea kayaking, this is the catalog to get—many of the packages are geared toward paddlers. For further information call (907) 463–3466, or e-mail artour@alaska.net. The Web site is www.alaska.net/~artour.

The **Juneau International Hostel,** located at 614 Harris Street, is a particular pleasure for fans of hosteling. It's located in a large, historic, rambling house on the side of a hill called Chicken Ridge. Clean, spacious, and handicapped accessible, it's just a few blocks above downtown Juneau. In spite of its relatively large capacity (forty-eight beds, sitting room with fireplace and library, laundry), it's filled almost all the time in the summer. Reservations are a must. The cost is $10 for adults. Call (907) 586–9559.

If your plans call for a trip between Juneau and Sitka, one of the most pleasant ways to travel between the two ports is via the **Alaska Marine Highway ferry** LeConte. The advantage of sailing on this vessel, as opposed to one of the larger ships of the fleet, is that the *LeConte* stops along the way at **Hoonah, Tenakee Springs** (most trips), and **Angoon.** Of course, you don't have to be heading to Sitka to visit these small communities; you can, if you like, simply take a round-trip from Juneau to one or all three, then return by ferry or small plane to Juneau. Call (800) 642–0066 for information or reservations. On-line reservations can be made at www.dot.state.ak.us/external/ambs/home.html.

Located on the northeast shore of Chichagof Island, about 40 miles and three ferry hours north of Juneau, lies **Hoonah,** a thriving village of mostly Tlingit Indian people. If you're not laying over, check with your ship's purser and see if you have time to mosey into the village (about a fifteen-minute walk). If you don't, at least take the time to visit the graveyard right across the highway from the ferry dock. You'll find some graves there that are quite old, others new, some traditional with angel figures, others marked with the distinctive Russian Orthodox Church's cross with two cross beams, and still others with cast figures from the Tlingit Indian totemic tradition.

Southeast Alaska Trivia

Early on October 24, 1918, the S.S. Princess Sophia, *a passenger vessel carrying 350 people, went aground on Vanderbilt Reef in Lynn Canal. Forced off the reef the following evening by storm and high tides, the* Princess Sophia *sank and all aboard perished.*

In town you'll find two restaurants plus lodging, grocery, gift, and general merchandise establishments. Overnighters will find **Hubbard's Bed and Breakfast** (in the woods but only a mile from downtown) clean and pleasant. Rates are $85 for a double; call (907) 945–3414 for reservations. Want to see a genuine brown (grizzly) bear while you're in the area? Check out the village garbage dump (honest), about 2 miles from town. But do not walk to the site. Get someone to drive you, or hire a cab. These critters are big and wild.

Between Hoonah and Sitka, the ferry *LeConte* stops occasionally at **Tenakee Springs,** long enough sometimes for passengers to run with towel in hand to the community's hot springs for a quick, relaxing soak. The springs, incidentally, provided one of the principal reasons for the community's founding back in 1899. Miners would journey to the site every winter when cold weather shut down their "diggin's" and they'd stay for weeks or months. The tradition continues, sort of. Lots of Juneauites, Sitkans, and other Southeast Alaska residents still come to take the waters, both winter and summer. Interestingly, there are posted hours for men's bathing and other hours for women. But never the twain meet, at least in the 5-by-9-foot bathing pool. You'll find several overnight options in Tenakee Springs, including furnished cabins for rent from longtime Alaskans Elsie and Don Pegues' **Snyder Mercantile Company** (907–736–2205). Rates are $40 per night for a one-room cottage and $65 for a deluxe, two-bedroom minilodge. Bring your own sleeping bag. Another option is to book a sportfishing package from **Tenakee Hot Springs Lodge** (907–736–2400). Rates start at $2,590 for five days and nights including air from Juneau, fishing boat charter, and home-cooked meals as well as lodging. Fishing in the area is first rate; beachcombing and hiking are likewise, and chances are you'll see sea life in the water—humpback whales, seals, sea lions, and otters. The one-way ferry trip from Juneau to Tenakee Springs costs $22. Airfare is approximately $73.

The Tlingit village of **Angoon** offers yet another offbeat destination from Juneau. Located on the northwest coast of Admiralty Island, the community is accessible by ferry and by air from Juneau, which is 60 air miles away. Two very comfortable lodging possibilities at Angoon—the **Favorite Bay Inn** and the **Whalers' Cove Sportfishing Lodge**—provide all the comforts with easy access to sportfishing, kayaking, canoeing, and simple sight-seeing. Worth a visit: nearby Tlingit Indian village. The islands and waters of Kootznahoo Inlet and Mitchell Bay are prime kayaking locales. To contact the inn or lodge, call (800) 423–3123. Rates at the inn are $89 for a single. For information on the lodge visit www.whalerscovelodge.com. Call for sportfishing package rates. A one-way trip from Juneau to Angoon costs $24; airfare is $80.

Here's one of the most economical day cruises you can experience in Alaska. Twice a month on Sunday mornings, the smaller ferry **LeConte** departs from Auke Bay terminal (about 14 miles north of Juneau) for the picturesque fishing village of **Pelican,** on the northwest corner of Chichagof Island. The route takes you through Icy Straits, past prime whale-watching waters off Point Adolphus. Along the way you may view sea lions, seals, bears, deer, eagles, and other wildlife. Arrival at Pelican is at midday, and you have an hour and a half to walk along the town boardwalks, stroll around the commercial fishing docks, and watch as commercial fishers unload halibut, salmon, crab, and black cod at the cold storage plant. You can have lunch at the local cafe or your choice of two bar and grill establishments, including **Rosie's** (907–735–2265), sort of a Southeast Alaska institution among fishermen. The return ferry departs midafternoon and arrives seven hours later in Juneau. If that's too much time afloat, you can fly back on **Alaska Seaplane Service** (907–789–3331) for $100 one-way, or charter a plane from **Wings of Alaska** (907–789–0790 or www.wingsofalaska.com), starting at $440. Call the Alaska Marine Highway System (800–642–0066) for latest scheduling information. If you lay over, the **Otter Cove Bed & Breakfast** (907–735–2259) offers beach and streamside privacy within a few minutes' walk on the boardwalk to "downtown." Rates begin at $75. E-mail is ottercove@hotmail.com; the Web address is www.northernlightsdesign.com/seaotter.

The people of **Haines** will tell you, perhaps with some justification, that their community has the best summer weather in Southeast Alaska. The warmer, drier air of the Yukon interior regions, they say, flows over

Chilkat Pass into the Chilkat Valley and brings with it more sunshine and less rainfall than other panhandle communities experience. Whatever the reason, Haines and vicinity does offer the visitor a pleasurable place to perch for a day or a few days.

Sadly, many visitors pass Haines by. They're in such a toot to get off the ferry and rush north to the main body of Alaska, they miss many of Haines's considerable pleasures—pleasures like the Tlingit Indian dancing and cultural exhibits at old Fort William Henry Seward; like the old fort itself (now a National Historic Landmark), with its rows of elegant officers' homes and its traditional military parade ground; like a fascinating museum of Southeastern Alaskana, a new museum of natural history, and a state park that many rank among America's most pleasurable.

You get to Haines aboard the ferries of the Alaska Marine Highway System, either from Skagway, an hour's sailing from the north, or from Juneau, about four and a half hours from the south.

Passengers-only water taxis makes several round-trips daily between Haines and Skagway. Or you can drive to Haines over the 151-mile Haines Highway, which joins with the Alaska Highway at Haines Junction, Yukon Territory, Canada. You can also fly to Haines. Several excellent small-plane carriers provide frequent scheduled flights from Juneau and Skagway. Rugged coastlines, thickly forested islands, high-rising mountains, and Davidson and Rainbow glaciers are only a few of the sights you encounter along the way.

Once in Haines, a good place to stop for advice, a map, and literature is the Visitor Information Center (907–766–2234) on Second Avenue South, about a block from the Haines downtown business district. Only a few minutes' walk from the visitor center is the *Sheldon Museum and Cultural Center* (907–766–2366), on the harbor end of Main Street. This museum literally had its start in 1893, when Steve Sheldon, at the ripe old age of 8, purchased a piece of the original transatlantic cable and began a lifetime of collecting. He arrived in Haines from his native Ohio in 1911 and met and married a woman from Pennsylvania, also an avid collector. Their family hobby has resulted in what is now the Sheldon Museum, a collection that encompasses Tlingit basketry and totemic art (including a rare, unfinished Chilkat ceremonial blanket), mementos of Fort Seward (later called Chilkoot Barracks when it housed the only U.S. troops in Alaska), photos of colorful Jack Dalton, plus pack saddles and other gear Dalton used to clear the Dalton Trail toll road to the Klondike. You can also see the shotgun he kept loaded behind the bar of his saloon. The museum is open 1:00 to 5:00 P.M. daily, plus mornings and evenings when cruise ships are in port. Admission is $3.00.

Another museum recently has opened, the **American Bald Eagle Foundation**'s collection of Southeast Alaska natural history. Displayed in a beautiful diorama of taxidermy are the animals, birds, and fish of the region. The foundation is a block from the Visitor Information Center, at the intersection of Second Avenue South and the Haines Highway.

Haines's premier attraction is unquestionably **Fort William Henry Seward,** established in 1904, renamed Chilkoot Barracks in 1922, and deactivated in 1946. The government sold the entire fort to a group of World War II veterans in 1947, and although their plans to create a business cooperative did not fully work out, the fort's picturesque buildings have been largely preserved. You can, in fact, sleep and dine in any of several grand old officers' quarters, which now serve as hotels, motels, or B&Bs. Other old structures still at the fort include warehouses, the cable office, and barracks. One large building now houses the **Chilkat Center for the Arts,** where some nights you can watch the award-winning, nationally recognized **Chilkat Indian Dancers** during evening performances. For a schedule of performances call (907) 766–2160. In still other fort buildings you can see contemporary Tlingit craftsmen of **Alaska Indian Arts** (AIA) fashion large and small works of traditional totemic art from wood, silver, fabric, and soapstone. Totem poles carved and created by AIA on the fort grounds can be seen all over Alaska and, indeed, the world. You'll see totemic art, too, at the **Totem Village Tribal House,** also on the fort parade grounds. Adjacent to the structure is a traditional trapper's log cabin of the kind you might find in Alaska's bush country.

Adjacent to the fairgrounds at the northern edge of the city (Haines is home to the **Southeast Alaska State Fair** each August), you'll come to some gold rush–era buildings that may seem vaguely familiar. These buildings, now called **Dalton City,** served as the set for the Walt Disney movie *White Fang,* based on Jack London's novel. When the moviemaking ended, the Disney company donated the set to the community. The buildings may be of recent origin, but they present an authentic picture of a gold-rush community during the tumultuous time of the Klondike gold stampede. Picture-taking opportunities abound.

A site often overlooked by visitors is **Chilkat State Park,** about 8 miles south of town on Mud Bay Road. You don't have to be a camper to enjoy this forested wonderland on the Chilkat Peninsula. For visitors seeking just an afternoon outing, there are ample trails, saltwater beach walks, and gorgeous views of Davidson and Rainbow glaciers. The state charges $6.00 for camping here.

In the late fall and early winter, throngs of eager birders arrive to visit the *Alaska Chilkat Bald Eagle Preserve,* just a few minutes' drive from the city. There, 2,500 to 4,000 American bald eagles gather each year to feast on a late run of Chilkat River salmon. This is the world's largest concentration of bald eagles, and the spectacle is easily seen from turnoffs alongside the highway. A number of eagles and many other bird species can be seen there year-round, and other wildlife is frequently spotted, especially during summer float trips down the stream.

Chilkat Guides, Ltd., offers daily *Bald Eagle Preserve Raft Trips* through some of the most spectacular portions of the Chilkat River and the preserve. This is a gentle float in spacious 18-foot rubber rafts. Eagles, bears, moose, even wolves, if you're lucky, may be seen during the four-hour trip. The tour begins with a van pickup near the old army dock, and includes a 30-mile drive to the preserve. Then comes the float downriver to a haul-out spot near the Indian village of Klukwan. The price is $75 for adults. For more details call (907) 766–2491; e-mail raftalaska@aol.com, or visit www.raftalaska.com.

Both *Chilkat Guides* and Juneau-based *Alaska Discovery* package float trips down the magnificent *Alsek and Tatshenshini Rivers,* which flow out of the Canadian interior. These trips (which Chilkat Guides does in ten and thirteen days, respectively, and which Alaska Discovery schedules for ten and twelve days) open up some of the world's most awesome mountain/glacier/wild river country. Exciting whitewater, relaxing floats, abundant wildlife, and wild country treks are only a few of the features of these premier experiences, which begin in Haines and end at Yakutat, for a jet flight back to Juneau. Prices for the Tatshenshini trip vary from $1,975 to $2,250; for the Alsek, from $2,400 to $2,650. Contact Chilkat Guides at the number above; Alaska Discovery can be reached at (800) 586–1911, www.akdiscovery.com, or akdisco@alaska.net.

Don and Karen Hess's *River Adventures* combines van (or bus) touring with a jet boat ride. The result is a half-day, four-hour outing 25 miles up the Haines Highway through the Chilkat Bald Eagle Preserve to a boat dock, where passengers transfer to river craft for 44 miles of wilderness, wildlife, and birdlife watching. Moose and bear are often seen, and during a smoked salmon snack break there's time to use a high-powered spotting scope to view game on nearby mountainsides.

The cost is $70 for morning and afternoon trips. Call (907) 766–2050 for more details or e-mail k.hess@eudoramail.com.

"Everything is negotiable." That's Kathi Rose's motto for her family-run business, *The New Other Guys Taxi & Tours.* This company offers sight-seeing trips in a twelve-passenger van to just about any place the van can go. And if that's still not far enough out for you, they'll pack you in a four-wheel-drive vehicle and take you even further. For a look at brown bears, moose, eagles, or Rainbow and Davidson Glaciers, try the two-and-a-half-hour van ride to *Chilkat State Park.* That trip is $35 per person, but group rates can drop the price to $25 per person. For an all-day excursion, pack a lunch and a gold pan and head to *Porcupine Mine* for a day of gold prospecting. The truck holds up to three people, at $100 each, for this trip. For more information call Rose at (907) 766–3257.

Bicyclists can join other pedalers on day rides or longer tours through *Sockeye Cycle* of both Haines and Skagway. In Haines they're located on Portage Street uphill from the dock in Fort Seward. Their excursions

Bold and Beautiful Lituya Bay

*I*n 1958, an earthquake rattled the land in Southeast Alaska along the Fairweather fault, and a huge chunk of earth—40 million cubic feet of dirt and rocks—broke off from a piece of mountainside and landed in a picturesque T-shaped body of water known as Lituya Bay. It's hard to say there is a "prettiest" place in Alaska. Snow-tipped mountains, aquamarine glaciers, forested hillsides, and broad sweeping rivers all have a way of capturing the eye. But Lituya Bay, on the passage north from Cross Sound to the community of Yakutat, might just qualify.

On this day though, July tenth to be exact, you would not have wanted to be in Lituya Bay. As the landslide thundered into the water, it caused a giant wave—called a splash or seiche wave—that surged to the opposite side of the bay at the alarming height of 1,740 feet, taller than even the 1,250-foot Empire State Building.

The wave plucked the trees along the bay like a gardener pulling weeds. It scoured the soil down to bedrock. Surely any animals in the wave's path were swept out to sea and gone forever. Later, the unearthed trees floated in the bay like match sticks, stripped of their bark and branches, and twisted into splinters. Even loggers couldn't salvage the useless debris.

The Lituya Bay seiche wave set a record that has never come close to being broken. The second-highest recorded seiche wave was a mere 230 feet, caused by a landslide in a lake in Norway.

include the one-day or overnight *Chilkat Pass* bicycle adventure into the newly created *Tatshenshini/Alsek Provincial Park,* a part of the largest protected United Nations International Wilderness Area in the world. The price per person is $120 for the day trip and $320 for the overnighter, which includes four meals. Even more challenging is a 350-mile nine-day *Golden Circle Tour* north from Haines up the Haines Highway to Canada's Yukon, east to Whitehorse in the Yukon Territory on the Alaska Highway, then south on the Klondike Highway to Skagway. The trip costs $1,850. Rentals are $6.00 for an hour, $20.00 for a half day, and $30.00 for a full day. For details about these and other trips, call (907) 766–2869 in Haines, (907) 983–2851 in Skagway. E-mail is cycleak@ibm.net, and the Web address is www.haines.ak.us/sockeye.

Shane and Janis Hortons' *Chilkoot Lake Tours* (800–354–6009; Eagles_Nest@wytbear.com; www.eaglnest@wytbear.com) offers easy-going, quiet tours and fishing excursions that take in some of Southeast's most scenic lake and wildlife-viewing country. Two hours of sight-seeing cost $50 per person; a three-hour fishing trip for Dolly Varden and sockeye salmon runs $75. The Hortons also operate *Eagle's Nest Motel,* near the center of town, and *Eagle's Nest Car Rental.* Doubles at the motel cost $75; auto rentals start at $45 a day.

For some of the best local seafood, stop by the *Hotel Halsingland* (907–766–2000, halsinglan@aol.com; www.haines.ak.us/halsingland) for full dinners starting at about $19. The hotel also offers rooms starting at $89 for a double. Economy rooms are available, starting at $50.

It's pleasant simply to stroll by the *Chilkat Restaurant and Bakery* (907–766–2920), on Fifth Avenue between Main and Dalton Streets, just to savor the smells of baked goods and cooking that wafts from within. It's even more pleasant still to stop in for a breakfast of waffles, omelettes, or sausage gravy and hot biscuits. Lunch can be as light as soup and a burger, or it can be a full meal. Among dinner specialties: halibut, salmon, and Klondike stew and biscuits. Roberta Lane describes this as a family restaurant (no smoking) and a "from-scratch bakery," featuring Alaska sourdough and farm breads. Breakfasts cost from $4.50, lunches from $5.00, and dinners somewhat higher, though the luncheon menu is available through the dinner hour.

The historic building that houses the *Fort Seward Lodge, Restaurant, and Saloon* was constructed in the early 1900s as the fort's post exchange. In those days it included a gym, movie house, library, and two-lane bowling alley as well as a soda fountain. The latter was a popular place with tourists, who enjoyed watching the soldiers' pet bear (named

Three Per, for three percent beer), who would beg for ice cream cones when she couldn't entice the soldiers to give her beer. Three Per has long since gone to bear heaven, but the building is still popular with visitors, who can enjoy all-you-can-eat crab dinners in season, rent rooms with private or shared baths, and savor a favorite libation in the bar. Rooms start at $50; meals and saloon charges are in the moderate range. For more information phone (907) 766–2009 or (800) 478–7772.

Also on fort grounds: Norman and Suzanne Smith's **Fort Seward Bed and Breakfast,** house number 1 on Officer's Row, features stately Jeffersonian rooms with fireplaces, cable TV, and awesome views of Lynn Canal. Full sourdough pancake breakfasts are included in the $85 rate for two. For information phone (907) 766–2856 or (800) 615–NORM, or visit www.haines.ak.us/norm. Also on the parade grounds in Officers' Row are **Fort Seward Condos,** owned and operated by Ted and

The Chilkoot Trail of the Great Gold Rush Days

*M*y husband and I are planning a trip on the famed Chilkoot Trail, which during the 1898 Klondike Gold Rush was the route gold-seekers toiled up to Lake Bennett in Canada. It is a famous trail; old sepia-toned prints captured hordes of laden prospectors making their way up "The Scales," which seemed to climb straight to heaven. So it is with anticipation that I look forward to this trip. As long as my husband doesn't repeat his antics of the last time he was on this trail—more than twenty years ago when he was but a young lad of 16.

He was a Boy Scout—the Scout law is "trustworthy, loyal, helpful, friendly, courteous, kind, obedient, cheerful, thrifty, brave, clean, and reverent"— and he traveled with Troop 211. It was a three-day trip in which the Scouts would do like the gold miners, hauling their packs and themselves clear to the top. All seemed to be going well, until a

Scout of large proportions, we'll call him Norm, began to complain about all the weight he must carry (including the double-burner Coleman stove he had insisted earlier that he must have in order to cook his canned food). Scoutmaster Mr. Weston, tired of hearing Norm's complaints, made the rest of the Scouts take Norm's belongings and redistribute the weight evenly among themselves. Obviously, moans and groans ensued, but like good Scouts they followed their orders.

It wasn't until Norm had reached the top of the great pass that he realized the joke was on him. Bent on revenge, the "trustworthy, loyal, helpful, friendly, courteous, kind" Scouts had discreetly filled Norm's pack with rocks so that the poor child never got relief after all.

Remind me not to complain during our trip.

Mimi Gregg. These completely furnished bedroom apartments come with fully equipped kitchens. The Greggs were among the original purchasers of the fort back in the '40s and have a wealth of memories and history to share. Rates start at $85 per night. Call (907) 766–2425. Dave Nanney's **Chilkat Eagle Bed and Breakfast** sits next to the Chilkat Center for the Arts. It's small, intimate, and was built in 1904 as NCO quarters. Hospitality is practiced here in four languages: English, Spanish, French, and Japanese. The rate is $75 for a double. Call (907) 766–2763, e-mail eaglebb@kcd.com, or visit www.kcd.com/eaglebb.

If you want to stay on the waterfront, check out **A Sheltered Harbor Bed and Breakfast.** There are five rooms with private baths, and breakfasts are a tasty, filling affair. Prices range from $75 for a single to $115 for the suite. For more information call (907) 766–2741.

At mile 8.5 on the Haines Highway, situated on a cliff that overlooks the Chilkat River and the Chilkat Mountains, the **Chilkat Valley Inn** offers a wilderness and wildlife-viewing setting only minutes from town. Lois Gammill and Don Quan heat their units with cozy wood stoves, as many Alaskans do. Call (907) 766–3331 or (800) 747–5528. The rate is $80 per night for a single.

Bear Creek Camp and International Hostel (907–766–2259) offers a lot of options—regular cabins, cabins with bunk beds, campsites, plus a separate shower house and bathrooms. There's also a kitchen for guests' use in another cabin. The camp and hostel is situated among trees and mountains about a mile from downtown. If you don't have wheels, call owners Brian and Laura Johnson and they'll come and pick you up at the ferry for $3.00 (or look for Brian's gold taxi van in town). The nightly fee is $14 for a bunk in the hostel, $38 for a cabin, or $8 for a campsite. To get there head out Mud Bay Road. When you come to Small Tract Road, turn left and drive for about 3/4 mile. It's around a corner and on the left.

You can reach the **Weeping Trout Sports Resort,** on the shores of Chilkat Lake north of Haines, only by boat, but it's well worth the effort for travelers looking for rejuvenation in quiet surroundings or golf in the most unlikely of places. Accommodations are modest but more than adequate, with rooms available in the main lodge or in cabins. Boats, rafts, and canoes are available for exploring, but the most intriguing feature of the place is the par-three, nine-hole golf course, whose fairways boast such names as Devils Club (154 yards), Cut Throat Cut (181 yards), and minuscule Lake Lob (45 yards). Call (907) 766–2827 for prices and further information. E-mail is weepingt@kcd.com; Web site is kcd.com/weepingt.

Deishu Expeditions rents kayaks and organizes tours ranging from half-day local paddling to six days between Juneau and Haines. Their shoreline trip beside *Chilkat State Park* is a particular delight, especially in June when kayakers can paddle out to *Strawberry Island* for berry picking and poking around the old homestead there. Rentals for single kayaks are $25 a half day, $35 a full day; guided tours are $85 for a half day, $125 for a full day. Lots of tours to choose from. Call (800) 552–9257 for more information, or visit the Web site at www. seakayaks.com.

Pardon the bad play on words, but this outfit is for the dogs. Sled dogs, that is. *Chilkoot Sled Dog Adventures* features Southeast Alaska's only live presentation about mushing, plus a daily drawing that awards one visitor a summer dogsled ride on wheels. A shuttle to the site leaves the downtown visitors center Monday, Wednesday, and Friday at 1:00 P.M. Call (907) 766–3242 for details.

When you're ready to leave town, if you're Skagway-bound and don't have a car, you should consider the Haines–Skagway *Water Taxi and Scenic Cruise,* a one-hour narrated boat excursion that features more than twenty waterfalls plus the possibility of viewing seals, sea lions, porpoises, bald eagles, and other creatures. The "taxi" is the eighty-passenger, 50-foot *Sea Venture II,* which operates between the two cities twice daily. The fare is $20 one way, $32 round-trip. In Haines call (907) 766–3395 for information and reservations. In Skagway call (907) 983–2083.

In the annals of the nineteenth-century American frontier, no town had a more frantic, frenzied, fascinating history than *Skagway.* This city at the northern end of Lynn Canal, some 90 miles north of Juneau, was packed to overflowing during the "Days of '98," when thousands of would-be gold seekers poured into the community to outfit themselves for treks to the Klondike gold fields. It was one of the most lawless towns under the American flag. Jefferson "Soapy" Smith and his gang of toughs and con men controlled the city, prompting the superintendent of the Canadian North West Mounted Police across the border to call it "little better than hell on earth." Amazingly well preserved, with many structures from late in the last century and early in this one still standing and in use, much of the town today comprises the *Klondike Gold Rush National Historical Park.* And there's still a lot of violence in this town . . . but it's all make-believe, a nightly reenactment of the July 8, 1898, shoot-out between "good guy" citizen Frank Reid and "bad guy" desperado Soapy Smith. (Both men died in the encounter.)

There's more to Skagway than gold rush structures and shoot-outs, though. There is, for instance, the **White Pass & Yukon Route.** Declared an International Historic Civil Engineering Landmark by the American Society of Civil Engineers, a designation achieved by only fourteen other projects, including the Eiffel Tower in Paris and the Statue of Liberty in New York, the narrow-gauge railway provides one of North America's premier rail experiences. Construction of the line between Skagway and Whitehorse, Yukon, began, against horrendous grades and incredible natural obstacles, in 1898. The builders clawed and blasted their way to the 2,885-foot White Pass in 1899 and to Whitehorse the following year. The WP&YR today carries visitors from Skagway, at sea level, to the pass in the incredibly short distance of only 20 miles. Riders have three options: a three-hour round-trip, taking in the most spectacular of the cliff-hanging mountain and lush valley sights as far as the summit; a 28-mile trip to Fraser on the Klondike Highway, where Whitehorse-bound travelers transfer to motor coaches; or a five-and-a-half-hour round-trip excursion to Lake Bennett, where some 20,000 stampeders camped during the winter of 1898 after climbing and crossing the Chilkoot Pass. (They then proceeded by boat and raft through additional lakes, rapids, and riverways to the Klondike.) WP&YR round-trip fares start at $78. For reservations or information call (800) 343–7373.

And speaking of the railroad, the headquarters and information center of the **Klondike Gold Rush National Historical Park** is located in the restored old **WP&YR Depot,** at Second Avenue and Broadway. You'll find historical photos, artifacts, and film showings there plus visitor information about the town and current conditions on the Chilkoot Trail. Walks through the downtown historic district guided by Park Service rangers leave from the center several times daily. The National Park Service, at substantial effort, has restored a number of Skagway's most historic buildings, including the **Mascot Saloon,** Third Avenue and Broadway, built in 1898, and the **Trail Inn and Pack Train Saloon,** Fourth Avenue and Broadway, constructed in 1908. **Captain Benjamin Moore's cabin,** 1/2-block west of Broadway between Fifth and Sixth Avenues, goes back all the way to 1887; the good captain was there, waiting for the gold rush to start, when the first stampeders clambered ashore a decade later. Call (907) 983–2921 for walking tour schedules. The tours are free of charge.

The city also has a free self-guided walking tour that takes in downtown businesses as well as some of the Victorian-style homes in the community. Maps are available at the visitors center. For further information call (888) 762–1898.

Other worthwhile stops in Skagway include the *Corrington Museum of Alaska History,* at Fifth Avenue and Broadway, with exhibits from prehistory to modern-day Alaska, and *Gold Rush Cemetery,* about 1½ miles north from downtown, where Frank Reid and Soapy Smith lie buried.

The *Arctic Brotherhood Hall,* at Second Avenue and Broadway, has at least three claims to fame: It's old, having been built in 1899 to house "Camp Skagway Number 1" of a once thriving Alaska–Yukon fraternal organization of gold seekers. It now houses the city's *Trail of '98 Museum,* and therefore provides a wealth of gold rush information. And its curious, false-fronted facade is covered with more than 20,000 (count 'em, 20,000) individual pieces of big and little rounded pieces of driftwood.

The collection includes "good guy" Frank Reid's will, the tie "bad guy" Soapy Smith was wearing during the shootout, an Eskimo kayak and Indian canoe, an authentic Chilkat blanket, a faro gambling table, and an assortment of prospecting gear. Admission is $2.00. For further information call (907) 983–2420.

During the Klondike gold rush, Skagway was the jumping-off place for the White Pass "Trail of '98" horse and wagon route to the Yukon. For stampeders who couldn't afford either pack horses or wagons, the nearby community of Dyea (pronounced Dy-EE) was the starting point for the famous *Chilkoot Trail* to the gold fields. The trail today is part of the Klondike Gold Rush National Historical Park and, like trekkers of old, you, too, can hike from Dyea (accessible by gravel road, 9 miles north of Skagway) to Lake Bennett. It's a three- to six-day walk, with some shelters along the way. For details from the park superintendent's office, call (907) 983–2921.

Although the Chilkoot Trail is the best known trail in the area, the hiker with limited time can enjoy several other hiking options, including the easy, woodsy *Lower Dewey Trail,* less than a mile long. You'll find the *Skyline Trail and A. B. Mountain* longer (more than 3 miles to the summit), more strenuous, but greatly rewarding. ("A. B.," incidentally, stands for Arctic Brotherhood, a gold rush fraternal organization.)

A new Chilkoot Trail map and maps of area hiking destinations are available at the city and Park Service visitor centers.

While in Skagway, don't pass up the chance to see a true piece of history on Seventh Avenue and Spring Street. Built in 1900, the McCabe Building is the first granite building in the state of Alaska, and it was originally intended to be a women's college. The building is undergoing a major facelift these days, but soon the **Skagway City Hall** (temporarily at Twenty-second Avenue and Main Street) will call this historic site home. Bring your camera, too. Outside, an old Baldwin steam locomotive makes a perfect photo backdrop.

Even if you're lodging elsewhere, take the time to stroll through the lobby of the **Golden North Hotel,** Alaska's oldest hotel, built in 1898 during the gold rush boom. The hotel recently has undergone a $1.2 million renovation and features lovingly furnished rooms with period pieces contributed by pioneer Skagway families. Each room is a minimuseum in itself, and the stories of the families who once lived in Skagway are on the walls in the form of photos, documents, and news headlines. Proprietors Dennis and Nancy Corrington also lay claim to another "oldest," the oldest microbrewery in Alaska. Originally established in 1897, **Skagway Brewing Company** brewed the premier beers for the Gold Rush stampeders. The company boasted its Red Star Amber and its Blue Top Porter. Today the Corringtons produce the products again, including Red Star, Blue Top and thirteen other brews. For further information on the hotel or the brewery, call toll-free (888) 222–1898, visit www.alaskan.com/goldennorth, or e-mail corrington@msn.com.

Another new addition to Skagway is **The White House Bed and Breakfast,** a beautifully renovated Victorian-style home that was almost destroyed by fire in the late '70s. Owners Jan and John Tronrud have done an excellent job decorating the home. Rates start at $99. For further information call (907) 983–9000, or visit www.skagway.com/whitehouse.

Historic **Skagway Inn Bed and Breakfast,** at Seventh and Broadway, traces its origins to 1897 and its days as a brothel providing "services" for lonely gold stampeders. Today the inn contains twelve rooms restored to Victorian charm. Baths are shared. Innkeepers Karl and Rosemary Klupar offer full breakfasts, home-baked muffins, fresh-ground coffee, piping-hot tea, courtesy van service (including transportation for hikers to the start of the Chilkoot Trail), and Alaskan expertise to share. Rates start at $95 for a single. Call (907) 983–2289. E-mail is sgyinn@ptialaska.net; Web site is located at puffin.ptialaska.net/~sgyinn. In the evening, incidentally, you can purchase dinner at the restaurant there called **Olivia's at the Skagway Inn.** This is probably Skagway's most expensive restaurant, but expect it to be worth the tariff. It is a fine-dining experience.

Skagway Hostel, at 456 Third Avenue, is the home of Frank Wasmer and Nancy Schave and accommodates up to twelve hostelers in beds in the main house. There's additional space in a backyard bunkhouse. The charge is $15.00; for an additional $5.00 donation you can join Frank and Nancy and other hostelers for a family dinner that features fresh veggies from Nancy's garden. For further information call (907) 983–2131. Reservations will be accepted with a $15.00 deposit.

Perhaps the strangest "cabin" in the U.S. Forest Service wilderness cabin network is the retired *White Pass & Yukon Route Caboose,* located 5½ miles north of Skagway. The view, a stunner, takes in the Skagway River and the Sawtooth Mountains. Visitors may rent this unit for $25 a night, just like most others in the system, but instead of flying, hiking, or boating in you reach the caboose by—you guessed it—taking the train! For information call the U.S. Forest Service in Juneau at (907) 586–8751.

For a truly off-the-beaten-path camping experience, travel 9 miles down the road to the *Dyea Campground.* There are many things about this hidden treasure that make it so special. First, it is free. Second, it is located among lush green trees, which make the air feel particularly clean and clear. And third, if you're like me and enjoy a closer-to-nature experience, there are only the basics—pit toilets, water from a simple pump, and lots of space to spread a tent and enjoy the surroundings. No humming generators here! For further information on the campground, call the Park Service at (907) 983–2921.

For bicyclists, *Sockeye Cycle,* of Skagway and Haines, offers a *Klondike Summit to Sea Cruise,* a tour that provides a van ride to the 3,292-foot summit of the White Pass, then a 15-mile guided coast downhill to town with jagged mountains, forests, and glacier views along the way. The price is $69. For information call (907) 983–2851 in Skagway, (907) 766–2869 in Haines. E-mail is cycleak@ibm.net; Web site is www.haines. ak.us/sockeye/.

Skagway is the southern terminus of the *Klondike Highway,* which extends into British Columbia and Canada's Yukon Territory. Each fall, on a designated weekend in September, the highway becomes less a highway and more a race course as hundreds of running teams from all over the United States and Canada arrive to race in stages all the way to Whitehorse, 108 miles away. For dates and information about the *Klondike Trail of '98 Road Relay,* contact the Skagway Convention and Visitors Bureau at (907) 983–2854.

Glacier Bay National Park and the Community of Gustavus

No question about it. *Glacier Bay National Park and Preserve* is one of the extraordinary parks of the nation. Home to sixteen massive, glistening saltwater glaciers and the site of hundreds of huge and little valley and mountaintop ice masses, Glacier Bay National Park is all about the power of ice in shaping a land. It's a place where the relentless grinding force of glaciers has carved deep, steep-walled saltwater fjords and U-shaped mountain valleys, and it's a place of stark, barren, rocky expanses where glaciers have only recently receded. It's also a land of mature, lush spruce and hemlock forests, where the ice receded decades ago. It's a place where the word *awesome* comes frequently to mind.

Glacier Bay National Park lies some 60 miles west of Juneau, accessible by cruise ship, yacht, jet, or light aircraft. Visits can be as short as a day trip out of Juneau or as long as a week or more. The community of **Gustavus,** easily reached by air, abuts the park and provides a rich variety of guiding, fishing, lodging, and supply services.

If you want lodging accommodations within the park boundaries, your only choice (though highly pleasurable) is *Glacier Bay Lodge* on the shores of Bartlett Cove. The lodge is a fifty-six-room resort located 10 miles from the community of Gustavus. It contains fully modern guests rooms, a dining room, cocktail lounge, small gift shop, and the *National Park Service Glacier Bay Visitor Center.* Rooms begin at $82.50 per person per night. If that's too rich for your budget, you may want to consider men's or women's dorm rooms with beds, which can be rented for $28 per night. For a brochure or reservations call (800) 451–5952.

The sight-seeing yacht *Spirit of Adventure* departs Bartlett Cove daily for a full day, which includes close-up looks at glaciers, thousands of birds, and good prospects of viewing brown bears and mountain goats on land plus whales, porpoises, and seals in the water. Park Service naturalists accompany each sailing. The fare, including lunch onboard, is $156.50. Package tours are available that include one or two nights at the lodge. Bartlett Cove is also base for the Glacier Bay Tours and Cruises vessel *Wilderness Explorer,* which serves as a floating camp for kayakers on overnight tours within the park and elsewhere. Prices for a five-night, six-day adventure start at $1,480 from Juneau. For information about both vessels, call (800) 451–5952.

Now about *Gustavus,* next door to the park. Funny place this town. Except it's not a town, because the 300 strong-willed, individualistic citizens who live there have voted repeatedly not to become any sort of official city with trappings like mayors or government. But Gustavus is a definable community because these same people—as friendly and sharing and helpful as they are fiercely independent—manage to provide everything that they need in order to happily reside there. They're equally prepared to provide travelers with everything they need to happily visit for a few days or a season. The setting is awesome, bounded on three sides by the snow-capped peaks of the Chilkat Range and the Fairweather Mountains and on the fourth by smooth, sandy, saltwater beaches. The community spreads itself sparsely over miles of flat countryside and includes boundless opportunities for berry picking, hiking, bicycle riding, kayaking, golfing, whale watching, freshwater and saltwater angling, beachcombing, birding, and just gawking.

For such a small community, Gustavus has no shortage of fine lodging opportunities. The first place that comes to mind is the *Gustavus Inn,* once a rural homestead and now a comfortable, inviting inn for road- (or plane or boat!) weary travelers. The home was originally built in 1928 and served a pioneer family with nine children. In 1965 the new owners—Jack and Sally Lesh—did some renovations and opened their doors to guests. Today, one Lesh generation later, David and JoAnn Lesh carry on the tradition. The food continues to be the inn's strongpoint, with fresh seafood in great quantity. And there still are ample opportunities to borrow a bicycle and go for a ride, fish from the banks of the nearby Salmon River, hike on the many trails and backroads, or just wander your way into relaxation. Rates start at $135 per adult, $67.50 per child, including all meals. For more information call (800) 649–5220 and (913) 649–5220 October to April.

Gustavus's second inn, the *Glacier Bay Country Inn,* likewise offers a very Alaskan, high-quality experience in a setting of verdant forests and majestic mountains. Here, too—in a distinctive structure with multiangled roofs, dormers, decks, and log-beamed ceilings—informally gracious living and fine dining are trademarks. The charge is $183 for a single, $352 for a double, including three full meals. The Marchbanks family, who owns the inn, also books stays at the *Whalesong Lodge,* about 4 miles away. The Whalesong features one three-bedroom condo, ideal for families or parties, and four rooms, each with a private bath. Lodging here comes with a continental breakfast. The condo rents for $110 per person with a three-person minimum;

the rooms go for $99 per person. If you'd like a meal plan, the March-bankses say they can work out an arrangement. Another Marchbanks enterprise **Grand Pacific Charters,** features overnight trips on sight-seeing vessels, plus fishing and whale-watching packages. For further information or reservations, visit the business's Web site at www.glacier-bayalaska.com, or send an e-mail to gbci@thor.he.net. The phone number is (800) 628–0912.

Yet a third delightful inn to check out is **Alaska Discovery Inn.** The five-room inn is right off Main Street and has rooms with shared and private baths. The private-bath rooms are $105 for a double; the shared-bath rooms are $95 for a double. There is a $10 charge for each additional person in your room. For further information call (800) 586–1911, or visit www.akdiscovery.com on the Web. E-mail is akdisco@alaska.net.

A Puffin's Bed and Breakfast—among several travel services offered by Chuck and Sandy Schroth's Puffin Travel, Inc.—is centrally located within walking distance of a grocery, cafe, and shops. Each cabin has its own private bath or shower, but you walk down a lighted path to get to all but two of them.

Guests gather for a full breakfast at a new central lodge, where activities can be planned for the day, including fishing or biking—fishing poles and bikes are available to guests. Rates start at $75 for a double. The Schroths also book a wide variety of fishing and sight-seeing tours. For more information visit the Puffin Web site at www.puffintravel.com, e-mail puffin@compuserve.com, or call (907) 697–2260.

Glacier Bay, with its protected arms and inlets, provides ideal kayaking waters for sight-seeing at sea level. **Glacier Bay Sea Kayaks,** operated by longtime Alaskans Bonnie Kaden and Kara Berg, has been renting these craft to visitors for many years, by the day for short excursions around Gustavus or for taking aboard larger vessels for drop-off at camping locales in the national park. Prices start as low as $35 a day. Call (907) 697–2257 for information, or visit www.he.net~kayakak/. E-mail is kayakak@seaknet.alaska.edu.

Newer to the kayak-renting scene yet equally as qualified is **Sea Otter Kayak Glacier Bay,** across from the store on Dock Road. Owners Maureen Moore and Ted Bond will pick you up at the airport or dock, outfit you with a kayak and all the necessary gear, and deliver kayaks to their appropriate destination. Rates begin at $25 for a single and $35 for a double for a half day and $40 and $50, respectively, for a full day. For more information call (907) 697–3007, e-mail seaotter@he.net, or visit www.he.net/~seaotter/ on the Internet.

Award-winning *Alaska Discovery* operates water and hiking tours in the park, catering to both one-day visitors with or without outdoor experience and to knowledgeable kayakers and rafters who seek a more rigorous wilderness adventure. Call (800) 586–1911 for more details (Web site: www.akdiscovery.com; e-mail: akdisco@alaska.net).

Another sea kayaking option is offered by John "Rusty" Owen and his wife, Pamela Jean Miedke, who together operate *Seawolf Wilderness Adventures.* Kayak excursions can be arranged anywhere in Southeast Alaska, including the Inside Passage and Outer Coast. The couple will transport you on their 65-foot yacht/floating lodge, the *Seawolf,* for overnight trips as well as four- and five-day trips. You can combine kayaking with the trip or just lounge on the yacht and take in the sights. You even can listen to the whales sing on the hydrophones supplied on deck. To rent the entire boat will cost anywhere from $1,800 to $3,000, depending on your destination. A per person rate runs about $300 to $350 per day. For more information call Seawolf at (907) 697–2416, e-mail seawolfak@hotmail.com, or visit www.seawolf-adventures.com on the Internet.

Spirit Walker Expeditions offers a variety of tours from a one- or two-day trip by kayak to nearby (and aptly named) Pleasant Island to their eight-day expedition among the (also aptly named) Myriad Islands, where hundreds of tiny isles make up a miniature Inside Passage. Prices for these trips range from a $115 day trip to a $2,350 weeklong Myriad Island adventure, which includes bush plane airlift from Gustavus. Call (800) KAYAKER for more details or visit www.he.net/~kayak on the Internet.

The 70-foot *Steller,* formerly a state research vessel, provides a floating base for kayakers and motor skiff sight-seers on *Glacier Bay Adventures'* four-day trips. The main search is for humpback whales, but the vessel frequently encounters Steller sea lions, sea otters, porpoises, seals, and minke whales. Visitors usually spend one day in Dundas Bay, where a shore visit allows anglers to sample freshwater fishing in the Dundas River. For more details call Dan Foley at (907) 697–2442. The inclusive rate is $1,500 per person, including air from Juneau.

Jim Kearns's *Fairweather Adventures* offers lodging and marine wildlife tours at the mouth of Glacier Bay, on the banks of the Salmon River. Kayak trips, sportfishing, beach excursions, and exploring are all available. The cost runs approximately $2,000 for an inclusive full week's adventure. Phone (907) 697–2334 for details or e-mail saiw@ seaknet.edu.

When you're ready to leave Gustavus, call *Air Excursions,* which is the primary airplane carrier for the community. Fares are about $55 one way to Juneau. For more information call (907) 697–2375.

For more information in general on the community of Gustavus, call (907) 697–2245.

PLACES TO STAY IN SOUTHEASTERN ALASKA

GUSTAVUS

Alaska Discovery Inn, off Main Street; (800) 586–1911, www.akdiscovery.com.

Glacier Bay Country Inn and the Whalesong Lodge; (800) 628–0912, www.glacierbayalaska.com. A distinctive inn and a three-bedroom condo, respectively.

Glacier Bay Lodge; (800) 451–5952. A fifty-six room resort on the shores of Bartlette Cove; dorm rooms also available for thrifty travelers.

Gustavus Inn; (800) 649–5220. Comfortable, inviting inn.

A Puffin's Bed and Breakfast; (907) 697–2260, www.puffintravel.com. Private cabins; breakfast served in a central lodge.

HAINES

Captain's Choice Motel; (907) 766–3111, www.kcd.com/captain. Forty-room hotel with a view of Lynn Canal.

Chilkat Eagle Bed and Breakfast, 67 Soap Suds Alley; (907) 766–2763, www.kcd.com/eaglebb. Near Lynn Canal.

Chilkat Valley Inn, mile 8.5 on the Haines Highway; (907) 766–3331 or (800) 747–5528.

Fort Seward Bed and Breakfast, house number 1 on Officer's Row; (907) 766–2856, (800) 615–NORM, or www. haines.ak.us/norm. Awesome views of Lynn Canal.

Fort Seward Lodge, Restaurant, and Saloon; (907) 766–2009 or (800) 478–7772.

A Sheltered Harbor Bed and Breakfast; (907) 766–2741. On the waterfront.

HOONAH

Hubbard's Bed and Breakfast; (907) 945–3414. In the woods but only a mile from downtown.

HYDER

Grand View Inn; (250) 636–9174, www.myhome.net. On Highway 37A, Hyder's main road.

JUNEAU

Driftwood Lodge, 435 Willoughby Avenue; (907) 586–2280, www.alaskan.com/drift-woodlodge/. A popular lodging establishment for lawmakers in the state capital for the legislative session.

Inn at the Waterfront, 455 South Franklin Street; (907) 586–2050. Accommodations and gourmet food at this historic structure.

Silverbow Inn, 120 Second Street; (907) 586–4146. Historic hotel with modern accommodations.

Westmark Baranof Hotel, 127 North Franklin Street; (907) 586–2660, www.westmarkhotels.com. In historic downtown Juneau.

JUNEAU AREA

Pearson's Pond Luxury Inn; (907) 789–3772. A B&B inn.

Sepal Hollow Bed and Breakfast, 10901 Mendenhall Loop Road; (907) 789–5220.

KETCHIKAN

Blueberry Hill Bed and Breakfast, 500 Front Street; (907) 247–2583, www.ptialaska. net/~blubrry.

Gilmore Hotel, 326 Front Street; (907) 225–9423. Has a commanding view of Ketchikan's frantic waterfront.

KETCHIKAN AREA

Eagle's Roost Bed and Breakfast, 410 Knudson Cove Road; (907) 247–9187, www.cruising-america. com/eagles.html/. Fourteen miles north of Ketchikan, perched just above Knudson Cove harbor and marina.

Great Alaska Cedar Works Bed and Breakfast, 1527 Pond Reef Road; (907) 247–8287. Eleven miles north of Ketchikan. Two beachfront cottages.

Yes Bay Lodge, on the Cleveland Peninsula, north of Ketchikan; (907) 225–9461 in Alaska or (800) 544–5125 out of state.

PORT ALEXANDER

Laughing Raven Lodge; (907) 568–2266, www.portalexander.com. A secluded getwaway for wildlife viewing, hiking, kayaking, and fishing.

SITKA

Alaska Ocean View Bed and Breakfast, 1101 Edgecumbe Drive; (907) 747–8310 or www.wetpage.com/ocean-view. The name says it all.

Burgess Bauder's Lighthouse; (907) 747–3056. Located on an island a few minutes by boat from downtown Sitka; use of skiff included.

SKAGWAY

Golden North Hotel, Third and Broadway; (888) 222–1898, www.alaskan.com/golde-north. Alaska's oldest hotel, built in 1898, and lovingly restored with period pieces from pioneer Skagway families.

Skagway Hostel, 456 Third Avenue; (907) 983–2131.

Skagway Inn Bed and Breakfast, Seventh and Broadway; (907) 983–2289, www.puffin.ptialaska. net/~sgyinn. Twelve rooms restored to Victorian charm.

White House Bed and Breakfast; (907) 983–9000, www.skagway. com/whitehouse. Beautifully renovated Victorian–style home. Two blocks from downtown.

WRANGELL

Harbor House Lodge; (970) 636–4020, www.kenwyrick.com/ harborhouse. Adjoining Wrangells main's harbor and a 2–block walk to downtown.

Old Sourdough Lodge, 1104 Peninsula Avenue; (800) 874–3613, www.akgetaway.com. Rustic lodge with comfortable accommodations.

Rooney's Roost Bed and Breakfast, 206 McKinnon Street; (907) 874–2026. Just a block from downtown.

Stikine Inn; (888) 874–3388, inn@stikine.com, or www.stikine.com. Wrangell's largest hotel, with thirty-three rooms, restaurant, and meeting rooms. One block from ferry terminal.

Wrangell Hostel, 220 Church Street; (907) 874–3534. Operated by the First Presbyterian Church mid-May through Labor Day.

PLACES TO EAT IN SOUTHEASTERN ALASKA

GUSTAVUS

A Bear's Nest Café;
(907) 697–2440,
www.freeyellow.com/members2/thebearsnest/. Features organic breads, soup, seafood, salad.

HAINES

Bamboo Room Restaurant and Pioneer Bar, near corner of Second and Main; (907) 766–2800, www.kcd.com/bamboo. Breakfast, lunch, and dinner, and full bar.

Chilkat Restaurant and Bakery, Fifth Avenue between Main and Dalton Streets; (907) 766–2920.

Fort Seward Lodge, Restaurant, and Saloon; (907) 766–2009. All-you-can-eat crab dinners in season.

JUNEAU

Armadillo Cafe,
431 South Franklin;
(905) 586–1880.
Tex-Mex cuisine.

Douglas Cafe,
918 Third Street;
(907) 363–3307.
Perhaps the only restaurant in Juneau that features amber clams and amber mussels; all that and (arguably) Alaska's best clam chowder, too.

Fiddlehead Restaurant and Bakery,
429 West Willoughby;
(907) 586–3150. Outside city center, but a local favorite.

Mike's Fine Food & Spirits;
(907) 364–3271.
Fine dining at affordable prices.

Westmark Baranof Hotel,
127 North Franklin Street;
(907) 586–2660,
www.westmarkhotels.com.
Fine dining in historic downtown Juneau.

KETCHIKAN

Annabelle's Famous Keg and Chowder House, 326 Front Street; (907) 225–9423.

PELICAN

Rosie's; (907) 735–2265. A Southeast Alaska institution among fishermen.

SKAGWAY

Olivia's at the Skagway Inn, Seventh and Broadway; (907) 983–2289, www.puffin.ptialaska.net/~sgyinn. A fine-dining experience. Pricey, but worth it.

WRANGELL

Hungry Beaver,
274 Shakes Street;
(907) 874–3005. Locally famous pizza; restaurant and lounge.

Canada's Yukon

S o, you may be asking, what is a chapter about part of Canada doing in an Alaska guidebook? Actually, there are a couple of reasons.

First of all, if you're driving from Southeast Alaska to Alaska's interior, you have to go through a small sliver of Canada's British Columbia and a big hunk of Canada's Yukon. From Haines or Skagway at the northern end of the Southeast Alaska ferry system, you can drive the 152-mile Haines Highway or 98 miles of the Klondike Highway to junctions with the Alaska Highway. From there your route lies northwesterly through Canada's Yukon Territory to the rest of Alaska.

Second, from the traveler's point of view, visiting Canada's Yukon is really part of the North Country experience. Aside from a few artificial differences, like Canada's metric road signs, or gasoline pumped in liters instead of gallons, you'll notice few distinctions between the Yukon and Alaska's interior region. Both are lands of rolling hills, majestic mountains, fish-filled lakes, and vast, untrammeled wilderness areas teeming with moose, caribou, bears, and wolves.

In both interior Alaska and the Yukon, you'll marvel at a sun that nearly doesn't set during the summertime, and in both you'll find friendly, helpful, outgoing folk who revel in their Native heritage, their gold rush past, and their present-day frontier lifestyle.

> ## Yukon Trivia
>
> *Work on the White Pass and Yukon Route railway began in 1898. By July 6, 1899, the rails topped the summit and reached Lake Bennett. The narrow-gauge railway connected Carcross and Whitehorse in June 1900, and on July 29, 1900, the golden spike was driven at Carcross, marking completion of the entire line.*

The main arterial road of the Yukon Territory is the Alaska Highway, referred to by many tourists—but few Alaskans or Yukoners—as the Alcan. (It's rather like calling San Francisco "Frisco." Everyone will know what you're talking about, but knowledgeable visitors will observe the local preference.) The fabled road begins at Dawson Creek in British Columbia, meanders through the Yukon Territory to the Alaska border, and ends at Delta Junction, Alaska—a total journey of 1,422 miles.

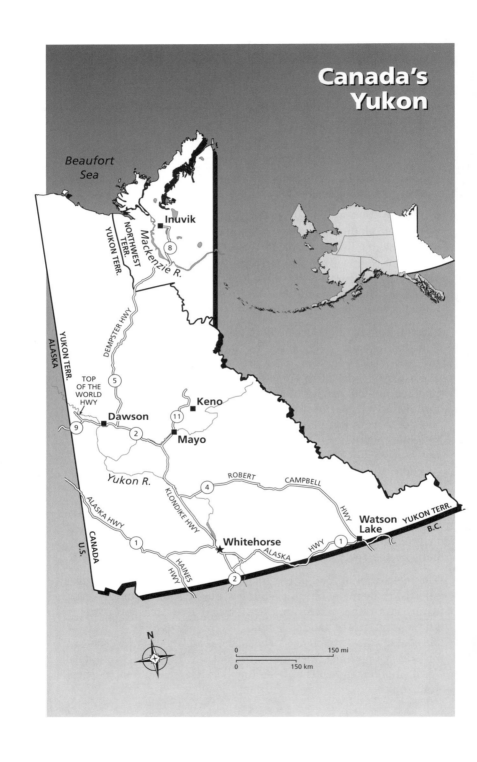

Canada's Yukon

CANADA'S YUKON

TOP 10 PLACES IN CANADA'S YUKON

Kluane Lake

Takhini Hot Springs

*Alaska Chilkat
Bald Eagle Preserve*

*Inn on the Lake
Bed and Breakfast*

Sign Post Forest

S.S. Klondike

Jack London's cabin

Eagle

Midnight Dome

Herschel Island

The two largest cities of the Yukon are White-horse, present-day capital of the territory, and Dawson City (not to be confused with Dawson Creek, B.C.). It was near the present site of Dawson City, in 1896, that the discovery of gold on a tributary of the Klondike River set off one of the world's wildest stampedes.

In both Alaska and the Yukon, you'll see numbers on frequent mileposts or kilometer posts beside the highways. These numbers represent miles or kilometers from a highway's beginning. Home and business addresses and even cities are often referenced in miles or kilometers. Whitehorse, for instance, is shown in a Yukon government guide-book as being located at kilometer 1,455.3 on the Alaska Highway. In this Canadian section of this book, we'll identify most sites by their kilometer post markings, although in discussing short drives and distances, we'll frequently refer to miles, since most U.S. residents have a better feel for mileage measurements. When, in the next chapter, we're back in Alaska, U.S.A., highway references will be in miles.

Here's a word of explanation about the layout of this chapter. It assumes you'll be traveling northerly through the Yukon to Interior Alaska either from Skagway (over the southern half of the Klondike Highway), Haines (over the Haines Highway), or Dawson Creek at the start of the Alaska Highway. So, to start with, the chapter discusses sights and options along each of these three northbound approaches to Whitehorse. After a discussion of things to see and do in Whitehorse, the chapter describes the northern portion of the Klondike Highway from near Whitehorse to Dawson City. After suggesting a round trip on the Dempster Highway from Dawson City to Inuvik in Canada's Northwest Territories, it deals—still Alaska-bound—with the Top of the World Highway north and west from Dawson City to the point where it crosses the border and meets Alaska's Taylor Highway. The Taylor, in turn, is described from northernmost Eagle to Tetlin Junction on the Alaska Highway, 80 miles northwest of the Alaska border.

Finally, the chapter backtracks to Whitehorse and lists your Alaska Highway options between that city and the point where you cross into Interior Alaska and the United States again. Of course, if you're departing Interior Alaska and heading southerly to southeast Alaska or Dawson Creek, British Columbia, follow the listings in reverse.

The Klondike Highway: Skagway to Whitehorse

Don't let the start of the **Klondike Highway** out of Skagway scare you. The first 10 or 11 miles climb at a pretty steep grade, from sea level to 3,000 feet plus, but after that the going's relatively level and certainly no worse than other mountain roads in the Lower Forty-eight and elsewhere. The road is two lanes wide, asphalt paved for its 98-mile (159-kilometer) length, and roughly parallels the historic Trail of '98 from Skagway to the Klondike gold fields. It rises from lush, thickly vegetated low country to high rocky mountain and lake terrain.

You come to **U.S. Customs** just beyond mile 6, but there's no need to stop unless you're southbound, heading for Skagway from Canada. The actual **U.S.–Canada border** lies just before mile 15. Advance your watch one hour, from Alaska to Pacific time. The Alaskan mileposts beside the road now become Canadian kilometer posts. You come to **Canada Customs** and the White Pass & Yukon Route's Fraser Station near kilometer 36. If you're northbound, you have to stop and check in with the Canadian authorities.

At kilometer 43, take the turnout to the east for a spectacular view of **Tormented Valley,** with its little lakes, stunted trees, and rocky landscape of big and little boulders. The historic remains of an ore-crushing mill for the **Venus Mine** can be seen and photographed at kilometer 84. Twelve kilometers farther there's a spectacular view of **Bove Island** and a portion of the Yukon's southern lakes system.

The community of **Carcross,** on the shores of Lake Bennett, lies at kilometer 106. Formerly called Caribou Crossing, the town has hotel accommodations, a general store, gas station, RV campground, cafe, and a **visitor reception centre** in the old White Pass & Yukon Train Depot (867–821–4431) where you can get tourist information— including, if you're into gutsy adventures, details about local skydiving lessons. This also is a good place to pick up maps and an Alaska ferry schedule.

If time permits, turn right at kilometer 107 and head northeast on the paved 34-mile Tagish Road to **Tagish,** Yukon Territory, then head south on the good, but mostly gravel 60-mile Atlin Road to **Atlin,** British Columbia. The drive takes a little more than two hours. Atlin is a favorite getaway for Southeast Alaskans, many of whom have summer cottages there. Atlin Lake is a huge, meandering, spectacular body of water with lots of recreational opportunities. In the community itself you can visit the **Atlin Historical Museum** in the town's original one-room schoolhouse. September through June the museum is open weekends; it's open daily in summer. Phone (250) 651–7522. While there, for a small donation you can tour the **MV Tarahne,** which once carried freight and passengers across Atlin Lake to Scotia Bay. Tours of the drydocked vessel are available at 3:00 P.M. daily during summer. Time your visit for Sunday and a brunch is served on-board. Phone (250) 651– 0076. Also worth noting in town is the cold, bubbly water at the mineral springs under the gazebo at the north end of town. You can rent motorbikes or houseboats, take flight-seeing excursions around the area, or engage a guide for excellent lake and stream fishing. The community has a hotel plus several B&Bs and inns, including **Noland House,** which can accommodate four guests in luxurious, historic rooms. The rate is $85 for a single, $95 for a double; call (250) 651– 7585. When you leave, you can avoid duplicating about a third of your route back to Carcross by joining the Alaska Highway at Jake's Corner (about 60 miles north of Atlin).

Happy Trails, an outdoors shop at the south end of Second Street, is the place to go if you want to go fishing or hiking in the area. Fishing licenses, gear, and tackle as well as maps and mountain bike rentals are available. Phone (250) 651–7662.

Back on the Klondike Highway, a few minutes' drive beyond Carcross lies **Frontierland Heritage Park,** a six-acre theme park with gold mining, live Dall sheep, an old-time trapper's cabin, the only mounted sabre-toothed tiger in existence, the world's largest mounted polar bear, plus a cafe and gift shop. On the same property, but in a separate building, is the **Museum of Yukon Natural History,** a privately owned collection of mounted Yukon wildlife in authentic dioramas. Admission to Frontierland is $4.00; admission to the museum

Yukon Quest Sled Dog Race: Held each February, this 1,000-mile race goes from Whitehorse to Fairbanks and reverses directions each year. (867) 668–4711; yukonquest@yknet.yk.ca.

Yukon Sourdough Rendezvous Festival: Held in late February in Whitehorse, this weird and wacky festival is designed to "combat cabin fever." (867) 667–2148; YSR@yukon.net; www. rendezvous.yukon.net.

Gertie's International Dart Tournament: Held every May in Dawson City. Drawing some of the world's best darters. Call the Klondike Visitors Association at (867) 993–5575.

Yukon International Storytelling Festival: Whitehorse, June. Put on by Friends of the Northern Storytelling Festival. Storytellers from around the circumpolar world. (867) 633–7550.

Yukon Gold Panning Championship: Held in July in Dawson City as part of Canada Day festivities. Call the Klondike Visitors Association at (867) 993–5575.

Fireweed Festival: In Faro each August. A horticulture show, triathlon, squash tournament, dance, and Yukon folk songs. (867) 994–2375.

is $4.00; combined admission is $6.50. Call (867) 821–4055 or e-mail frontier@yknet.yk.ca. Hours for both are 8:30 A.M. to 6:00 P.M. daily.

Here's a Yukon superlative for you—a "smallest," not a "biggest." At kilometer 111 you pass the *Carcross Desert,* at 260 hectares (640 acres), the smallest desert in the world. Glaciers and a large glacial lake originally covered the area, and when the glaciers retreated they left sand deposits on the former lake bottoms. The well-named *Emerald Lake,* nestled in the hills farther along at kilometer 120, is incredibly green and colorful, the subject of thousands of photo exposures each year.

At kilometer 157, 98 miles beyond its starting point at Skagway, this portion of the Klondike Highway junctions with the *Alaska Highway.* You're just a few minutes' drive south of Whitehorse. The northern portion of the Klondike Highway, which extends all the way to Dawson City, recommences just north of Whitehorse.

The Haines Highway: Haines to Haines Junction

The Haines Highway (which several Canadian publications call the Haines Road) runs 152 miles (246 kilometers) from the water's edge in Haines, Alaska, to Haines Junction on the Alaska Highway, west of Whitehorse. They're spectacular miles, sometimes paralleling the path of the old Dalton Trail to the Klondike. In the process they traverse thick green forests in the Chilkat Valley at lower elevations and high, barren, mystical plains once you've climbed over Chilkat Pass. Your travel log will record frequent views of piercing sawtooth mountains plus lakes that contain monster-sized trout. The road is two-lane, asphalt, and open year-around.

About 9 miles from Haines, you enter the *Alaska Chilkat Bald Eagle Preserve* where, in winter, thousands of American bald eagles gather to feast on the still-abundant salmon of the Chilkat River. If you want to stop, use pullouts and viewing areas about 10 miles farther down the road.

At mile 40 you'll arrive at *U.S. Customs,* but if you're Canada-bound you don't have to stop until you cross the *U.S.–Canada border* and come to *Canada Customs and Immigration* a couple of minutes farther on. (Remember, kilometer posts now replace mileposts in metric-minded Canada.)

You'll cross *Chilkat Pass* (elevation 1,065 meters; 3,493 feet) at kilometer

Yukon Facts

The Yukon Territory comprises 193,380 square miles.

The population of the Yukon Territory is approximately 33,500.

Herschel is the Yukon Territory's only island.

102 and come to **Million Dollar Falls Campground** at kilometer 159. There's pleasant camping and fishing here, and it's an excellent picnicking choice, even if you don't want to spend the night.

Approaching kilometer 188, you come to the **St. Elias Lake Trail,** a novice- and intermediate-friendly hiking trail through subalpine meadows. It's a 6⁴/₁₀-kilometer (4-mile-plus) trek that offers a good chance to spot mountain goats beyond the lake.

You have another camping and fishing opportunity at big, long **Dezadeash Lake** (pronounced DEZ-dee-ash), home to lake trout, northern pike, and grayling at kilometer 195.

At kilometer 202 you can hike **Rock Glacier Trail,** in **Kluane National Park,** a half-hour walk to the rocky residue of a former glacier and a panoramic view. Rock glaciers are a unique landform created when glacial ice and frost-shattered rock mix and flow downhill.

Haines Junction, Yukon Territory, lies at Haines Highway kilometer 246, nearly 153 miles from the road's start in Haines, Alaska. Whitehorse lies about 100 Alaska Highway miles east.

The Alaska Highway: Watson Lake to Whitehorse

Amazingly, the 2,233-kilometer (1,388-mile) **Alaska Highway** was constructed and connected in eight months and twelve days as a military road during World War II. Construction started March 8, 1942, and ended October 24; it was one of the most amazing road-building feats in modern history. The road, then and now, commences in **Dawson Creek, British Columbia,** originating at the huge, picture-worthy **Milepost 0 Monument,** on Tenth Street in downtown Dawson Creek. It ends at Delta Junction, Alaska. It's an asphalt road all the way, though the quality of the pavement varies, and you'll likely encounter gravel detours from time to time as road crews strive to improve the highway and your vacation experience.

The first major Yukon Territory (Y.T.) community you'll come to (and, therefore, our starting point in this book) is **Watson Lake,** at kilometer 1,021. The **Alaska Highway Interpretive Centre,** at the junction of the Alaska and Campbell Highways, is a good place to pick up the latest data on road conditions as well as visitor attractions in the area—including the mind-blowing *Sign Post Forest,* which started in this way: Back in 1942, the American soldier Carl K. Lindley of Danville, Illinois, one of thousands of U.S. servicemen constructing the highway, got homesick and erected a sign indicating the mileage back to his hometown. Others did the same, and a tradition took hold. Later, after the war, civilian motorists started driving along the road from the Lower Forty-eight states to Alaska, and they erected signs, too. Among the more than 27,000 signs there, you'll find one license plate, from Virginia, that reads AAW–7191. How do I know? I put it there.

Yukon Trivia

The 1,422-mile-long Alaska Highway, stretching from Dawson Creek, British Columbia, to Delta Junction, Alaska, was built in 1942 by the American military in a period of eight months.

Just beyond kilometer 1,162 you cross the Continental Divide, separating lands that drain into the Pacific Ocean from those that drain into the Arctic Ocean. Just off the highway at kilometer 1,294, you arrive in the mostly Native community of Teslin, originally a summer home for Tlingit Indians from Southeast Alaska and British Columbia. The *George Johnston Museum,* open from 9:00 A.M. to 7:00 P.M., houses the largest Tlingit Indian artifact collection in the Yukon. You'll see dioramas, rare historical photographs, George Johnston's 1928 Chevrolet, and many post-European and early Yukon exhibits. The museum honors Johnston, a Tlingit Indian who was born in 1884 and died in 1972. An expert photographer, Johnston brought the car, a first in these parts, to Teslin. Admission is $3.00 for adults. Phone (867) 390–2550, or visit www. yukonweb.com/community/teslin/museum.

Nine miles north of Teslin, at kilometer 1,306, *Mukluk Annie's Salmon Bake* (867–667–1200) serves up salmon and barbecued ribs, steaks, and pork from 11:00 A.M. until 9:00 P.M. There are also houseboat rides on Teslin Lake every evening at 8:00 P.M., free to salmon bake customers and guests at Mukluk Annie's motel there. *Jake's Corner* and access to the Atlin Road lies beyond kilometer 1,392; you come to Whitehorse city limits at kilometer 1,455, about 40 miles later.

Whitehorse is the Yukon Territory's "big city," a modern community of 27,850. It's home to about two-thirds of all the Y.T.'s residents and serves as its hub and transportation center. The town's origins lie in the construction of the White Pass & Yukon Route Railway from the ocean port of Skagway early in the century. Its economy today relies on government, trade, and tourism plus minerals and mining activity.

CANADA'S YUKON

If you're driving, make the *Yukon Visitor Reception Centre,* at kilometer 1,473.1 on the Alaska Highway, your first stop in the Whitehorse area. It's operated by Tourism Yukon and contains lots of good information and laser disk visuals, especially about Yukon national parks and historic sites. It's also one of your best sources for up-to-date highway data. Call (867) 667–2915. Located beside the centre is the *Yukon Transportation Museum* (867–668–4792), which features North Country transport, from dogsleds and stagecoaches to a WP&YR railcar replica and vintage aircraft. Admission is $3.00. Another source of visitor information, particularly for sites in and around Whitehorse, is the *Whitehorse Chamber of Commerce Information Centre* in town, at 302 Steele Street (867–667–7545).

Perhaps your best source of information, though, is Jeanette Bringsli at the *City of Whitehorse* at 2121 Second Avenue. She can tell you, practically off the top of her head, just about anything you want to know about Whitehorse, and she'll do it with a smile to boot. I hope she's still there when you visit. Phone (867) 667–6401, or visit www.city.whitehorse.yk.ca.

Not to be missed is the *MacBride Museum* (First Avenue and Wood Street; 867–667–2709; macbridemus@yknet.yk.ca), 5,000 rambling but fascinating square feet of artifacts, historic photographs, maps, and exhibits that cover the Yukon from ancient prehistory to the present. The real Sam McGee's cabin (of Robert Service fame) can be seen here, as well as horse wagons and steam engines. Admission is $4.00. The museum is open daily, in the summer, from 10:00 A.M. until 6:00 P.M.

The Bishop Who Ate His Boots

*T*he well-known Gold Rush story "The Bishop Who Ate His Boots" was the inspiration for the famous scene in Charlie Chaplin's movie The Gold Rush. *Lost at 40 below and out of provisions, Bishop Stringer decided to boil his and his companion's sealskin-and-walrus-sole boots for seven hours, then drink the broth. According to the bishop, it was "tough and stringy, but palatable and fairly satisfying." Bishop Stringer lost fifty pounds during the ordeal, but eventually found his way to a Native village, where he was nursed back to health.*

Everybody does a tour of the *S.S. Klondike,* the largest stern-wheeler to ply the Yukon River, and you should, too. It's located literally on the shores of the Yukon River, near the Robert Campbell bridge. The 210-foot ship was built in 1929, sank seven years later, but was refloated and rebuilt in 1937. It continued in service until the fifties. Now designated a National Historic Landmark, it's been restored to reflect one of the North Country's prime methods of travel during the late 1930s. Admission is $3.50. Call (867) 667–4511.

You'll probably never have a better chance to see Yukon wildlife than during a drive-through tour of the *Yukon Wildlife Preserve.* (Contact Gray Line at 867–668–3225.) In hundreds of acres of forests, meadows, and marshlands you can view caribou, elk, bison, moose, mountain goats, sheep, musk ox, mule deer, snowy owls, and rare peregrine falcons. Admission is $15. The *Yukon Conservation Society* sponsors free guided hikes around the Whitehorse area during the summer, providing an opportunity to learn about the unique northern flora and fauna as well as the natural history and geology of the land. Call (867) 668–5678 for schedules.

An interesting dining experience can be had at *Klondike Rib and Salmon BBQ* at Second Avenue and Steele Street downtown (867–667–7554). Here you can sample such exotics as Alaska salmon and halibut, Texas-style barbecue ribs, English-style fish and chips,

Stern-wheeler S.S. Klondike, Whitehorse

plus their specialty—arctic char, caribou, and musk ox.

For the traveler in search of art, the **Yukon Arts Centre,** at Yukon Place off Range Road (867–667–8575), offers a spectacular view plus the territory's largest art gallery, a theater, and an outdoor amphitheatre. There is no charge, but donations are accepted. The centre is open weekdays 11:00 A.M. to 5:00 P.M., and Sundays 1:00 to 4:00 P.M. A **Yukon Permanent Art Collection**—showing northern landscapes and lifestyles as portrayed by prominent Canadian artists—is displayed in the foyer of the Yukon Government Administration Building, on Second Street. Open weekdays only, 8:30 A.M. to 5:00 P.M.

June through August, escorted **Whitehorse Heritage Buildings Walking Tours** originate every hour on the hour, 9:00 A.M. to 4:00 P.M., Monday through Saturday at the Donnenworth House, 3126 Third Avenue. Phone (867) 667–4704. There is a $2.00 fee. If you can't join an escorted tour, pick up the self-guided "Walking Tour of Yukon's Capital" from local merchants.

You don't have to be Anglican (Episcopal) to visit the **Old Log Church** located a block off Main Street on Elliott Street and Third Avenue. The sanctuary building, constructed in 1900 for the Church of England, and the log rectory next door are rich in Yukon's history. Exhibits, artifacts, and relics tell the story of the Yukon's history from precontact life among aboriginal peoples to early exploration and beyond. Admission is $2.50. Tours are conducted Monday through Saturday, 9:00 A.M. to 5:00 P.M.; Sunday, noon to 5:00 P.M.

Takhini Hot Springs lies twenty to thirty minutes from downtown Whitehorse; don't miss it. You get there by driving roughly 9 miles north of the Yukon Visitors Reception Centre on the Alaska Highway, then nearly 4 miles north on the Klondike Highway to the Takhini Hot Springs Road. You then travel about 6 miles west to the well-marked springs area. This place offers some of the most pleasant soaking and swimming waters you'll find in the North Country as well as the opportunity to chat in really relaxing surroundings with Yukoners, Alaskans, and fellow travelers. Facilities here are fully modern, with changing rooms, showers, and a coffee shop on-site. If you're RV camping or tenting, plan to stay in the campground there. Activities, besides bathing and swimming, include hiking and horseback riding. The charge for the hot springs is $4.00; for camping, $10 to $12. For information call (867) 633–2706.

Another option just outside town is *Inn on the Lake Bed and Breakfast,* which is a unique and special place. If you don't want to just sit around during your visit, take advantage of the inn's complimentary golf passes, or go mountain biking, kayaking, canoeing, or wind surfing. There is a Jacuzzi suite and personal steam rooms, and, to top it all off, the food is great.

In town, there are many other options, among them *Historical House Bed and Breakfast,* originally built for none other than Sam McGee. The place features antique furniture, which is priceless and perfect for the setting. While there, be sure to converse with the proprietor, Bernie Phillips, who also happens to be the city councillor. Bernie will be glad to entertain you on his caribou horns—just ask. Rooms are $75 for a double in the summer. Phone (867) 668–3907.

Longtime Yukoners Carla Pitzel and Garry Limbrich operate *Hawkins House Bed and Breakfast* at 303 Hawkins Street, overlooking a city park and swimming pool. They describe their B&B as Victorian luxury, offering such amenities as a 1905 loveseat and bubble baths in a claw-foot tub when you stay in the Victorian Tea Rose Room and stained-glass windows of old Montreal in the French Room. There's a balcony view of Canyon Mountain and the paddle wheeler S.S. *Klondike.* Rates begin at $109 for a double. Call (867) 668–7638, e-mail cpitzel@internorth.com, or visit www.hawkinshouse.yk.ca.

If getting on the Yukon is your goal, the *Canadian Yukon Riverboat Family* tour offers day trips or cruises in a luxurious houseboat from Whitehorse to Dawson City. Gourmet meals are provided. Call (867) 633–4414.

Or for something a little more adventurous, there's *Go Wild Tours'* Gold Rush Raft and Float tours, which depart daily through scenic Miles Canyon. Daily hikes and Yukon artist tours also are available through Go Wild. Phone (867) 668–2411.

From Whitehorse, if you're driving, you have two choices for travel north and west to the main body of Alaska. You can continue on up the Alaska Highway, driving west and then northwest to Haines Junction, Kluane National Park, Beaver Creek, and the U.S. border, or you can drive northerly on the Klondike Highway to Carmacks, Minto, Stewart Crossing, and Dawson City, where you can connect with the Top of the World Highway to the Alaska border.

The Klondike Highway:
Whitehorse to Dawson City

The northern portion of the Skagway-to-Dawson City Klondike Highway starts at kilometer 1,487 on the Alaska Highway, about 9 miles beyond Whitehorse. The first major stop along the way is Carmacks, at kilometer 357. (Remember, kilometer posts show the distance from Skagway.) The community is historically important as a stern-wheeler steamboat stop on the Yukon River route between Whitehorse and Dawson City. *Experience Yukon Inc.* in the Carmacks Hotel will take you through Five Finger Rapids, a scenic, splashy, fun experience. It's a six-hour round-trip for three persons at $100 each. Call (867) 863–6021 for information about this and overnight tours, canoe rentals, or pike and lake trout fishing or e-mail expyukon@yknet.yk.ca. At kilometer 380.5 you can see the rapids from an observation deck built as part of the Five Finger Rapids Day Use Area of trails and picnic sites.

For campers or picnickers, the Yukon government's *Minto Landing Campground,* located at the end of a short road that meets the Klondike Highway at kilometer 431.3, is situated right on the grassy banks of the Yukon. An old abandoned log cabin on the site is particularly picture worthy. Overnight camping costs $8.00. Phone (867) 667–5340.

At kilometer 537 you come to *Stewart Crossing,* where you have the opportunity to take a side excursion (about 150 miles round-trip) over the *Silver Trail* through scenic woods and water country to the mining communities of *Mayo, Elsa,* and *Keno City.* If you plan to overnight here, the Yukon government *Five Mile Lake Campground,* just east of Mayo, offers generous campsites, kitchen shelters, launch sites, a swimming beach, and an obstacle course where kids can work off energy. The charge is $8.00 per night. *Country Charm Bed and Breakfast,* near the same lake, offers a quiet country setting, biking, and hiking. The rate for doubles is $55. Call (867) 996–2918, or e-mail swood@klondike.com.

The *Mining Museum* at Keno City is a particular delight, with displays that vary from old-time mining equipment to baseball uniforms the local teams wore. There's no admission charge. Hours are 10:00 A.M. to 6:00 P.M. If the museum piques your prospecting interests, drive down Duncan Creek Road south of Keno City for a guided tour of Duncan Creek Gold-dusters. There, you'll also be able to try a little gold-panning of your own.

Back on the Klondike Highway at kilometer 715, a few minutes before you arrive in Dawson City you come to a private RV park and gold-panning

The Rush Is On

George Washington Carmack is credited with discovering gold at Bonanza Creek, setting off the great rush north for Klondike gold.

It was in 1896 that Carmack and two brothers, Tagish Charlie and Skookum Jim, went looking for gold in the Klondike region. Another prospector, Robert Henderson, reported good color on Gold Bottom Creek but said he didn't want any "Siwashes" (Jim and Charlie were Indians) on Gold Bottom.

So the three partners went looking for their own creek and staked Rabbit Creek, soon to be known as Bonanza Creek. Their strike was the richest in North America and made them wealthy men. They shared their bounty without dispute. They didn't tell Henderson of their discovery, and he did not share in the riches.

area with the unlikely name of *GuggieVille.* If you're interested in panning for Yukon gold, you can do it here on the massive dredge tailings of the former Guggenheim mining camp. Call (867) 993–5008.

The high point (literally) of a Dawson City visit comes when you drive the Dome Road from its junction at Klondike Highway's kilometer 717 to the top of *Midnight Dome* for a panoramic view of the city, the Yukon and Klondike Rivers, the Bonanza gold fields, and the Ogilvie Mountains. Awesome.

Dawson City, of course, is where it all began— the frenzied, frantic, fabled stampede for North Country gold. It started in 1896 when George Carmack, Skookum Jim, and Tagish Charlie found "color"—lots of it—in a Klondike River tributary called Rabbit Creek, later renamed Bonanza Creek. The rush catapulted into international prominence when the vessel *Portland* steamed into Seattle on July 17, 1897, and the *Seattle Post-Intelligencer* screamed "Gold! Gold! Gold!" in its banner headline. A "ton of gold" was proclaimed in the story that followed. The rush was on.

Tens of thousands of gold seekers (most of them ill prepared and without the slightest concept of the rigors they would face) crowded aboard almost any boat that would float out of West Coast ports and headed for Skagway and the White Pass, Dyea and the Chilkoot Pass, St. Michael on the Yukon River, or any of a number of other gateways to the Klondike. Their common goal was Dawson City and the rich gold country around it. It's said that 100,000 gold seekers set out for the Klondike. Some 30,000 made it.

Today the rush to the Klondike continues, but it's a vastly more comfortable odyssey. Travelers come not to extract riches but to see the place where all the excitement happened. Thanks to eleventh-hour rescue restorations by the national and territorial governments, Dawson City looks remarkably as it did a near-century ago, when it sprang up on the Yukon River shores. Old buildings and landmarks were saved from certain rot and destruction, including the magnificently refurbished 1899 *Palace Grand Theatre* and *Diamond Tooth Gertie's,* where you can legally gamble away your "poke" at real gaming tables as many a prospector did in '98. At the historic old *1901 post office,* at Third Avenue and King Street (open noon to 6:00 P.M.), your first-class letters and postcards will be canceled the old fashioned way—by hand. Collectors can purchase special commemorative stamps.

Before beginning a foray to any of these sites, it's probably wise to stop by Tourism Yukon's *Dawson Visitor Reception Centre,* at Front and King Streets (867–993–5566), to get oriented. While you're there, take time to view some Yukon attractions on laser video disk players and maybe even take part in one of the free *Dawson City walking tours* that originate at the site several times daily. If you plan to extend your trip to Inuvik and Canada's Northwest Territories via the Dempster Highway, cross the street from the Dawson reception centre and get highway and other information from the *Northwest Territories Information Centre* (867–993–6167).

At *Jack London's cabin* near Grant Street and Eighth Avenue, you can take part in interpretive tours, daily at 1:00 P.M., that showcase London's cabin that was discovered in the Yukon wilderness. The structure was carefully disassembled, and half the logs were used to re-create the writer's cabin at its present site in Dawson City. The other half went into the construction of an identical cabin at Jack London Square in Oakland, California. Admission is $3.00. At Eighth Avenue and Hanson you'll find the *Robert Service cabin* where poetry is recited at 10:00 A.M. and 3:00 P.M. daily. The cabin is open 9:00 A.M. to noon and 1:00 to 5:00 P.M. Admission is $6.00.

> ## Yukon Facts
>
> *The Yukon Territory's Mount Logan, at 19,550 feet, or 5,959 meters, is Canada's highest mountain.*
>
> *The Yukon Territory's official flower is fireweed.*
>
> *There are about 250 active mines in the Dawson gold fields.*

For a really in-depth look at Dawson's history, visit the old *1901 Territorial Administration Building,* where the Dawson City Museum and Historical Society houses its collection of gold-rush era artifacts, paleontological remains, cultural exhibits of the Han Native people, even a collection of narrow-gauge steam locomotives. There are also vintage film showings and lectures. Admission is $4.00. Call (867) 993–5291, or e-mail demuseum@yknet.yk.ca.

For some real adventure while you're in Dawson City, contact Sebastian Jones and Shelly Brown for their *40-Mile Dog Tours,* a true North

Country experience. They're so far off the beaten path, you should reach them by mail, P.O. Box 666, Dawson City, Yukon YOB1GO, Canada.

Likewise, Leo Boon's **Big Bear Adventures** offers day trips, rentals, and multiday camping, bicycling, and paddling trips that showcase this beautiful part of the country. Seven-day bicycling trips start at $1,050. Canoeing on the Snake River for seventeen glorious days is $3,650, or try the Yukon River for eight days at $1,195. This historic river journey will give you a feel for what the gold stampeders experienced. Kayaking and hiking trips also are featured. Call (867) 633–5642, or e-mail bear@yknet.yk.ca.

Bear Creek, a gold mining industrial complex of some sixty-five buildings that operated from 1905 to 1966, is now open for visitors. Parks Canada interpreters, under the auspices of Klondike National Historic Sites, conduct guided tours daily. The complex, open 9:30 A.M. to 5:00 P.M. daily, is located about 6²/₁₀ miles east of Dawson City. Visitors are greeted in the former general manager's residence, and during the course of a tour they see an intact blacksmith shop and the Gold Room, where the precious metal was cleaned, melted down, and cast into bullion. Mining artifacts include a Keystone prospecting drill, a large turn-of-the-century steam-operated water pump, and a hydraulic monitor. Admission to Bear Creek is $5.00. E-mail the complex at Daw_info@pch. gc.ca.

It's not far off the beaten path (in fact, it sits on Front Street and First Avenue, on the banks of the Yukon between King and Queen Streets), but it's a must-see if you value restored historical artifacts. We're referring to the **Steamer Keno,** built in 1922 in Whitehorse for service between Stewart City and Mayo Landing. It's typical of the breed of shallow-draft riverboats that served the North Country from early gold-rush times until well into the twentieth century.

The largest wooden-hull, bucket-line gold dredge in North America—old **Gold Dredge #4,** two-thirds the size of a football field long and eight whopping stories high—can be seen south of town near the spot where it ceased operations in 1960. The site is beside Bonanza Creek off Bonanza Creek Road, about 7⁸/₁₀ miles south of the Klondike Highway. About 2¹/₂ miles farther south you'll find **Discovery Claim** (and a monument to mark the spot) on Bonanza Creek, where George Carmack, Skookum Jim, and Tagish Charlie made their history-making discovery.

At the **Dawson City Bed and Breakfast,** at 451 Craig Street, you're situated in a quiet, beautiful setting overlooking both the Klondike and Yukon Rivers. Breakfasts are full service. The owners will pick you up at the airport, bus, or waterfront if you don't have your own wheels. Rates are $85 for a double with a shared bath, $95 for a private bath. Call (867) 993–5649, e-mail dawsonbb@dawsoncity.net, or visit www.yukon. net/dawsonbb.

White Ram Manor Bed and Breakfast is within walking distance of most Dawson City attractions. Look for the pink house at Seventh Avenue and Harper Street. Accommodations include full breakfasts, use of kitchen facilities for other meals, a hot tub, barbecue, and picnic area. Rates start at $85. Call (867) 993–5772, e-mail accomodations@dawsoncity.net.

Another option is the newly built **Bonanza Gold Motel and RV Park**, with fifty-two service sites and fifteen suite rooms with Jacuzzi. The establishment is 1 mile from the city center by the Klondike River bridge. The motel restaurant, **Blackbird Bistro,** specializes in tasty Mexican cuisine and is open in summer. Call (867) 993–6789, e-mail accomodations@dawsoncity.net, or visit www.yukon.net/bonanzagold/.

If you've got a computer handy and want to search for your own lodging options, a good site to check out is the **Northern Network of Bed and Breakfasts,** at www.nnbandb.com. The site keeps track of more than fifty bed-and-breakfasts in the Yukon and beyond, and it is updated daily.

Dredge No. 4

*H*uge, earth-devouring machines once chewed their way up and down the creek beds of the Yukon River valley, gobbling up everything in their paths, right down to bedrock, processing it all in their complex innards, and spitting out mounds of rubble behind them. Their trails can be traced across the valley floors like giant worm tracks 50 feet high.

The dredges all are gone save one. Dredge No. 4 is now a Parks Canada Historic Site. This 3,000-ton monster made three passes up and down the valley, averaging 22,000 grams a day.

In 1960 it sank and was neglected for thirty-two years.

In 1992 it was resurrected, and today you can tour its rusting interior. There were seventy-two buckets, each weighing two and one-half tons, in a continuous chain that pulled material up from the creek bed and dumped it into the dredge's internal gold-sluicing works. Those who remember when it was in operation say that the vibration of the dredge in action was so great that it could be heard 11 miles away and felt 9 miles in any direction.

A nice day trip from Dawson City is the one-and-a-half-hour **Yukon River Cruise and Pleasure Island narrated tour,** which includes the Dawson waterfront, Han' Native village at Mooshide, a sled dog exhibit, and complimentary coffee. You can choose between a cruise-only option and a two-and-a-half-hour all-you-can-eat king salmon barbecue and cruise to the island. Call (867) 993–5482.

When you're ready to leave Dawson City, you have three driving choices. You can retrace the Klondike Highway south to the place just outside of Whitehorse where it meets the Alaska Highway, then continue north on the Alaska Highway to the main body of Alaska. Or you can take the Top of the World Highway to the place at the Alaska border where it meets the Taylor Highway, which, in turn, also connects with the Alaska Highway in Alaska. Or you can keep going north and west via the Dempster Highway to Inuvik, in the Mackenzie Delta, not many miles from the shores of the Arctic Ocean. (Of course, when you've made it to Inuvik, you have to turn around and drive back the way you came. The Dempster doesn't meet or loop with any other highway.)

The Dempster Highway: Dawson City to Inuvik

The **Dempster,** the third choice, definitely deserves consideration. It stretches 741 kilometers (460 miles) from its starting place about 41 kilometers (25 miles) south of Dawson City on the Klondike Highway. It ends in **Inuvik,** Northwest Territories, surely one of the most literally colorful communities in North America, with almost every hue of the rainbow represented on homes and buildings.

Along the highway you pass sometimes through valleys bounded by great granite mountains, at other times over high flat plains, with rolling hills in the distance. Sometimes your route is the legendary trail of the valiant North West Mounted Police who patrolled the region by dogsled in the days before the highway was built.

Accommodations and service stations are rare along most of the route, so top off your tank every chance you get. Halfway to Inuvik, you come at kilometer 364 to Eagle Plains and the **Eagle Plains Hotel and Restaurant,** which offers thirty-two comfortable rooms, groceries, vehicle services, gas, and a restaurant that serves the tastiest, most satisfying sourdough pancakes this side of the Canadian border. Take the time to examine the display of historic photos on the walls of the restaurant.

They tell the tragic story of the Mounties' "Lost Patrol" in 1910 and of Inspector W.J.D. Dempster's finding and retrieval of their frozen bodies. Other pictures relate the murderous exploits of the "Mad Trapper of Rat River" and the manhunt organized against him in 1932. The Mounties, as always, got their man. Rooms cost $99 to $121. Call (867) 993–2453.

At kilometer 403 you cross the **Arctic Circle** (take pictures of the monument), and at kilometer 471 you leave the Yukon Territory, and enter the Northwest Territories. From now on, kilometer posts show the distance from this point. At kilometer 86, turn off the highway to visit the nearby community of **Fort McPherson.** You can fill up on gasoline as well as visit the church graveyard where the hapless Lost Patrol members lie buried. Also, if you're in the market for a backpack, duffel bag, or an attaché case, visit the **Fort McPherson Tent and Canvas** factory. The workmanship is first rate, and almost certainly no one in your hiking club back home will have one with the company's distinctive emblem. Call (867) 952–2179 for information.

At kilometer 269 and the community of **Inuvik,** don't fail to visit the igloo-shaped **Catholic Church.** Igloo-shaped? It sounds hokey, but the effect when you see it is breathtaking, and the paintings inside, created by Inuvialuit painter Mona Thrasher, are more than inspirational. Take

Igloo-shaped Catholic Church, Inuvik

time to see, as well, **Ingamo Hall,** a log friendship center with a great hall that has the feel of a baronial mansion.

If you'd enjoy an Arctic country setting for your overnight accommodations, consider the **Arctic Chalet,** a B&B lakeside home and cabins. Olav and Judi Falsnes offer simple but nutritious breakfasts and complimentary canoes. (Caution: Saturday check-ins must be prearranged.) Rates begin at $85 for a double and $80 for a single. The Web address is www.yukonweb. com/tourism/arctic-chalet. Call (867) 777–3535. If you're camping, go to the **Chuk Campground,** about 2 miles from town on the Airport Road. Its hilltop location presents a worthwhile view of the Mackenzie Delta, and its breezes tend to discourage mosquitoes. Rates are $12 for a primitive campsite and $15 with electric hookup.

For the really ultimate in far north travel, fly to **Herschel Island,** off the Arctic Coast about 150 miles to the northwest (a Yukon territorial park, but accessible from Inuvik) for wildlife viewing as well as a look at the native Inuvialuit culture from prehistory through the nineteenth-century whaling era. Several air carriers offer the trip. You also can arrange your trip through **Arctic Nature Tours,** which offers nature, cultural, adventure, and custom tours by plane and boat. Visit the village of Tuktoyaktuk on the Arctic Coast, or go fishing on the Mackenzie River. Phone (867) 777– 3300, e-mail arcticnt@permafrost.com, or visit www.arcticnaturetours.com.

The Top of the World Highway: Dawson City to the Alaska Border

ack to Dawson City and the second choice mentioned earlier, driving on the **Top of the World Highway** to the Taylor Highway. Yes, that's the official name of the road. It begins with a free car ferry ride over the Yukon River and heads west toward the Alaska border and Alaska's Taylor Highway for 127 kilometers (79 miles). The road, you'll find, really lives up to its name. Much of the time you're on ridge tops looking down on deep valleys. Lots of good scenic photo ops here. It's a good gravel road, but slippery in heavy rains. About 105 kilometers (66 miles) beyond Dawson City, you'll cross the U.S.–Canada border. Stop at the United States border station if you're heading westerly for Alaska and at Canada Customs and Immigration if you're eastbound for Dawson City.

The Taylor Highway: Jack Wade Junction to Eagle and Teltin Junction

W e're now going to talk about part of Alaska again, even though this chapter deals largely with the Canadian Yukon. Travel on the Taylor Highway is so logically connected with the Top of the World Highway from Dawson City, it just doesn't make sense to have you jump pages into other sections of the book.

At *Jack Wade Junction,* where the Taylor and the Top of the World Highways meet, turn north on the Taylor Highway and drive 65 miles to visit *Eagle,* a small but historically important community in the Alaska scheme of things. Still standing is the **Wickersham Courthouse** where Judge James Wickersham dispensed frontier justice during Eagle's gold rush days early in the century. Still intact as well are the old Waterfront Customs House, a military mule barn, water wagon shed, NCO (noncommissioned officers) quarters, and other structures that were part of old Fort Egbert. The federal Bureau of Land Management (BLM) has renovated and restored portions of the old fort where, incidentally, Captain Billy Mitchell once served a tour of duty. The Eagle Historical Society (907–547–2325; EHSmuseums@aol.com) conducts daily tours of the community, starting at 9:00 A. M. at the courthouse. The cost is $5.00. You can visit the National Park Service headquarters for the *Yukon–Charley National Preserve* (907–547–2233; pat_sanders@nps.gov) on the banks of the Yukon near Fort Egbert. Staffers will show you a video about the national preserve and answer any questions.

> **Yukon Trivia**
>
> *About 3 percent of the Yukon Territory is covered by wetlands, a much lower percentage than the rest of the country. The Yukon's inland waters comprise 1,792 square miles, or 4,481 square kilometers.*

Gray Line of Alaska's luxury river vessel **Yukon Queen** operates between Eagle and Dawson City, Yukon. The company transports passengers between Eagle and Anchorage or Fairbanks by motor coach. Call (800) 544–2206 for details. The **Kathleen,** operated by Upper Yukon Enterprises, offers Yukon and Porcupine River luxury sight-seeing expeditions. Call (907) 547–2254.

After your Eagle visit, backtrack south on the Taylor Highway to Jack Wade Junction. The distance from Jack Wade Junction to Tetlin Junction, and the Alaska Highway, is about 96 miles. When you've gone about 30 of those miles, around mile 66, slow down and look for *Chicken.* No, this isn't a joke; it's a town . . . sort of. It's said the community got its name because the miners back in the gold rush days couldn't spell *ptarmigan,* which some called an Alaska chicken anyway. The original mining camp is now abandoned private property and is closed to general traffic. If you turn off the Taylor Highway at the Airport Road, you'll come to the *Chicken Creek Cafe,* known for its pies and baked goods and the gathering place from which tours depart daily at 1:00 P.M. for old Chicken. Nearby you'll find the *Chicken Saloon* and *Chicken Mercantile Emporium,* where you can buy a Chicken hat, a Chicken pin, and, naturally, a Chicken T-shirt. *Chicken Discount Gas and Propane* gives you yet another opportunity to keep your gas tank full.

The Taylor Highway ends (or begins, depending on which way you're traveling) at Tetlin Junction, mile 1,302 on the Alaska Highway, where there's lodging, food, and gas if you've perilously coasted in without buying fuel on the Taylor Highway.

The Alaska Highway: Whitehorse to the Alaska Border

Back in Canada's Yukon and beyond Whitehorse about 90 miles lies Haines Junction, at the junction of the Haines Highway from Haines, Alaska, and the Alaska Highway at kilometer 809. The community calls itself the Gateway to Kluane. Kluane (pronounced clue-AW-nee) is the Yukon's biggest lake. Its namesake, *Kluane National Park* (867–634–7250; kluan_info@pch.gc.ca; www.harbour.com/parkscan/ kluanel), is one of the preeminent wilderness national parks of North America.

Especially for the hiker, mountain climber, canoe enthusiast, kayaker, and river runner, Kluane National Park is a place to spend days, not hours. To get oriented, visit the park's *visitor reception centre,* about $2/10$ mile east of the junction with the Haines Highway and just off the Alaska Highway. There you'll see an international award–winning audiovisual presentation about the park, and you'll be able to pick up information about long and short hiking trails and canoe-kayak routes. Summer hours are 8:00 A.M. to 8:00 P.M. daily; call (867) 634–2345.

At *Kluane Helicopters,* you can take a flight-seeing tour over the park or get really adventurous and go heliskiing or helihiking. Phone (867) 634–2224.

For a double treat, stay at *Dalton Trail Lodge,* at Dezadeash Lake bordering the park. The rooms are luxurious, and the double treat comes at dinner time with scrumptious Swiss cuisine. Meals and accommodations are $100 per person. Overnight adventure and fishing packages are $1,110 and $1,300, respectively. Phone (867) 667–1099, or e-mail richard@yknet.yk.ca. The Web address is www.yukonweb.com/tourism/dalton/.

The Yukon River and its tributaries drain almost one-third of Alaska.

If you just need a quick place to camp, the *Cottonwood RV Park and Campground* is a good choice. It's right on the road, but I'll always have fond memories of the place after spending a beautiful July Fourth camped overlooking Kluane Lake, when a rainbow seemed to shine right in the tent. Cabin rentals also are available. Phone the Mobile Operator at 2M3972, Destruction Bay Channel, or call (867) 634–2739. E-mail rwilson@yknet.yk.ca or visit www.yukonweb.com/tourism/cottonwood.

About 35 miles beyond Haines Junction, at kilometer 1693, the Sias family (six generations of Yukoners) operate *Kluane Bed and Breakfast.* Accommodations are heated A-frame cabins with mountain views, showers, cooking facilities, and a beach. Expect full family-style breakfasts here with pancakes and the Siases' own farm-fresh eggs. To call contact the Whitehorse Mobile Operator 2M3924 on Destruction Bay channel.

At the *Sheep Mountain Visitor Centre,* kilometer 1706.8, you can frequently spot a herd of Dall sheep on the nearby slopes. An interpretive trail leads to Soldier's Summit, which was the site of the opening ceremony for the Alaska Highway on November 20, 1942.

The Bayshore Lodge and Oasis Restaurant, at about kilometer 1712, offer an unexcelled pristine setting (and a giant lakeside hot tub) on the shores of Kluane Lake. The Bumbleberry pie in the restaurant is legendary. Call owners Jim Stocco and Shirley Steele at (867) 841–4551.

At the village of Burwash Landing, kilometer 1061.5, the *Kluane Museum of Natural History* (867–841–5561) contains major new natural history exhibits featuring wildlife of the region as well as Indian artifacts, costumes, and dioramas. Admission is $3.00.

Here's another North Country travel superlative: *Beaver Creek,* at kilometer 1,934, is Canada's westernmost community. Tourism Yukon's *visitor reception centre* features a special display of wildflowers and dispenses tons of visitor information especially for visitors entering Canada from Alaska. The *Beaver Creek Canada Customs and Immigration Office* at kilometer 1,937.5 is a required stop for visitors entering Canada. At kilometer 1,967.5 you arrive at the *Canada–U.S. border.* Set your clocks back an hour (from Pacific to Alaska time), and start thinking again in miles and gallons.

PLACES TO STAY IN CANADA'S YUKON

DAWSON CITY

Aurora Inn, Fifth Avenue and Harper Street; (867) 993–6860.

Bonanza Creek Motel and RV Park, (867) 993–6789; www.yukon.net/bonan-zagold. One mile from the city center by the Klondike River bridge.

Dawson City Bed and Breakfast, 451 Craig Street; (867) 993–5649, www.yukon.net/dawsonbb.

White Ram Manor Bed and Breakfast, Seventh Avenue and Harper Street; (867) 993–5772, www.yukon.net/WhiteRam.

Westmark Inn Dawson City, Fifth Avenue and Harper Street; (800) 544–0970, www.westmarkhotels.com.

EAGLE PLAINS

Eagle Plains Hotel and Restaurant, kilometer 364 Dempster Highway; (867) 993–2453.

HAINES JUNCTION

Dalton Trail Lodge, (867) 667–1099; www.yukonweb. com/tourism/dalton. Bordering Kluane National Park.

Cottonwood RV Park and Campground, kilometer 1717 Alaska Highway; (867) 634–2739, www.yukonweb.com /tourism/cottonwood.

INUVIK

Arctic Chalet, (867) 777–3535; www.yukonweb.com /tourism/arctic-chalet. Lakeside B&B home and cabins within walking distance of downtown.

MAYO

Country Charm Bed and Breakfast, (867) 996–2918; www.nnbandb.com. Five miles north of Mayo and close to Five Mile Lake. Open May 15 to September 15.

WHITEHORSE

Hawkins House Bed and Breakfast, 303 Hawkins Street; (867) 668–7638, www.hawkinshouse.yk.ca.

Historical House Bed and Breakfast, 5128 Fifth Avenue; (867) 668–3907.

Inn on the Lake Bed and Breakfast, 20 miles outside Whitehorse. Call the chamber of commerce at (867) 667–7545 for details.

Westmark Klondike Inn, 2288 Second Avenue; (867) 668–4747, www.westmarkhotels.com.

PLACES TO EAT IN CANADA'S YUKON

CHICKEN

Chicken Creek Cafe, Airport Road (around mile 66 Taylor Highway). Known for pies and baked goods.

DAWSON CITY

Blackbird Bistro, (867) 993–6789; www.yukon.net/ bonanzagold. Great Mexican food. One mile from the Klondike River bridge.

EAGLE PLAINS

Eagle Plains Hotel and Restaurant, kilometer 369 Dempster Highway; (867) 993–2453. Great pancakes; halfway to Inuvik from Dawson City.

HAINES JUNCTION

The Oasis Restaurant, kilometer 1712 Alaska Highway; (867) 841–4551. On the shores of Kluane Lake.

TESLIN

Mukluk Annie's Salmon Bake; (867) 667–1200. Nine miles north of Teslin.

WHITEHORSE

Klondike Rib and Salmon BBQ, Second Avenue and Steele Street; (867) 667–7554. Alaska salmon and halibut, Texas-style barbecue ribs, English-style fish and chips, arctic char, caribou, and musk ox.

Southcentral Alaska

More than half the population of Alaska lives, works, and plays in Southcentral Alaska, a region of magnificent glaciers, big lakes (one of them even named Big Lake), forests, fertile river valleys, and many of the tallest mountains in North America. Brown (grizzly) bears, moose, Dall mountain sheep, mountain goats, and wolves thrive hereabouts, and, happily, you'll find no small number of hiking trails and vehicular back roads that offer access for viewing these creatures in their native terrain.

Fact is, there are more miles of asphalt highways, marine highways, byways, airways, and railways in Southcentral than in any other portion of the state. In square miles the region occupies perhaps a fifth of the mainland mass of Alaska. In shape Southcentral Alaska is a roughly 250-mile-deep arc of land and waters bordered on the south by the Gulf of Alaska, on the north and west by the curving arc of the Alaska mountain range, and on the east by the Canadian border—except at the very bottom, where the Southeast Alaska panhandle comes up to join the main body of Alaska.

Before the arrival of Europeans in the eighteenth century, this region and Alaska's interior were the domain of mostly Athabascan Indians, a tough, resourceful people who lived by hunting moose, caribou, and bear as well as lesser game and birds. They harvested fish from saltwater shores and freshwater streams. Among their many skills was working in leather, sometimes richly adorned with beads fashioned from hollow porcupine quills and other natural materials. Those skills survive today, especially in the form of colorful decorative beadwork—greatly prized by visitors and residents alike—sewn onto moccasins, vests, and other leather goods.

> ## Southcentral Alaska Trivia
>
> *The first hint of Alaska's rich gold reserves was uncovered by Russian mining engineer Peter Doroshin, who discovered gold on the Kenai Peninsula in 1850.*

Southcentral's modern history began in 1741 with the arrival of Russians sailing for the czars (Vitus Bering and Alexei Chirikov), followed by the

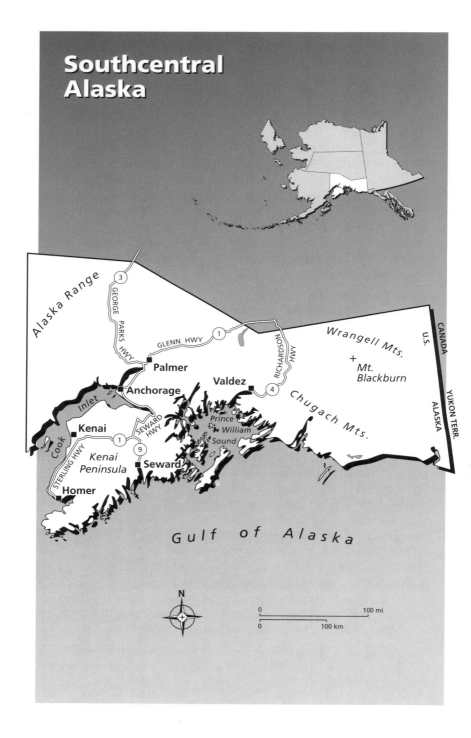

Southcentral Alaska

Alaska Range

GEORGE PARKS HWY

③

GLENN HWY

①

RICHARDSON HWY

④

Wrangell Mts.

+ Mt. Blackburn

Palmer

Valdez

Chugach Mts.

Anchorage

Cook Inlet

SEWARD HWY

Prince William Sound

Kenai

①

Kenai Peninsula

⑨

Seward

STERLING HWY

Homer

CANADA

U.S.

YUKON TERR.

ALASKA

Gulf of Alaska

N

0   100 mi

0   100 km

**TOP 10 PLACES IN
SOUTHCENTRAL ALASKA**

Homer

Halibut Cove

Resurrection Trail

*Clam Gulch State
Recreation Area*

*Captain Cook State
Recreation Area*

Swanson River Canoe Trail

Hatcher Pass

Prince William Sound

Tony Knowles Coastal Trail

Matanuska Glacier

English (Captains James Cook and George Van-
couver) and other Europeans in the 1800s. After
the Alaska Purchase of 1867, Americans came
sporadically to the region seeking gold and other
resources. But it was not until 1915 and the beginning of construction of the Alaska Railroad from
Seward to Fairbanks that the area began to come
into its own. Anchorage—a city created as construction and managing headquarters for the
line—came into being. It later boomed, especially
during and after World War II, when military
installations swelled the population. In recent
years the development of Alaskan petroleum
resources has created additional growth in
Anchorage and other communities.

Visitors find the weather surprisingly mild in this region of Alaska.
Around Anchorage, for instance, summertime temperatures range in
the comfortable mid-sixties and seventies. Thanks to the sheltering
heights of the Alaska Range, wintertime temperatures usually hover
between ten and twenty-five degrees—above zero—although they
occasionally plunge to twenty or more degrees below. Whenever you
come, be prepared for an extraordinary vacation in this part of Alaska.
It teems with opportunities both on and off its major roadways.

Anchorage

S ince Anchorage is the transportation hub of Southcentral Alaska,
this chapter treats it as the hub, as well, for planning trips in the
region. After first describing the city and its immediate environs the
chapter describes the water world and marine highway routes of Prince
William Sound to the southeast, the more southerly highways (including the Seward and the Sterling) of the Kenai Peninsula, then the highways (George Parks, Glenn, and Richardson), which head northerly
toward Denali National Park and other points in interior Alaska.

Anchorage is Alaska's "Big Apple," a large (for Alaska) metropolitan, cos-
mopolitan community of oil executives, college professors and students,
business and transportation managers, tradespersons, artists, and no
small number of working stiffs who keep the wheels of all this commerce turning. Curiously, Anchorage is Alaska's largest Native village as
well; thousands of Indian, Eskimo, and Aleut Natives have chosen to live
and work in Alaska's largest city.

Anchorage is also the transportation hub of Alaska. Jet flights go and come at Anchorage International Airport from every region of Alaska, from the other states of the United States and from Asia and Europe. The state-owned Alaska Railroad headquarters here and extends southerly to Seward, on Resurrection Bay, and Whittier, in Prince William Sound, and north to Denali National Park and Fairbanks. Three major state highways begin in or near Anchorage: the Seward Highway to the Kenai Peninsula, the Glenn Highway to Tok and the Canadian border, and the George Parks Highway to Denali National Park and Fairbanks. Off these arterials you'll find scads of lesser roads that lead to remote villages, near–ghost towns, backwoods lodges, and lots of wilderness terrain for exploring, fishing, photography, and fun.

First, within Anchorage itself: Number-one stop on any offbeat traveler's itinerary should be the *Alaska Public Lands Information Center,* at Fourth Avenue and F Street downtown (907–271–2737; www. nps.gov/aplic/center). Housed in the old Anchorage Federal Building, circa 1939, the center contains scores of really helpful state and federal exhibits, videos, wildlife mounts, transportation displays, and even a trip-planning computer to assist in organizing your travels. Once you have finished there, head diagonally across the street to the Anchorage Convention and Visitors Bureau's *log cabin visitor information center* (907) 274–3531. Within the cabin's main room, as well as in the adjacent downtown center, you'll find friendly local volunteers and tons of printed material to assist you in planning your stay in the city. Visit the visitors bureau Web site at www.anchoragecvb.net.

By all means, ask for the visitors bureau's excellent free visitor's guide, which contains more than one hundred pages of tourist information, including a better-than-average walking tour of the downtown vicinity. Among more than two dozen sites noted are the *Alaska Railroad Depot* and old locomotive *Engine Number 1,* built in the early 1900s and used in constructing the Panama Canal as well as the Alaska Railroad; *Elderberry Park* and the *Oscar Anderson House,* the city's first (1915) wood frame home, open for viewing; and *Oomingmak Musk Ox Producer's Coop,* where you can see and purchase garments made from Arctic musk ox qiviut (pronounced KEE-vee-ute), the softest yet warmest wool-like material on earth.

Anchorage is a great place to be if you're an aviation buff. At 4721 Aircraft Drive, near the International Airport, is the *Alaska Aviation Heritage Museum,* which includes twenty-five rare, historical bush planes and dozens of photographs and memorabilia exhibits. While there, you can watch aircraft being restored, view a bush-plane pioneer

TOP ANNUAL EVENTS IN SOUTHCENTRAL ALASKA

Fur Rendezvous: *This yearly February winter event in Anchorage gets cabin-weary Alaskans out and about. Featuring sled dog races, carnival rides (yup, even in the winter) and canning, cooking, baking, brewing, arts and crafts competitions, and more. For information contact (907) 274–3531 or www.anchoragecvb.net.*

Iditarod Trail Sled Dog Race: *As Alaska's state sport, dog mushing is celebrated with the premier sled dog race, the Iditarod, the first weekend of every March. The ceremonial start to this 1,049-mile-plus race begins in Anchorage. For information contact (907) 376–5155, iditarod@iditarod.com, or www.iditarod.com.*

Kachemak Bay Wooden Boat Festival and **Kachemak Bay Shorebird Festival:** *Usually held in conjunction with each other, these May festivals showcase two groups common to Homer–varied and beautiful birds and hand-crafted and well-kept wooden boats. The boat festival is held on Homer's spit, while the bird-watching takes place across the community. For information contact (907) 235–7740 or www.xyz.net/~homer.*

Mount Marathon Race: *Spend July Fourth in Seward watching the best of the best race to the top of Seward's backdrop, Mount Marathon, then back down again in this grueling, tough-as-nails event. Accompanied by festival booths, food, and fireworks. For information contact (907) 224–8051 or chamber@seward.net.*

Alaska State Fair: *The state's largest fair in the heart of farm country, Palmer, in the Matanuska Valley. Held each September, the fair includes carnival rides, arts and crafts booths, animal exhibits, giant vegetables, quilting and canning competitions, and more. For information contact (907) 746–5000, info@alaskavisit.com, or www.alaskavisit.com.*

film, and even take a vintage seaplane ride for $50. This also is an excellent place to watch Anchorage's many seaplane pilots come and go from the largest floatplane base in the world, **Lake Hood**. Admission is $5.75 for adults and $2.75 for children. For more information call (907) 248–5325.

Speaking of unique flying opportunities, a local airline, **Era Aviation,** offers a Nostalgic Air Cruise aboard an elegant, fully equipped DC-3. This truly unique experience takes you back to the '40s, while you pass over some of Alaska's most beautiful sights. Flight attendants are dressed in period costumes, and they serve you champagne in glass stemware or, if you prefer, Classic Coke or other beverages. Your front seat pocket will have vintage magazines, and the piped-in music will be that of the big-band era. The price for this air adventure is $139 per person, with a 7:00 P.M. departure time. If you like a most-different experience, don't miss it. Call (800) 866–8394 (or 907–266–8394 locally) for more information.

The **Tony Knowles Coastal Trail** (named after former Anchorage mayor and now Alaska governor Tony Knowles) merits special mention. This wide asphalt trail starts at the west end of Second Avenue and follows the meandering shore of Cook Inlet for 10 scenic miles around woods, inlets, and lakes to **Kincaid Park.** Best of all, the Coastal Trail connects along the way with other segments of Anchorage's outstanding network of bike and pedestrian paths. Ask for a trail system map at the visitor center.

Although downtown Anchorage is brimming with shops touting the best buys and most unique pieces in Alaska Native arts, the best place to find truly artistic works of art is at the gift shop in the newly constructed **Alaska Native Medical Center,** off the corner of Tudor Road and Bragaw Street. It's not within walking distance of downtown, but a trip there will be worth the time and effort. Artists from the **Alaska Native Arts and Crafts Association** sell their wares there from 10:00 A.M. to 2:00 P.M. Monday through Friday and the first Saturday of every month. The medical center itself is a work of art; while there, peruse the hallways for a free art tour. Call (907) 729–1122 for more information.

The **Anchorage Museum of History and Art,** at Seventh Avenue and A Street also has a small shop with tasteful, authentic art objects for sale. The gift shop number is (907) 343–6195. The museum is one of Anchorage's showcases, so it's not very off the beaten path, but a visit to the city isn't complete without checking it out. The museum's exhibits on Alaska history, flora, and fauna, as well as its art exhibits, rival those of metropolitan areas. For more information about the museum, call (907) 343–6173.

Another very Alaskan shopping opportunity exists in the open-air **Saturday Market,** staged each week in summer at the Lower Bowl parking lot at the corner of Third Avenue and E Street. You can pick up made-in-Alaska arts and crafts, antiques, fresh produce, fish, and garage sale items. Hours run from approximately 10:00 A.M. until 6:00 P.M. No charge for admission.

The **Fort Richardson Alaskan Fish and Wildlife Center,** located in Building 600 on the Fort Richardson Military Reservation accessible off the Glenn Highway about 7$\frac{1}{2}$ miles northeast of town, isn't just for soldiers and their families. You, too, can view some 250 mounts of Alaska wildlife, including bears, moose, caribou, sportfish, birds, and other critters. The center is open

---

Southcentral Alaska Trivia

Eagle River, which flows 9 miles north of Anchorage, heads at Eagle Glacier and was named in 1916. Before that, miners and trappers called it Glacier River and Sitk Creek. Before that, Alaska Natives called it Yukla-ina. Today a thriving community lies along the banks of Eagle River, about 15 miles north of Anchorage.

year-round, with free admission. Call (907) 384–0431 for hours. The *Elmendorf Wildlife Museum,* which has 200 game and bird species, is at the Air Force base north of the city and similarly opens its doors to the public in Building 4–803. To reach the base turn north on Reeve Boulevard from the Glenn Highway, about 7/10 mile from the highway's start at Medfra Street. Turn right on Post Road and proceed to the base entrance. The hours are noon to 5:00 P.M. Friday and 3:00 to 4:45 P.M. Tuesday through Thursday. For information call (907) 552–2282.

One of the best things the Alaska legislature ever did was set aside *Chugach State Park,* nearly half a million acres of wild and wondrous mountain valleys and alpine country, right smack dab next to Anchorage. From numerous gateways along city roads and state highways, you'll find access to gentle and tough trails to hike, lakes to fish, rivers to kayak or canoe, and wildlife to see and photograph. Among the latter are moose, Dall mountain sheep, mountain goats, plus brown (grizzly) and black bears. For maps and more information, call (907) 345–5014.

You'll find Anchorage one of the most pleasant communities in Alaska to be hungry in. For dinner it's almost impossible to beat *Marx Brothers,* located downtown in one of Anchorage's oldest houses, at 627 West Third Avenue. It can be pricey (entrees range from $15 to $35), but where else will you find the likes of Alaska halibut in macadamia nut crust with coconut curry and mango chutney? Phone (907) 278–2133. If your taste buds run to Greek or Italian cuisine, try *Villa Nova Restaurant,* at 5121 Arctic Boulevard (907–561–1660).

You can devour great hamburgers at the *Arctic Roadrunner* from two locations: 2477 Arctic Boulevard (907–279–7311) and 5300 Old Seward Highway (907–561–1245). For chicken done fast and right, the *Lucky Wishbone,* at 1033 East Fifth Avenue (907–272–3454), is a favorite among Anchorage folk.

You absolutely, positively cannot miss the best pizza this side of the Mississippi at Anchorage's *Moose's Tooth Pub & Pizzeria,* named after one of Denali's more-treacherous-looking ridges. You can order everything from a halibut pie to a Popeye, a spinach-laden special, to a traditional meat-lover's favorite. This is my all-time favorite place to go (the

Caesar salad is especially delicious) because the pizza's fresh, the beer is home-brewed and the atmosphere is kid-friendly, yet adult-oriented. This is a favorite among locals, and it's usually crowded at peak times, so come early if you can. The restaurant is in a tricky location, at 3300 Old Seward Highway, but it's worth the trip. For more information call (907) 258–2537.

Gwennie's Old Alaska Restaurant is sort of outrageous, but it, too, is a favorite among locals for breakfast, lunch, and dinner. The big, rambling structure features lots of historical photos and relics on the walls and a menu that features Alaskan reindeer omelettes, smoked salmon, and king crab. Prices are moderate. It's located at 4333 Spenard Road. Phone (907) 243–2090.

Visitors often feel intimidated by the place and pass it by, but if you want to rub elbows (literally) with Alaskans in a frontier saloon setting, drop by ***Chilkoot Charlie's,*** Anchorage's best known watering hole. Called Koot's by the locals, it's located at 2435 Spenard Road. Forget reservations. Just come out, and they'll shoehorn you in somehow. Phone (907) 272–1010.

Alaska state and federal employees stretch their per diem dollars in Anchorage by staying at the small (thirty-eight rooms) ***Voyager Hotel*** downtown, at 501 K Street. The ample rooms each have a queen-size bed and a couch that makes up into a twin, full kitchen facilities, and TV. They serve fresh complimentary coffee in the lobby each morning. To stay at the Voyager, you'll need reservations almost any time of year. Call (800) 247–9070 or (907) 277–9501.

In the alternative-lodging category, you'll find no shortage of options in the Anchorage area. Here are a few of my favorites:

My husband and I had our wedding reception at the breathtakingly beautiful ***Alaskan Frontier Gardens Bed and Breakfast*** in South Anchorage. This spacious cedar-wood home offers comfortable rooms, a full breakfast, an eight-person hot tub, and lots of Alaska artifacts to look at in the main living room. The landscaping on this three-acre pine-studded lot looks like it came out of a magazine. Hanging baskets adorn the large porches, and colorful gardens adorn the entire lawn. Hostess Rita Gittins promises that you'll love your stay. Rooms start at $100 in the summer. For more information check out www.AlaskaOne.com/akfrontier, or e-mail afg@alaska.net. Phone (907) 345–6556.

Downtown is the wonderful ***Earth Bed and Breakfast,*** operated by Netherlands-born Margriet van Laake, who, by the way, speaks six

Southcentral Alaska Trivia

Anchorage's Lake Hood is the busiest seaplane base in the world. During summer as many as 800 take-offs and landings can take place in a single day.

Pop singer Jewel grew up on her family's homestead near Homer, on Kachemak Bay.

languages! Her rooms are comfortable and the rates are reasonable, starting at $79 in the summer. The sunny garden is tastefully landscaped, and the bed-and-breakfast is conveniently located close to the downtown area and bike paths. Margriet also operates **Earth Tours,** an agency with an emphasis on hiking, canoeing, and camping. Call (907) 279–9907, or visit www.AlaskaOne.com/earthtrs on the Web. Margriet's e-mail is earthtrs@alaska.net.

And now, for one of the most unique places to stay and, I might add, most fun, try Angie and Tom Hamill's **Birch Trails Bed and Breakfast** at 22719 Robinson Road in the Anchorage bedroom community of Chugiak. I say "most fun" because at the Hamills place you can meet dogs—lots of dogs, Alaskan huskies, in fact, true sled dogs. And being a musher myself, I'm pretty partial to sled dogs. The Hamills offer their entire downstairs to guests, and it is complete with private entrance, two bedrooms, shared bath, stocked kitchenette, game and exercise area, library, and deck with hot tub and views of the Chugach Mountains. Besides great meals they also offer hiking, river rafting, and fishing packages. The other part of their business is **Birch Trails Sled Dog Tours.** If you're traveling in the winter, you can join the Hamills and their twenty-seven dogs to get a taste of the state sport—sled dog mushing. See how the dogs live, romp, and play, and learn how to harness the dogs and ride the runners. The Hamills offer everything from 2-mile rides to half- and full-day rides as well as Learn to Mush programs. Call (907) 688–5713, or e-mail thamill@micronet.net.

Anchorage International Hostel, at Seventh Avenue and H Street (practically downtown), is quite large for Alaska, but since Anchorage is the travel hub for most of the state, its ninety-five beds fill up early. Reservations are a must; request them by mail from 700 H Street, Anchorage 99501. Bring your own sleeping bag if you have one; otherwise you can rent one. There are showers, a kitchen, sitting rooms, storage, and phones. The hostel is wheelchair accessible. The rate is $16 per night for members; $19 for nonmembers. For information call (907) 276–3635 or e-mail hipat@servcom.com.

Two other hostels operate out of Anchorage: the **International Backpackers Inn/Hostel,** at 3601 Peterkin Avenue (907–274–3870), and **Spenard Hostel International,** at 2845 West Forty-second Place (907–248–5036, spnrdhstl@alaskalife.net). Reservations are recommended at both places.

Remember the Coastal Trail that was mentioned earlier? One of the best ways to see the trail is by bicycle, and one of the best places to rent a bicycle is right downtown, only 5 blocks from the trail. **Downtown Bicycle Rental** offers hybrid, mountain, touring, and children's bikes for $12 for up to three hours and $15 for five hours. You'll get a free lock, helmet, and map of Anchorage's extensive trail system. The shop is at the corner of Fifth Avenue and C Street. Phone (907) 279–5293.

Here's another quality bike tour, this one offered by **Alaskan Bicycle Adventures.** They call it Bicycle Alaska, and it is an eight-day, eight-night adventure through some of Alaska's most beautiful country. There are six days of cycling, with an average of 65 miles per day, and the trip is topped off with a cruise in the glacier-studded Prince William Sound. The cost for this adventure is $2,445. If you want an equally long trip, but with a little less pedaling and a little more variety, try the **Hike and Bike Alaska** package, also priced at $2,445. In this trip you'll take daily hikes, canoe trips, or river raft floats, and you'll cycle an average of 15 miles on four of the trip's eight days. This trip, too, is topped off with a Prince William Sound cruise. For more information on this and other options, call (800) 770–7242, e-mail bicycle@alaskabike.com, or visit www.alaskabike.com.

If you're a winter fan, Anchorage can be particularly fun. Organized sled dog races take place virtually every January and February weekend at the Tozier Sled Dog Track on Tudor Road. And nobody, but nobody, fails to feel the excitement when the biggest winter sled dog racing events of the year roll around in February and March.

First is the **Anchorage Fur Rendezvous,** staged in mid-February. This "Mardi Gras of the North" runs through two weekends and includes the World Championship Sled Dog Race, which begins and ends right downtown on Fourth Avenue. Literally thousands of cheering Alaskans line the way. The "Rondy" also features some rather outrageous activities among its hundreds of scheduled events, including an outhouse race, featuring privies being pushed and pulled on skids. Another riotous event is a canoe race—down the icy slopes of a hill since all the water in the area is long since frozen over. There are also snowshoe obstacle races put on by senior citizens, snow machine races, ice sculpting competitions, Eskimo blanket tosses, a grand parade, dances, Native crafts fairs, and outdoor fur auctions. Call (907) 277–8615 for more details.

Several tour companies have created tours built around the Fur Rendezvous as well as Alaska's premier sled dog race, the 1,049-mile **Iditarod Trail Sled Dog Race,** running from Anchorage to Nome on the

Bering Sea. *Alaska Sightseeing/Cruise West* offers a seven-day, six-night package that culminates with the start of the Iditarod. Other features include visits to the Iditarod Trail Museum, excursions around Anchorage and Turnagain Arm (including Portage Glacier), the Matanuska Valley, and the Iditarod Trail Mushers banquet. Prices start at $995 per person, double occupancy. For details call (800) 666–7375 or (907) 276–1305, or visit www.alaskatravelstore.com.

Far North Tours offers several ways to experience the Iditarod, including a $60 Iditarod Restart tour that takes clients out to the official race restart at Wasilla, in the Matanuska Valley. (The downtown Anchorage start is largely ceremonial.) The company also offers a $195 Fly the Iditarod Trail tour. It includes an Alaska bush plane trip to Skwentna, one of the official checkpoints along the trail. Most ambitious is a seven-day affair that includes the Mushers banquet, the start in Anchorage and restart in Wasilla, the bush plane trip to Skwentna, plus a personal dogsled tour. It costs $1,500, double occupancy. Call (800) 478–7480.

Prince William Sound

Curious thing about Prince William Sound. It took the nation's all-time most awful oil spill—the *Exxon Valdez* disaster of 1989—for most people to learn about one of the continent's most gorgeously pristine regions. The vessel, you'll recall, went aground on Bligh Reef, ruptured its hull, and spilled more than 11.3 million gallons of North Slope crude oil onto more than 1,500 miles of coastline. The deadly pollution, killing uncounted thousands of birds and sea mammals in its path, extended as far as the Alaska Peninsula, 600 miles away. Yet there's some good news. Although the sound will continue to suffer from subsurface oil contamination for decades to come, from a visual perspective it has largely recovered. Myriad glaciers, islands, and mountains await visitors aboard huge cruise ships, tiny kayaks, day boats, and state ferries. Whales of several species spout, roll, and sound in the waterways. Hundreds of thousands of birds again inhabit the trees and cliffside rookeries throughout the region. Bears wander along otherwise deserted beaches. Mountain goats frolic high (but visibly) on the peaks overhead.

As in Southeast Alaska, Prince William Sound's communities are not connected by road, but many who live there consider that a virtue. Actually, you can drive to the sound by first taking the Seward Highway from Anchorage to Portage, then piggybacking your car aboard the Alaska Railroad's short shuttle through mountain tunnels to Whittier (although a road to Whittier, currently under construction, may soon

Southcentral Alaska Facts

Between 1911 and 1938, one billion tons of copper were mined from the Kennecott Copper Mine.

The northernmost rain forest in Alaska is in Girdwood, about 26 miles south of Anchorage on the Seward Highway.

The largest king salmon taken with sportfishing tackle weighed 97 pounds, 4 ounces and was caught by Les Anderson in the Kenai River in 1985.

The highest mountain in the Chugach Mountain Range is Mount Marcus Baker at 13,176 feet. It is located at the tips of Matanuska and Knik glaciers.

change this scenario). For particulars see the Seward Highway, in the Kenai Peninsula section. Or you can drive on portions of the Glenn and Richardson Highways to Valdez. Cordova, the third of Prince William Sound's three principal communities, can't be reached by regular highway, but the state ferry *Bartlett* regularly calls there as well as at Whittier and Valdez. Call (800) 642–0066 for more information.

Here's a rundown on these towns: **Whittier** is principally a jumping-off (rather, a sailing-off) place. The community, in reality, comprises an excellent dock and wharf area, a few waterfront buildings and—dominating the scene—two very tall and prominent buildings (that are skyscrapers by Alaska standards) called Begich Towers and the Buckner Building. The U.S. Army built the structures during World War II to house servicemen and their families stationed at the site. Today the fourteen-story Begich Towers has been converted into condos and about half the population of Whittier lives there. The Buckner Building is now vacant. Another building, Whittier Manor, houses a good share of the rest of Whittier's residents.

The **Alaska Marine Highway System** operates the state ferry *Bartlett* between Whittier and Valdez during the summer. Rates vary depending upon length of your vehicle. Passenger rates can be obtained by calling the ferry system at (800) 642–0066 or by visiting www.akms.com/ferry. *Take note:* Grab a book and a cup of coffee when making this call. The phone is forever tied up, and "the next available operator will be with you momentarily." Try to arrange these reservations well in advance. Commercial tour operators also operate between the two communities. Stan Stephens Cruises is one worth noting. Stephens offers the opportunity for an overnight at Growler Island in a permanent tent camp. (See "Valdez," in this section, for more details.)

If you don't plan to drive your car aboard the ferry for Valdez, don't bring it to Whittier on the rail shuttle. There's really no place for you to drive it there. On the other hand, if you'd enjoy a really different circle trip from Anchorage, drive your car aboard the shuttle train, bring it aboard the ferry to Valdez, then disembark for a drive up the Richardson and Glenn Highways back to Anchorage, or stay on the Richard-

all the way to Fairbanks. If time permits, take the *Bartlett* ferry all the way to Cordova before disembarking at Valdez. The highway ferry trip, of course, works either direction.

From the Port of Whittier, several cruise and charter operators offer round-trip day cruises of the sound or one-day excursions from Whittier to Valdez. Captain Brad Phillips operates his deluxe catamaran **Klondike Express** daily in these waters, into numerous coves and bays and past dozens of glaciers. Captain Phillips calls this tour Twenty-six Glaciers in One Day, but you'll actually see many more. The chances of spotting whales, mountain goats, and other wildlife are excellent. For information about this tour, priced at $119 from Whittier, call (800) 544–0529, visit www.26glaciers.com, or e-mail phillips@alaskanet.com. *Major Marine Tours* packages an all-you-can-eat salmon dinner cruise from Whittier to Blackstone Glacier and back. The price is $89 per person. Call (800) 764–7300 for information, or visit www.majormarine.com.

Sound Adventure Charters operates Dude Fishing trips, which feature a hands-on commercial seine fishing experience aboard the 50-foot FV *Pagan.* Guests actually help with several salmon sets as well as check crab and shrimp pots. When the trip is over they take generous shares home. The cost is $500, plus $90 for an Alaska state commercial fishing license. The company's $150 per person Blackstone Glacier Day Cruise includes hot tubbing among icebergs as well as sight-seeing and sport-fishing. For details about these and other trips, call (907) 783–3153 or e-mail soundadv@customcpu.com.

Now about **Cordova.** For travelers who enjoy "untouristy" destinations, it is a great little place for poking around, mixing with the locals, exploring on one's own. Now mostly a fishing and fish-processing town, Cordova had its start as the saltwater port for shipping copper ore brought down on the Copper River & Northwestern Railway from the Kennecott mines.

You can drive about 50 miles to the face of one of Alaska's most accessible drive-up glaciers, *Childs Glacier,* on the Copper River Highway, east of town. You can also cross the historic *Million Dollar Bridge* (if you're game; it's been only "temporarily" fixed and sort of slanty ever since the 1964 Alaska earthquake) for a view of *Miles Glacier* as well. Childs Glacier, separated by a stream from the elevated, excellent U.S. Forest Service interpretive center there, is extremely active. If you wander down to the stream level and the glacier calves off a big hunk of ice, run for higher ground. The surge wave can be sizable and dangerous. On the drive out from town, keep your eyes alert for bears. Other sights along the way: beaver dams, picturesque marshlands, lakes and mountain vistas, silver salmon spawning streams, and trumpeter swans.

The **Reluctant Fisherman Inn** at 407/501 Railroad Avenue (complete with a photogenic mermaid sculpture) is located downtown, overlooking Cordova's busy harbor. The restaurant features locally caught seafood, and if you didn't bring wheels, you can rent a car there. The rate for a double with a harbor view is $115, and economy rates start at $75. Call (800) 770–3272, e-mail reluct@ptialaska.net, or visit www.cordova.ak.

Southcentral Alaska Trivia

The largest oil spill in U.S. history occurred on March 24, 1989, when the Exxon Valdez, *under the command of Captain Joseph Hazelwood, struck Bligh Reef in Prince William Sound and leaked more than 11.3 million gallons of North Slope crude oil into the sea.*

Cruises aren't too hard to come by when you're in a coastal community; the key is finding the one that's perfect for you. And if you happen to be a birder, this cruise, aboard the **Discovery Voyage,** is just right. Dean Rand, captain/naturalist of the twelve-passenger, 65-foot yacht *Discovery,* offers one of the finest wilderness cruises in Alaska. His was the first wilderness cruise to be offered in Prince William Sound, and it remains a popular ecotourism-oriented adventure today. The *Discovery* originally was built for the Presbyterian Missions service to the Native communities in Southeast Alaska and today is fully renovated to house passengers comfortably and enjoyably.

Trips aboard the *Discovery* range from a nine-day spring birding expedition for $2,200 to a seven-day fall whale-watching tour for $2,050. These are great times of the year to travel, Rand says, because you'll have the water practically to yourself—as long you don't mind sharing with thousands of seabirds, shorebirds, and whales. Rand also offers five- and seven-day packages, starting at $850. He carries kayaks and skiffs for landing parties, and the yacht is complete with private rooms, hot showers, and sumptuous food (including fresh seafood harvested on the trip). For more details call (800) 324–7602, e-mail info@discoveryvoyages.com, or visit www. discoveryvoyages.com.

The city of **Valdez** (Alaskans say "Val-DEEZ") calls itself the Switzerland of Alaska. Actually that's not too far off the mark. The range of Chugach Mountains that arch behind and around the city are certainly in a class with the Alps. But Valdez has at least one attribute the Swiss can only dream of—an ocean view of fish-filled waters and forested islands.

The town boasts at least one additional distinction. The 800-mile **Trans-Alaska Pipeline** from Prudhoe Bay, in the Arctic, terminates here in a major, 1,000-acre terminal operated by **Alyeska Pipeline**

Service Company. Alyeska loads more than a million gallons of crude oil daily onto huge oceangoing tankers docked at the site. For a two-hour bus tour of the facility, call Valdez Tours at (907) 835–2686. The cost is $15.

A good starting point for any visit to Valdez is the *visitor information center* (907–835–4636; valdezak@alaska.net; www.alaska.net/~valdezak) at 200 Fairbanks Drive downtown. You can view films about the 1964 Good Friday earthquake, which all but destroyed much of the old town near the water, and you can pick up a map showing the present location of historic homes from Old Valdez. Many were relocated when it was determined the old sites were no longer safe for occupancy. Nearby, at Chenega Street and Egan Drive, is the *Valdez Museum* (907–835–2764; vldzmuse@alaska.net; www.alaska.net/~vldzmuse/index.html), where exhibits range from slot machines to gold rush gear and a restored 1907 fire engine.

Operating vessels both from Valdez and from Whittier, *Stan Stephens Cruises* offers several cruising options, including some with a bountiful midcruise salmon, halibut, and chicken feast in the big dining hall on *Growler Island,* facing Columbia Glacier. Other trips offer overnights at Stephens's comfortable camp of large heated tents on the island. Depending on the cruise you take, excursions also sail past a shoreline gold mine, Bligh Reef, intriguing little bays and inlets, long silvery waterfalls cascading from high mountain cliffs, bears onshore, and whales, sea lions, and sea otters in the water. The last trip we took, on Stevens's *Nautilus II,* we saw three of the latter swimming peacefully at dockside before our trip even got under way. The company's cruise to and from Valdez, with one night on Growler Island, costs $188.50. For information call (800) 992–1297, or visit www.princewilliamsound.com. E-mail is ssc@alaska.net.

If you're into people-powered water sight-seeing, *Anadyr Adventures* of Valdez (800–865–2925; anadyr@alaska.net; www.alaska.net/~anadyr) provides deluxe charter boat–supported kayaking trips to remote and awesome parts of Prince William Sound. Trips range from one to ten days and can accommodate novices as well as expert paddlers. Three-hour local trips start at $59 a person, overnight excursions at around $275 per day, including transportation to the kayaking site and meals.

If you've traveled this far into Alaska and still haven't taken a river rafting trip, this may be the place to do it. Valdez-based *Keystone Raft and Kayak Adventures* (907–835–2606 or 800–328–8460; www.

alaskawhitewater.com; keystone@alaska.net) provides five trips daily down the nearby Lowe River through high-walled Keystone Canyon. The company also offers one-day floats through Class III and Class IV whitewater on the Tonsina River, four days on the Talkeetna River, five on the Chitina and Copper Rivers in the Wrangell Mountains, and kayak trips on waters around the state. Rates vary from $35 on the Lowe River to $1,150 for four to five days on the Tana River.

The Kenai Peninsula

Deep in the bowels of the Alaska Historical Library in Juneau resides a rare and treasured second edition of Jonathan Swift's *Gulliver's Travels,* an account written in 1726 about fictional Lemuel Gulliver's adventures in Lilliput, a nation of little people, and in Brobdingnag, the land of giants. What is especially intriguing about the book for Alaskans is Swift's map of Brobdingnag—a huge land mass extending westward from northern North America.

Remember that Vitus Bering and Alexei Shelikof, the men who discovered Alaska while sailing for the Russian czars, did so in 1741. The second edition of Swift's book is dated MDCCXXVII–1727, fourteen years before the Russian voyages of discovery. Yet Swift's map bears a resemblance (some say a close resemblance; others say, not really) to Alaska, complete with a little stretch of land that could be the Kenai Peninsula, extending from Southcentral Brobdingnag.

The comparison becomes more intriguing still when you realize that in modern Brobdingnag/Alaska roam many of North America's "most giant-sized" creatures, including record-sized brown (grizzly) bears, even bigger polar bears, and large concentrations of mammoth whales and walrus in adjacent seas. In addition, on the peninsula noted both in Swift's book and in modern guides, you can see and photograph huge moose.

The Kenai, probably more than any other locale, is where Alaskans themselves play and recreate. Lake, river, and saltwater fishing is superlative. Hiking trails are widespread and wide ranging. Moderate-sized and tiny communities offer traditional homespun Alaska hospitality. Access is easy by highway, rail, and air from Anchorage.

Because the Kenai is much used by Alaskans, particularly from Anchorage, it's wise to avoid weekend and holiday visits, when traffic on the only road access from Anchorage, the Seward Highway, can be horrendous.

Most of the time, however, the 127-mile asphalt road is more than pleasurable as it skirts saltwater inlets, circles around big and little lakes, and penetrates thick, vast forest expanses. It richly deserves its prestigious designation by the U.S. Forest Service as a National Forest Scenic Byway.

The Seward Highway: Anchorage to Tern Lake Junction

ollowing are some of the sight-seeing opportunities along the several highways that serve the peninsula, starting with the 127-mile **Seward Highway,** south of Anchorage. The Seward Highway mileposts you see along the side of the road, incidentally, measure the distance from Seward. So the parking area at Potter Marsh at mile 117.4, for instance, is 117^4/$_{10}$ miles from Seward and 9^6/$_{10}$ miles from Anchorage.

All along the highway, be on the lookout for wildlife, especially moose. The Kenai is home to a national wildlife refuge, and the abundant moose population is the reason for it. At mile 117.4 and at mile 116 you'll see turnoffs for **Potter Marsh,** a state wildlife refuge where you can view extensive waterfowl, shorebirds, arctic terns, and American bald eagles plus king, pink, and silver salmon. A boardwalk crosses the marsh. Between mileposts 106 and 110 on the Seward Highway, look frequently to the craggy tops of the rocky cliffs that rise from the road. If you look carefully, more often than not you'll spot mama **Dall mountain sheep** and their youngsters staring curiously down at you. Do not, of course, stop your car on the highway; there are several turnoffs where you can safely stop then walk back for easy viewing. In fact, if you are on the road for sight-seeing purposes, please respect your fellow travelers and obey the frequent signs asking slower vehicles to pull over. It is the law to pull over if more than five vehicles are behind you.

If you collect unusual critters to log in your life book of wild animals, stop at **Beluga Point,** at mile 110.3. Here, if you're just a little bit lucky, you may see the small white beluga whales that congregate in these waters. The best viewing is probably around high tide. At low tide the point is also a good place to witness a tidal bore. (See below.)

Bird Creek State Campground, just past mile 101, is not only a pleasant place to camp or picnic; it also provides one of the better vistas for watching one of Alaska's more spectacular natural phenomena—the **Turnagain Tidal Bore** that comes rushing through Turnagain Arm at low tide daily. Get a tide book (free at many service stations, sporting goods stores, and banks), and check the times for low tide at Anchorage. Then, to get the correct time for the Bird Creek overlook, add about two hours and fifteen minutes to whatever time is listed. What you'll see is a frothing, foaming wall of seawater—sometimes as high as 6 feet—come surging into the constricted inlet. Don't, by the way, even think of wading out onto the mudflats that are exposed in these and other Cook Inlet areas. The mud is like quicksand. Foolish waders have drowned during incoming tides after becoming mired in the muck.

At mile 90 the Seward Highway connects with the 3-mile Alyeska access road to **Girdwood, Alyeska Resort,** and **Crow Creek Mine.** Girdwood is less a city and more a still-woodsy gathering place of some 350 Alaskans, most of whom love to ski (usually at adjacent Alyeska Resort) and many of whom work at shops, stores, or eateries either at the resort (800–880–3880; www.alyeskaresort.com), in Girdwood or nearby. Many Anchoragites have condominiums here. The community isn't exactly planned or laid out, but it's small enough to be easy to wander around in. The residents are more than friendly and accommodating. At the resort (a world-class ski area in the winter months), you can take a tram ride ($15) 2,300 feet up the mountain for hiking, for casual but gourmet dining in the $16 to $20 range at **Seven Glaciers Restaurant** (907–754–2237), or for just taking in the sweeping view of Turnagain Arm.

At the Crow Creek Mine, you can pan for gold along creek beds still rich with the precious metal. The managers will even teach you how and point out likely areas for prospecting. Sure, it's sort of touristy, but there really is plenty of gold along these creek banks. Many Alaskans come here on weekends for recreational panning. Of course, you get to keep all the "color" you find. When you're through, you can refuel the body with sourdough pancakes or sandwiches in the **Bake Shop** (907–783–2831) at Alyeska Resort or partake of moderately priced pizza, pasta, or seafood at **Chair 5 Restaurant** (907–783–2500) in downtown Girdwood. The **Double Musky** (907–783–2822), with its huge (fourteen to twenty ounces) French pepper steak, at $24, is another favorite among locals and visiting Alaskans.

If you're overnighting in Girdwood, consider **Alyeska Bed and Breakfast.** Mark and Laura Lyle will even arrange custom breakfasts, in bed if you like, in their one- and two-bedroom suites. And by all means, partake of the hot tub. For details call (907) 783–1222.

Another good choice is **Alyeska View Bed and Breakfast,** on Vail Drive (907–783–2747). There are three comfortable rooms, all with a private entrance, and a big shared bath complete with a post-skiing, muscle-relaxing Jacuzzi. The rate for a room with two twin beds is $70. A room with a king-size bed or two full beds is $80.

Hostel enthusiasts can check out the **Alyeska Home Hostel** about ½ mile from the Alyeska Resort. This is a small, unpretentious, ten-guest cabin with a couple of rooms upstairs, another on ground level, a kitchen, woodstove, and small sitting room. There's no shower, but it does boast a sauna out back. The charge is $10 per person. To get there drive the Alyeska Road past Glacier Creek, make a right turn on Timberline Drive, then another right on Alpina for about ¼ mile. The hostel is on the right; you'll see the sign. For reservations call (907) 783–2099.

Back on the Seward Highway: If you're heading for the **port of Whittier,**

Active Ice

*T*here is something innately rewarding about climbing on ice in the middle of summer. I was raised in the South, where in the summer ice cubes in your tea melt within minutes. But here in Alaska, the ice remains, even in the summer. And while the ice is slowly receding, the deep-blue glaciers that cover a good portion of this state remain a presence.

Glaciers are so common, in fact, that you can literally touch them, even walk on them if you'd like. Six well-known glaciers are accessible by road in Southcentral Alaska.

Head south from Anchorage on the Seward Highway; 50 miles later you'll find the turnoff to Portage Glacier. You can view the glacier from the observation deck of the Begich-Boggs Visitor Center there, or you can hike to the nearby Byron Glacier—smaller, but equally impressive—if you want to actually touch the ice. (Warning: The ice is in constant motion, and giant pieces have been known to break off, injuring or even killing unsuspecting people. Be very careful of this, as well as crevasses that you could slip into.)

Keep driving on the Seward Highway; two hours later you'll find yourself in the town of Seward, which is the jump-off point for some of the best glacier-viewing in the state in Kenai Fjords National Park. Exit Glacier is accessible by road. Just drive the access road, pay an entry fee, and walk to the edge of the glacier. Again, be careful. Large chunks of ice frequently calve from the glacier.

My favorite glacier among those accessible by road is Matanuska Glacier, 46 miles northeast of Palmer, off the Glenn Highway, in the Chugach Mountains. My husband and I took my brother here once, and we spent a breezy afternoon exploring the glacier's terminus, climbing carefully across the ice.

For information on any of the other glaciers abundant in Southcentral Alaska, just ask at the Anchorage Visitor and Convention Bureau's visitor log cabin in downtown Anchorage. They'll get you pointed in the right direction.

on fabled Prince William Sound, watch for the pull-offs where you exit the highway to board the *Alaska Railroad "piggyback train"* at mile 80.3. What you do is drive your vehicle up a ramp and onto a railroad flatcar. (Railroad personnel will direct you.) Your car or RV will be secured, and you'll ride inside your own vehicle with a fabulous view during the forty-minute, 12-mile ride across valley floors and through two tunnels to Whittier. Call (907) 265–2607 for recorded schedules and information. For more information about things to see and do in the waters there, see the section on Prince William Sound. At mile 80 you'll come to a second ramp plus a parking area for your vehicle if you want to park and ride in a passenger railcar. By all means, leave your car at the lot if you're not taking the ferry from Whittier to Valdez. As noted earlier, there's really nowhere to drive in tiny Whittier. The cost for the piggyback option is $72 for the car and driver. The railcar option costs $20. For reservations and information call (800) 544–0552, 265–2494 locally, or visit www.akrr.com.

At mile 79 you can take a driving tour of *Big Game Alaska* (907– 783–2025; www.alaska.net/~jrrealty/biggame), the state's only drive-through wildlife park, to view moose, elk, buffalo, musk ox, caribou, and other North Country creatures from your own vehicle. Admission charge is $5.00 for adults.

Farther south on the Seward Highway, beyond mile 79, the highway connects with the Portage Glacier Road. This 5½-mile road leads to Alaska's most visited travel attraction, *Portage Glacier,* and perhaps Alaska's least known wildlife species, the glacier iceworm.

At the glacier the U.S. Forest Service operates *Begich-Boggs Visitor Center,* a comprehensive observation structure where, in good weather or foul, you can view the glacier, the frequently iceberg-clogged lake that the ice river flows into, and all kinds of interesting glacial exhibits. Each day a huge chunk of glacier ice is hauled into the center, where you can touch, rub, and pose with ice that fell as snow on the glacier perhaps a century ago. Incredibly, there are tiny but visible organisms, popularly called iceworms, that live in glacial ice. In the summer you can head out with U.S. Forest Service naturalists daily for an iceworm safari (no charge) to track down some of Alaska's littlest creatures. The center is open daily in summer 9:00 A.M. to 6:00 P.M. Call (907) 783–2326.

The Gray Line of Alaska sight-seeing vessel *Ptarmigan* makes frequent one-hour excursions from lakeshore to within ¼ mile of Portage Glacier's glistening face. This is Alaska's most economical ($25) glacier cruise. Forest Service naturalists accompany each trip. For information and reservations call (800) 478–6388.

At Seward Highway's mile 56.7 you have two somewhat confusing choices. If you're coming from Anchorage, turn right to access the **Hope Highway;** turn left to stay on the road to Seward. The Hope alternative is well worth exploring. The road leads to the community of **Hope** and one of Alaska's most celebrated backpacking experiences.

First, about the road and the community: At the turnout just beyond mile 2, you have at least a chance of seeing moose in the Sixmile Creek Valley below. Just past mile 11 there's a big, paved turnoff with a view of Turnagain Arm. At mile 16.5, turn on Hope Road for "downtown" Hope, a tiny picturesque community of year-round homes for a handful of residents and getaway cabins used by urban Alaskans. The road leads past the post office, then to the waterfront, a popular site for anglers. The town had its start as a mining center in 1896. Today it offers a secluded base for hiking, fishing, and just getting away from it all.

A Fall Ritual

*L*ike putting up wood for the winter or giving the house a twice-over in the spring, hiking the Resurrection Trail is a fall rite of passage for me. There is nothing like walking through a wilderness crisp with fallen leaves and pungent with overripe blueberries—and then getting to sleep right in the middle of it.

I make the annual trip in early September, when the blueberries are sure to be abundant. I bring a couple extra water bottles and fill them as I make my way along the 38-mile trail over the course of a weekend. The trail itself is unbeatable, only a couple hours' drive from Anchorage on the Kenai Peninsula. Within a half hour of hiking—save for the maintained trail— you feel as though you're the only person to have been here.

The last time I hiked the Resurrection Trail, I traveled with my brother, who was visiting for the first time from Virginia. We sat in the twilight on the steps of a U.S. Forest Service cabin we had reserved and listened to a bull moose grunting out its mating call from the other side of Juneau Lake.

Another time, my husband and I were treated to a wildlife sighting at just about every bend. We watched from our tent site as a porcupine made its way up a tree. The next day we stood stock-still after hearing a brown bear grunting in frustration; then, thankfully, we saw it run up over a ridge and disappear. On the last day we counted moose as if checking off out-of-state license plates on a road trip.

Same trail, different experiences. You can be sure I'll be back this fall.

Just past mile 16 and before you get to Hope, turn south on Resurrection Creek Road for the trailhead of the **Resurrection Pass Trail,** one of Alaska's finest backcountry hiking routes. I make a point of hiking this trail every fall, when the blueberries are ripe, but summer hiking is nice, too. It ends 38 miles later at about mile 53 on the Sterling Highway. In between, trekkers experience alpine ridges and lakes, scenic valleys, and vast panoramas plus the opportunity to observe moose, Dall mountain sheep, mountain goats, and bears. Spaced about a half-day's hiking distance apart are seven U.S. Forest Service rental cabins. (For information call 907–271–2599.)

Back on the Seward Highway, between miles 47.5 and 44.5, you'll find numerous turnoffs that offer excellent photo ops for pictures of Upper and Lower Summit Lakes and the spectacular mountains that rise behind them. If you're driving from Anchorage to Seward in one day, the log cabin **Summit Lake Lodge,** at mile 45.8, offers a good refreshment stop with moderately priced old-fashioned eggs-meat-and-potatoes breakfasts plus full lunch and dinner menus. And if you like pie, this is the best place ever to get the pie of your choice. You name it, they make it.

Just before mile 38, you come to Tern Junction, where the Seward Highway connects with the Sterling Highway. If you're Seward-bound, continue straight ahead on Alaska Highway Route 9. If you're headed for Soldotna, Homer, and other Sterling Highway points, turn right on Route 1.

The Seward Highway: Tern Lake Junction to Seward

*M*oose Pass, at mile 29.4, would be easy to miss if you blinked but it's an interesting little town (population about 150) and has a motel, general store, and restaurant. At Estes Brothers Grocery there's a big waterwheel that turns a working grindstone. If you collect pictures of unique signs, the one here reads MOOSE PASS IS A PEACEFUL TOWN. IF YOU HAVE AN 'AXE TO GRIND' DO IT HERE. If you're looking for an interesting spot to stretch your legs, there's a 1³/₁₀-mile paved biking and walking trail that skirts the edge of Trail Lake. Trail Lake Lodge (907–288–3101) offers a lakeside salmon bake plus a menu of steaks and seafood.

At Nash Road junction (mile 3.2 on the Seward Highway), turn left off the highway, then left again on Salmon Creek Road to find **The Farm Bed and Breakfast.** Host Jack Hoogland calls the rooms here elegantly casual. They come with private baths, decks, kitchenettes, and entrances.

The setting is one of trees and greenery. Rates are $65 to $100 for two with private bath; call (907) 224–5691, e-mail thefarm@ptialaska.net, or visit www.alaskan.com/thefarm.

The highway ends at mile 0 and the *city of Seward.* The community is relatively old by Alaska standards, having had its start in 1903, when railroad surveyors selected this site at the head of Resurrection Bay as an ocean terminal and supply center. Actually, there was a small Russian settlement there prior to 1903. Since 1923 the town has served as the far-thest-south point on the 470-mile route of the Alaska Railroad and prides itself today on being the "Gateway to Kenai Fjords National Park."

The four-hour *Alaska Railroad* trip from Anchorage to Seward, inci-dentally, is one of the North Country's most rewarding excursions for $86 round-trip. The journey departs Anchorage at 6:45 A.M. each morn-ing in summer and leaves Seward at 6:00 P.M. for the return trip. Sights along the way include the dramatic coast of Cook Inlet, major lakes and streams, forest country, deep gulches and gullies, and (at least every time I've made the trip) abundant wildlife, including moose and bears. During my last journey (northbound), the engineer had to stop the train just outside Seward because a big fat black bear sat resolutely on his haunches right in the middle of the track—and showed no inclina-tion to move. Finally he meandered to the side, much to the delight of photographers who were hoping for a better picture angle. For informa-tion about rail-only travel or rail/yacht combination tours that include cruising Resurrection Bay and Kenai Fjords National Park, call (800) 544–0552, e-mail reservations@akrr.com, or visit www.akrr.com.

To get a quick glimpse of old downtown Seward, the small boat harbor, and all the history in between, hop aboard the *Seward Trolley.* This sight-seeing bus departs from the railroad station and other points every half hour daily in summer. The fare is only $1.50 for adults or $3.00 for an all-day pass. It may be the cheapest tour in Alaska.

Two hiking destinations, among many others, are especially notable. From a trailhead at about mile 2 on the Lowell Point Road, you can walk, at low tide, along a 4½-mile forest and beach trail to *Caines Head State Recreation Area,* where World War II bunkers and gun emplace-ments serve as reminders of Alaska's strategic location during a time when a Japanese invasion of North America seemed plausible.

Mt. Marathon, which rises from the community's edge from just above sea level to 3,022 feet, offers another satisfying trek. But if you don't like crowds, avoid the peak on Independence Day. On July 4 each year the town continues a tradition begun in 1909 with a wager between two "sourdoughs." The bet: whether or not a person could run from mid-town to the top of the mountain and back in less than an hour. The outcome: Yes, it can be done—so far in a record time of forty-three minutes, twenty-three seconds. These days, competitors come from other towns, states, and even nations to scramble to the summit, then run, leap, slide, and fall during the helter-skelter descent witnessed by cheering crowds of spectators along the route.

A small but informative **National Park Service Visitor Center** with information on nearby **Kenai Fjords National Park** is located at 1212 Fourth Avenue, on the Seward waterfront. It sits among structures that house sight-seeing, charter, fishing, and souvenir shops. The center operates 8:00 A.M. until 7:00 P.M. daily in the summer, offering short slide shows, interpretive programs, other exhibits, and short walks.

You really won't find any hideaway eating places in Seward, but for lunch and dinner locals and visiting Alaskans often choose **Ray's Waterfront,** at 1316 Fourth Avenue at the small boat harbor (907–224–5606), especially for fish and seafood. Prices are in the $8.00 to $12.00 range for lunch, $15.00 to $25.00 for dinner.

Newer on the dining and lodging front in Seward, but no less appetizing, is the **Seward Windsong Lodge** and accompanying **Resurrection Roadhouse,** overlooking the Resurrection River on the way to Exit Glacier. The rooms are comfortable and secluded, and the food, well, let's just say the food rivals the views you'll see out the roadhouse's windows. Being a pizza enthusiast, I can say this: Try the white mushroom pizza—you won't regret it. For more information call (800) 208–0200, or visit www.sewardlodging.com.

And for coffee lovers, if you're wandering the streets of downtown Seward, be sure to stop at what looks like a church but actually is **Resurrect Art Coffee House Gallery,** on Third Avenue (907–224–7161). The name is a mouthful, but so are the tasty treats and espresso. This is a relaxing place to read a newspaper, visit with locals, or just admire the artwork that adorns the former church's walls.

Exit Glacier is one of the few glaciers in the North Country whose face you can actually approach on foot. It's located at the end of Exit Glacier Road, which junctions at mile 3.7 on the Seward Highway. En route to the glacier, you initially pass by small clusters of homes, then drive through thick forests and a steep-walled valley for about 8 miles to a National Park Service visitor parking area. A series of paths and trails lead to the snout of the 3-mile-long ice river. *Caution:* You'll see whole groups walking right up to the ice to pose for photos; that's a dumb thing to do. Huge pieces of ice can fall at any time. Stay safely back; you can still get some great pictures. If you're a hiker, you'll find options from short nature trails to an all-day trek to the Harding Icefield. There are bears and moose in the area, and, as at Portage Glacier, you can find ice-worms in the ice. Look for them in the early evening; they avoid the sun.

Of course, to really appreciate Kenai Fjords National Park, you need to see the fjords from the water. Several excellent day cruise operators offer half day or longer narrated excursions through Resurrection Bay to see whales, sea otters, a sea lion rookery, puffins, eagles, glaciers, mountains, and other features of the magnificent Kenai Fjords landscape. Times and rates vary.

You'll be surprised at the number of cruise ship operators in Seward, and their names are all so similar sounding that it's easy to get confused. You probably won't go wrong with any of these operators— they're all pretty reputable. But I've taken many a visiting relative on these various cruises, and there are two that I think really stand out.

Major Marine Tours offers a great half-day wildlife and glacier tour for $64 that is narrated by a National Park Service ranger. You'll have a chance to see puffins, sea otters, eagles, and all sorts of massive glaciers. For another $10, you can partake in the delicious all-you-can-eat salmon and chicken buffet. Other tours, including all-day tours, also are offered. Call (800) 764–7300, or visit www.majormarine.com.

My favorite cruise, though, is offered by **Allen Marine Tours,** and it's called the **Wildlife Quest.** This five-and-a-half-hour tour takes you by catamaran across Resurrection Bay to some of the best spots for viewing glaciers and wildlife. My mother marveled at the humpback whale that rose from the water, open-mouthed and feeding, just beside the boat. She'd never seen a whale before, and now this one was just 15 feet away. Moments later, a pod of orca whales skimmed the water, their fins giving us a graceful show. Then, to top it all, the boat maneuvered close to Columbia Glacier just in time for us to watch, and hear, a chunk of the giant ice field calve into the water. The tour is $99 and includes lunch and a pass to the Alaska SeaLife Center, which you'll read about later. Calling (888) 305–2515 or visiting www.wildlifequest.com will get you in touch with Allen Marine.

Clearly, the best way to see the natural beauty of this area is to be up close and personal. Resurrection Bay, and its surrounding smaller bays, offers some of the best kayaking the state has to offer. There are no shortage of kayak rental and tour companies to help you plan a memorable trip.

Sunny Cove Sea Kayaking Company offers day tours to three- and five-day guided sea kayaking and camping expeditions. The price ranges from $139 to $595. For more information call (907) 345–5339, or visit www.alaska.net/~kayakak.

A family-friendly outfit is *Kenai Fjords Kayaks,* which offers half-day, full-day, and multiday packages (800–992–3960).

Now, about the *Alaska SeaLife Center*. It isn't off the beaten path—in fact, it's one of the largest buildings in Seward. But it is a new facility, the crown jewel of this waterfront community, and it houses some of Alaska's most interesting animal life, so it is worth mentioning. A trip to this research and education center is $12 for adults, and there you'll be able to see puffins, sea lions, seals, and other marine wildlife up close. There are daily films, a viewing platform overlooking the bay, and all sorts of exhibits. For more information call the center at (800) 224–2525 or visit www.alaskasealife.org.

If you'd enjoy sleeping in a National Historical Site, book yourself into the *Van Gilder Hotel,* a small but comfortable hotel in the older business district in downtown Seward. It was built in 1916 as an office building but became a hotel in 1921. The rates begin at $75 for a room with shared bath. Call (907) 224–3079.

The Sterling Highway: Tern Lake to Homer

Seward, of course, is as far as you can go by road on the Seward Highway, which covers the eastern side of the Kenai Peninsula. At its Tern Lake junction with the Seward Highway at mile 37, however, the paved Sterling Highway heads west, then south along the western side of the Kenai. Strangely, the mileposts along the Sterling Highway measure distances from Seward, even though the road doesn't go there. The road ends at its southernmost point, at the tip of the Homer Spit at mile 179.5.

For the traveler who enjoys luxuries while traveling, the rustic but regal *Kenai Princess Lodge* (800–426–0500) is accessible from the road at mile 47.7. Activities include horseback riding, river rafting, flight-seeing, hiking, fishing, and touring from the lodge throughout the rest of the peninsula. Or just relax in a hot tub. Note the chandelier in the lobby made from deer antlers. Rates begin at $79 off season, $225 during peak season. The adjacent *Kenai Princess RV Park* (also 800–426–0500) provides one of the nicest private campgrounds in the state.

The small town of **Cooper Landing,** spread out along the road before and after mile 48, offers various visitor facilities, including fish guiding services, cabins, and shops.

Alaska Wildland Adventures offers a number of quality river trips from their launch site at mile 50.1. If you're looking for a bit of adventure, ask about their seven-hour Kenai Canyon Raft Trip through a remote, nonmotorized section of the Kenai River. It includes some spirited Class III rapids and a lunch on the shores of pristine Skilak Lake. The cost is $99. In case you prefer a more peaceful trip, the company offers a Kenai River Scenic Float through a portion of the Kenai National Wildlife Refuge, where there are frequent sightings of moose, eagles, Dall sheep, waterfowl, signs of beaver, and sockeye salmon. The cost is $45. Alaska Wildland also packages half- or full-day Kenai River Sportfishing trips, on which you can angle for salmon, rainbow trout, and Dolly Varden. Costs vary from $125 to $195. For details call (800) 334–8730, or visit www.alaskawildland.com.

Just down the road, at mile 50, Gary and Carol Galbraith's family-operated *Alaska Rivers Company* offers a half-day scenic float excursion for $42 or a full-day scenic, sometimes splashy, canyon experience for $85. Both trips include homemade picnic lunches, professional guides, and excellent wildlife viewing prospects. The Galbraiths also do guided hikes and have traditional Alaska log cabins—rustic but very comfortable—for rent on the shore of the Kenai River. The cost for two is $85; for three to four, the cost is $95. Call (907) 595–1226, or e-mail lrg@arctic.net.

At mile 58 you have a choice to make, and a *U.S. Fish and Wildlife Service information station* to help you make it. You can continue on the paved Sterling Highway westerly to mile 75.2, or you can take the southerly 19-mile gravel Skilak Lake Loop Road to its junction with the Sterling at mile 75.2. We recommend the latter. The gravel road isn't bad, and opportunities for photography, fishing, hiking, and wildlife spotting are excellent.

Hidden Lake, along the gravel road, is a particular delight, with a first-class U.S. Fish and Wildlife Service campground that features paved roads, campfire programs at an amphitheater, and a deck for spotting wildlife. *A warning note:* Beautiful **Skilak Lake,** like many of the large lakes on the Kenai, can be extremely dangerous. Horrific winds can arise suddenly on the water. If you plan to take out a small boat, stay close to shore and wear a life jacket.

After Skilak Loop Road connects with the Sterling Highway at mile 75.2, the Sterling Highway continues westerly to mile 83.4, where you have another off-highway choice. If you're transporting a canoe, the choice is an easy yes. The Swanson River and Swan Lake Roads head north, then east, for nearly 30 miles, accessing two of the most highly acclaimed canoeing routes in the North Country. The **Swanson River Canoe Trail** is 80 miles long and connects more than forty lakes with 46 miles of the Swanson River. Portages between lakes are short, less than a mile over relatively easy terrain. The **Swan Lake Canoe Trail,** separate from the Swanson River route, covers 60 miles and connects thirty lakes with forks of the Moose River. Both trails lie within the Kenai National Wildlife Refuge.

The opportunities for viewing wildlife—especially moose, eagles, trumpeter swans, and tundra swans—are enormous. For maps and additional information, call the refuge manager at the Kenai National Wildlife Refuge (907–262–7021), and ask for the free U.S. Fish and Wildlife Service pamphlet "Canoeing the Kenai National Wildlife Refuge." Information is also available at the USFWS cabin at mile 58, the Kenai National Wildlife Refuge Information Center in Soldotna, and at local information centers in Kenai and Soldotna.

At mile 94.2 you face still another vexing little decision. This time your options are three. You can continue westerly on the Sterling Highway to Soldotna (the city center is only a mile down the road), then keep driving southerly on the Sterling toward the end of the road in Homer. Or you can turn northerly at what is called the Soldotna Y on the Kenai Spur Highway to the city of Kenai, then drive on to Captain Cook State Recreation Area. The third choice is to drive on to Soldotna, visit that city, then backtrack the short distance to the Kenai Spur Highway. After you've finished exploring the spur road and the city of Kenai, you can then bypass Soldotna and drive southerly on the Kalifornsky Beach Road to rejoin the Sterling at mile 108.8. I recommend the third choice.

First, about **Soldotna:** If you want to fish the Kenai River for king salmon and other species, this community of about 3,700 offers a large number of charter boat fishing services. You can also fish on your own from the shores of the river; many do. Among the sights to see is the **Soldotna Historical Society Museum,** which includes a small "village" of historic log buildings, among them the 1958 territorial school, the last one built in Alaska before statehood. Damon Hall, at the village site, contains an excellent display of Alaska wildlife mounts. Still other mounted wildlife displays can be seen at the **Kenai National Wildlife Refuge Visitor Center** (www.r7.fws.gov/nwr/kenai/kennwr.html), at the top of Ski Hill Road. This is a prime location to get information about canoeing, hiking, camping, or just sightseeing in the refuge, which was established by President Franklin D. Roosevelt in 1941 as the Kenai National Moose Range.

Now retrace your steps back to the Y at mile 94.2 on the Sterling Highway, where the Kenai Spur Highway heads northerly. The city of Kenai lies about 11 miles up this road.

It's probably best to start a *Kenai* visit at the *Kenai Visitors and Cultural Center* (907–283–1991; www.visitkenai.com) near Main Street and the Kenai Spur Highway. There you'll find a cultural museum and wildlife displays as well as friendly staff to give directions around the far-flung community.

Kenai, you'll find, is one of those curious cities that don't really seem to have a downtown, yet this is a site where Native peoples and Russian fur traders have settled for centuries. The Russian heritage is dramatically expressed in the *Holy Assumption of the Virgin Mary Russian Orthodox Church,* not far from the visitor center. The original church was founded in 1846 by a Russian monk, Egumen Nicolai. The present three-domed structure was built a half century later and is one of the oldest Russian Orthodox houses of worship in Alaska. Tours are available, and in the summer you can usually walk right in. The nearby *St. Nicholas Chapel* was constructed in 1906 and covers the grave of the founding monk. In the same vicinity is *Fort Kenay,* a log structure built during the 1967 Alaska Purchase Centennial to commemorate the original 1869 U.S. Army installation. It housed some one hundred men and officers.

Walk to *Beluga Lookout,* at the end of Main Street, for possible sightings of the white beluga whales that visit these waters. Fishing for lunker king salmon, monster-sized halibut, and other species is, for many visitors, what Kenai is all about. Like in Soldotna, a large number of guides and charter boats call Kenai home.

Perhaps the best way to see the Kenai Peninsula and its surroundings is by plane, and the person to call for unique (and safe) flying is Michael Litzen of *Litzen Guide Service* (907–776–5868). Litzen specializes in custom packages, from guided hunt trips to fishing trips to, especially, ecotourism-oriented remote cabin drop-offs for those just wanting to get away from it all. And Litzen, who also uses his planes to do wildlife counts and radio tracking for state fish and game biologists, knows where the animals are for superb wildlife viewing that doesn't disturb the animals. A one-and-a-half-hour flight-seeing tour starts at about $300.

The *Captain Cook State Recreation Area,* at the very end of the Kenai Spur Highway, is one of Alaska's unsung and relatively undiscovered state parklands—probably because it's at the end of a single road. But especially if you're a camper, it's well worth the drive. *Discovery Campground,* near the end of the road, merits special mention. Here you'll find a locale of rolling hills, wooded spruce plateaus, and beautiful vistas of the Alaska Range across Cook Inlet. The volcanic peaks Mt. Spurr, Mt. Redoubt, and especially Mt. Iliamna stand out across the water (as do thirteen oil platforms).

Three warnings: On the tidelands, observe the warnings and don't let an incoming tide catch you off guard. Delicious berries are thick in the area, and they are there for the picking, but avoid the bright red or white poisonous baneberry. And third, if you get into a standoff with a bear, leave the site and the berries to him (or her). Don't even think of trying to shoo the bruin away.

After you've "done" the Kenai Spur Highway, you can retrace your travel to Kenai and the Soldotna Y at mile 94 on the Sterling Highway, then continue south down the Sterling. The more scenic choice, though, is to head west, then southerly on the Kalifornsky Beach Road down the coast to Kasilof, at mile 108.8 on the Sterling Highway.

A great place to stop for the evening here is *Deal's Den* at 26445 South Cohoe Loop Road. This bluffside retreat offers spectacular views of Cook Inlet and the distant Chigmit Mountains. Owners Bill and Peggy Deal are liable to welcome you with "Ciad mile failte," which is Gaelic for "100,000 welcomes." Once you step inside their home, the Irish charm won't stop. Their home is the ideal combination of Irish and Alaskan, with its bearskin rug and antler coffee table to the shillelagh and other Irish mementos hanging on the wall. There are nonsmoking rooms and a cabin available, and breakfast is a hearty sourdough pancake and reindeer sausage affair. The fishing on the nearby Kasilof River is great, and the Deals can match you up with some local fishing guides if you like. While there, be sure to ask the Deals about their precious twin grandsons, part of the large Deal clan and the cutest things ever to tackle a fishing pole.

If you're neither a hunter nor an angler, but you'd still like to do something very Alaskan, stop at mile 117.4 and head for *Clam Gulch State Recreation Area* (where there are 116 campsites) to join hundreds of locals on the shore for the grand old Alaska sport of razor clam digging. *Three caveats:* Don't drive down the extremely steep beach road to sea level unless you have a four-wheel-drive vehicle. Don't go digging without a valid Alaska sportfishing license, available at various sporting and retail establishments. And, again, don't get stuck offshore on an incoming tide. The best clamming occurs on minus tides and varies from month to month. Locals are more than happy to share their knowledge and technique. You'll find similar clamming opportunities at the Ninilchik Beach Campground, which is part of **Ninilchik State Recreation Area,** at mile 134.5.

At about mile 135 you'll come to a side road that leads to the old original **Ninilchik Village** and the beach. Take the time to explore this site, which includes a few old log buildings. A white Russian Orthodox

Homer Away from Home

I *had just returned from an outdoor writing workshop on the shores of Tutka Bay in Southcentral Alaska. The ferry had delivered the workshop participants to the dock at Homer, where our cars or our rides awaited us. I was in no hurry to leave, though. The sun was shining, the water was sparkling, and Homer—as I'd discovered soon after moving to Alaska—was my favorite place on Earth.*

Now, many years and countless visits to Homer later, it still remains my favorite place in all of Alaska. I've been to the far reaches of this state and still haven't found a place that makes me "feel" as good as Homer does.

So, after the workshop, I decided I wanted to keep that feeling. I'd always seen the Salty Dawg Saloon, with its telltale lighthouse tower and low log cabin, and I'd watched its customers— wiry-framed fishermen, unkempt deckhands, and rugged-looking old-timers—wander in and out of the place. It's a bar, a local's bar, and I had heard there were just wood shavings for a floor and old dollar bills plastered to the walls for wallpapering.

Tentatively, I walked in: a single, petite woman in a crowd of mostly intriguing-looking hardy Alaska men and a few equally hardy- and strong-looking Alaska women.

First of all, I wasn't shooed off. The barkeep was friendly and people smiled. Second, the beer was flowing so I felt compelled to order a cold draught and settle in. I liked this place. I really liked it. The wood-shaving floor was there, and the walls were littered with "stuff." It was dark and the ceiling was low. It felt like nighttime even though it was the middle of an Alaska August summer day.

The Salty Dawg has a rich history. It opened its doors in 1957. It changed hands in the '60s, '70s, and '80s, and it survived a near-miss when a nearby general store caught fire in 1994. It's been added onto, revamped, and remodeled.

But from what I could tell, those changes don't matter. This tough little Alaska bar, like the tough Alaskans who frequent it, will be here for years to come. And I'll make a point of being there every now and again myself.

church, still in use, overlooks the village from a photogenic hilltop setting. Modern **Ninilchik** stretches down the road from roughly mile 135.5. If you don't like crowds, avoid the area on Memorial Day and other holidays, when thousands converge for the fishing thereabouts.

At mile 157 on the Sterling Highway, the collector of superlatives will want to turn off the main highway and drive on the Old Sterling Highway past the Anchor River to another turnoff, this one on the Anchor River Beach Road. At the end of this road lies the **Anchor Point State Recreation Site.** There, on an overlook platform facing Cook Inlet, stands a big sign marking NORTH AMERICA'S MOST WESTERLY HIGHWAY POINT. You can't drive your car anyplace west of this point on the connected highways of the United States and Canada. Incidentally, more than a million razor clams are taken each year on the beaches between Anchor Point and Kasilof up the highway.

You come to **Homer,** my all-time favorite place in Alaska, at mile 172 and beyond, crossing onto the Homer Spit at mile 175. The Sterling Highway ends here just short of 142 miles from its beginning at Tern Lake Junction and nearly 233 miles from Anchorage.

The community, you'll find, enjoys mild and usually pleasant weather throughout the year. It's small enough to be cozy but large enough to have everything you need. The hiking, fishing, photography, and nature-watching opportunities are enormous. There's lots of Alaska history (and prehistory) here, and the people—though individualistic to the core—are as open and friendly as you'll find anywhere. No wonder author and radio personality Tom Bodett (of Motel 66 "We'll leave the light on for you . . ." fame) chooses to live here.

First, a little orientation: Most residences, city services (hospital, fire department, library, city hall), and government offices are located in what you might call Homer proper. The **Pratt Museum** (907–235–8635), which emphasizes natural and cultural diversity on the Kenai Peninsula, has a marine "touch tank" aquarium, a botanical garden, and a museum store. It's located at 3779 Bartlett Street in downtown Homer. Admission is $4.00, and children under age six are free. The hours are 10:00 A.M. to 6:00 P.M. daily.

Also located downtown is the world-renowned **Alaska Wild Berry Products** plant, where you can sample some of Alaska's tastiest berry products as well as other goodies. You can watch the processing and packing action through glassed observation windows and browse in the gift shop. It's open daily in summer at no charge.

Most visitor attractions and services are located on the 5-mile-long narrow gravel bar called the *Homer Spit.* The spit, which never sat very high above sea level, dropped 4 to 6 feet during the 1964 Alaska earthquake, but it nonetheless continues to be the site of countless visitor shops, eateries, commercial wharfs, docks for waterborne sight-seeing and fishing cruises, parking places, campsites, and a prime port for the Alaska Marine Highway System's oceangoing ferry *Tustumena.*

The *Salty Dawg Saloon,* one of Alaska's best known frontier bars, is located on the spit, as is *Homer Ocean Charters,* just a few doors down. Charter owners Roark Brown and Rick Swenson offer customized sight-seeing, bird-watching, bear-viewing, kayaking, and charter fishing trips throughout Homer's surrounding and scenic Kachemak Bay. Guided all-day kayak trips start at $125, which includes guide and water taxi into some of Kachemak's more scenic finger bays. Two-hour birding excursions run about $50. For more information call (800) 426–6212, e-mail hoc@xyz.net, or visit www.homerocean.com.

Here's one of my favorite trips to take while in Homer: the evening *Dinner Ferry* aboard the beautiful wooden boat, the *Danny J,* past *Gull Island* and on to the artist community of *Halibut Cove,* across the bay from Homer. You'll disembark there and explore the numerous boardwalks that connect the homes and galleries in this isolated community. On a sunny Alaska summer evening, you'll think you've entered a postcard. The last time we were there, we watched a seal slip in and out of the water onto a nearby dock and peer at us quizzically, as if it were playing peekaboo. To top your tour off, you'll eat dinner at Halibut Cove's sole restaurant, The Saltry, which has some of the best food you'll eat in Alaska—period. The seafood is, obviously, fresh-caught, and the salads taste like they were just picked from a nearby garden. My husband and I had unforgettable halibut ceviche that, despite many tries, we've never been able to replicate. The cost of the ferry is $21 per person, and meals are separate. For more information call (907) 296–2223; for reservations call Central Charters at (800) 478–7847.

If you enjoy nautical travel under your own steam, *True North Kayak Adventures* takes small groups of experienced and inexperienced kayakers into the wild beauty of Kachemak Bay for full-day close encounters of the sea otter kind (plus porpoises, sea lions, and shorebirds). Call Central Charters at (907) 235–7847 or Jakolof Ferry Service at (907) 235–2376 (www.xyz.net/~jakalof/home.html) for reservations and to arrange your water taxi ride from Ramp Number One behind the Salty Dawg Saloon to the kayak company's base across from Homer.

The price is $140, including all equipment, instruction, a hearty lunch, and the water taxi.

Rainbow Tours, on Cannery Row Boardwalk on the Homer Spit (907–235–7272), will book you for a guided *Kachemak Bay Natural History Tour* by boat and by foot, during which you'll observe 15,000 nesting seabirds on Gull Island, view sea mammals (including an occasional whale), explore beaches and intertidal areas, and learn about the marine life, local flora and fauna, and the Alaska Native prehistory of the locale. This is an all-day tour, 9:00 A.M. until 6:00 P.M. daily, priced at $63 for adults. Bring your own lunch, rubber boots, and rain gear.

Rainbow Tours also offers a scenic cruise to another isolated and picturesque waterfront community, Seldovia, for $45. Seldovia originated as a Russian sea otter hunting station. Today the community of "307 Friendly People and a Few Old Crabs"—as the city's Web site professes—relies on fishing, fish processing, some timber operations, and summer tourism. The city's picturesque boardwalk dates to the 1930s. Birders can collect lots of views of bald eagles here, as well as sea and shore birds, and sightings of sea otter from excursion boats are common. Check out *The Buzz* (907–234–7479) coffeehouse while you're there. Not only do they make some great warm beverages, but they also have some neat gift items for sale. My favorite pair of jade fish earrings came from there.

Homer, you'll find, abounds in charter boats, especially for halibut fishing. The town, in fact, calls itself the Halibut Fishing Capital of the World. You'll see incoming anglers hang their halibut on scales at the dock and record catches in the 50, 100, even 200 to 300 pound class.

Cranes' Crest Bed and Breakfast, at 59830 Sanford Drive (907–235–2969 or 800–338–2969) enjoys a 1,200-foot elevated view of Kachemak Bay, Homer Spit, mountains, glaciers, and coves—not to mention sandhill cranes, wild flowers, berry bushes, and moose. For adventurous youngsters in your party, proprietor Kate Gill can even provide a metal "igloo" where the young ones can "camp out" in their own sleeping bags.

Seaside Farm Hostel is many things: It's a large working homestead in the best Alaska tradition, a B&B, a campsite for tenters, a place to rent cabins—and a hostel with overnight accommodations in the main ranch house and a large cabin. There's an open-sided kitchen on-site for hostelers and campers. Hostel prices begin at $15.00, campsites cost $6.00, and cabins are $55. For reservations call (907) 235–7850.

George Parks Highway— Southern Section: Anchorage to Denali National Park

Now, back to Anchorage. Truth to tell, it's a little difficult some-times to know exactly which highway you're traveling on in Alaska. The *George Parks Highway* between Anchorage and Fairbanks is a good example because for the first 35 miles of the trip you're really on the Glenn Highway, which eventually takes you to Tok. The George Parks Highway starts at its junction with the Glenn at about mile 35 on the latter road, but the mileposts on both show the distance from Anchorage. To read about places to see and things to do on the first 35 miles out of Anchorage, see the discussion of the Glenn Highway–Tok Cutoff in the Glenn Highway section of this chapter.

The George Parks Highway, it should be noted, is among Alaska's best. You encounter some rough spots and frost heaves along a few portions (so keep road speeds within safe limits), but generally it is among the wider and most modern in the state. It cuts through some of Alaska's most urbanized country as well as some of the state's wildest and most scenic. You can see Denali (Mt. McKinley), North America's highest mountain, from a number of places, and the highway provides access to two of the state's most popular state and national parks.

At about mile 35.5 you can access the *Mat-Su* (for Matanuska-Susitna) *Visitors Center.* Especially if you plan a side trip to Palmer, a few miles east on the Glenn Highway, stop for information.

About mile 39.5 you come to the Wasilla city limits and shortly there-after Wasilla's Main Street. There your choices are several: Head north a block to 323 Main Street and visit the community's *Dorothy G. Page Museum* (907–373–9071), a visitor center, and historical park. Go north as well to access the Wasilla Fishhook Road to *Independence Mine,* or turn south across the railroad tracks to drive along the *Knik Road.* Especially if you're interested in learning more about sled dog racing, head left on this road and drive for a couple of miles to the *Iditarod Trail Committee Headquarters and Visitor Center.* (Look for the large, colorful sign.) You can view historical mushing exhibits and films, see sled dogs, meet a musher, and shop for mushing souvenirs. The center is open daily in summer and does not charge admission. Phone (907) 376–5155. At mile 13 visitors are welcome (by appoint-ment) at *Knik Kennels,* since 1948 the world's largest sled dog kennel and the home of numerous famous canine athletes. Admission is free.

Call (907) 376–5562. Nearly 14 miles down the road from the Parks Highway junction and about ½ mile after you come to the village of Knik, you'll find the **Knik Museum and Sled Dog Mushers' Hall of Fame.** In addition to mushers' portraits, mushing equipment, and Iditarod Trail historical exhibits, you can see artifacts from Knik village's gold rush (1898–1916) beginnings. The museum building itself dates back to that period. Admission is $2.00. Call (907) 376–7755. It's open from noon to 6:00 P.M. Wednesday through Sunday.

If your transportation preferences don't include pooch power, how about an airboat ride to Knik Glacier for a walk on the ice? The price is $65 for a four-hour tour. Or a llama trek into the back country? This option starts at $50. **Knik Glacier Adventures** offers these and other tours, plus log cabin rentals for $65 a night, at mile 7 on Knik Road. Call (907) 746–5133 for reservations, or e-mail knik@mtaonline.net.

If you want to overnight near Wasilla and still feel out of the mainstream, **Yukon Don's Bed and Breakfast Inn** features a fabulous 360-degree view of rural Iditarod Valley at mile 37.5 on Parks Highway. Proprietors Don and Beverly Tanner will welcome you into their home and can share many a story with you about life in this part of Alaska. Rates start at $75. For more information call (800) 478–7472, e-mail yukondon@alaska.net, or visit www.yukondon.com.

At mile 47, turn left on Neuser Drive for ¾ mile to the road's end at the **Museum of Alaska Transportation and Industry.** It features, in the words of the Mat-Su Visitors Bureau "ten acres of neat ol' stuff," including airplanes, locomotives, farm and construction rigs, plus "trucks and vehicles that built Alaska." Admission is $5.00 for adults, $12.00 for families. Call (907) 376–1211, or visit www.alaska.net~rmorris/mati1.htm. Hours are 10:00 A.M. to 6:00 P.M.

Just past mile 52 on the George Parks Highway, the Big Lake Road leads to (you guessed it) **Big Lake** and any number of lodges, B&Bs, eateries, service stations, shops, fishing supply stores, public and private RV facilities, and several smaller lakes joined to the big one. If you're interested in a different kind of overnight experience, consider **Big Lake Houseboat Rental,** located at the Klondike Inn on Northshore Drive, which will lease you a six-guest houseboat on which you can cruise more than 50 miles of shoreline. The rate is $165 to $250, depending on boat size. Call (800) 770–9187, e-mail houseboats@gci.net, or visit www.alaskaone.com/biglakeboat. *Suggestion:* Big Lake is one of Anchorage folks' favorite weekend getaway locales. Plan your own Big Lake visit Monday through Thursday to miss the madding crowd.

Lucky Husky (an Iditarod race viewing point), at mile 80 on Parks Highway, offers year-round sled rides, kennel tours, and a movie plus major mushing adventures in the winter. Kennel tour admission is $5.00; dogsled ride (on wheels) is $24. Phone (907) 495–6470, e-mail info@luckyhusky.com, or visit www.luckyhusky.com.

Nearing mile 99 from Anchorage, you come to a 14½-mile spur road to *Talkeetna,* one of several Alaska communities often compared to the once-popular mythical TV town of Cicely on *Northern Exposure.* There's a visitor center right at the Parks Highway junction, and 1 mile down the road lies *Mary Carey's Fiddlehead Farm,* reputedly the only one in the world. You can meet longtime Alaskan book author (and character) Mary Carey as well as purchase her gourmet pickled and frozen ferns, buy autographed copies of one of her fifteen books, and shop for ivory carvings, soapstone sculpture, and other Native arts. Phone (907) 733–2428.

Near the end of the spur road, stop in at the *Talkeetna Historical Society Museum,* located on the village airstrip, which is almost in the middle of town. Formerly a schoolhouse built in the middle thirties, the museum contains displays and information from its gold mining past as well as items commemorating the life of famed bush pilot Don Sheldon. Talkeetna is definitely a walk-around town, so pick up a walking tour map at the museum, then wander about, taking pictures of the community's WELCOME TO BEAUTIFUL DOWNTOWN TALKEETNA sign, the historic old *Talkeetna Roadhouse,* the old *Fairview Inn,* and various other log and clapboard houses and structures spread along Talkeetna's streets and paths.

Steve Mahay's *Mahay's Riverboat Service* offers two very different sight-seeing options out of Talkeetna: The McKinley Jet Boat Safari, priced at $45 for adults, and the McKinley Wilderness Safari for $95. The former is a leisurely two-hour, 10-mile adventure in which you will see how trappers lived at the turn of the century and visit an authentic trapper's cabin with its rustic furnishings. Your guide will display raw furs from the local area and demonstrate trapping methods. Naturalists will acquaint you with the wildflowers and plants that grow in abundance along the river system. The latter trip is four hours long and offers much the same as the first trip, only this one, Mahay says, is your best opportunity to see bears. Mahay operates two boats, the sixteen-passenger *Doria* and the fifty-passenger *Talkeetna Queen.* Call (907) 733–2223, or visit www.alaskan.com/mahays.

When they're not busy airlifting climbers to base camps on Denali (Mt. McKinley) in the spring and early summer, Talkeetna's several excellent bush flight services take visitors on airborne flight-seeing forays around North America's tallest mountain, sometimes even landing on a glacier's icy surface. Among the companies offering such services is Talkeetna-based **K2 Aviation** (907–733–2291), which offers statewide air tours and a variety of Denali Park air tour options. Prices for flight-seeing out of Talkeetna start as low as $95. The appropriately named **McKinley Climber Tour** takes you to 20,000 feet for a dramatic view of McKinley and Denali National Park and views of the Alaska Range extending north and west to the horizons. The two-hour tour is $185 per person.

<table>
<tr><td>

Southcentral Alaska Trivia

The popular skiing town of Girdwood was named for miner James E. Girdwood, who came to the area in 1896.

</td></tr>
</table>

Talkeetna's longest operating (since 1946) air taxi service is Cliff Hudson's **Hudson Air Service** (800–478–2321; hasi@customcpu.com; www. alaskan.com/hudsonair). The second generations of Hudsons can take you on scenic flights, land you on Denali's glaciers, and provide wildlife viewing excursions. Talkeetna, incidentally, is also accessible by daily summer Alaska Railroad train service from Anchorage or Fairbanks. Call (800) 544–0552 for information or visit www.akrr.com.

Denali National Park and Preserve, of course, gets lots of attention, and properly so. But there's another Denali Park, **Denali State Park,** which deserves more mention than it gets. You enter this park at mile 132 on the Parks Highway, and you're within its boundaries until mile 169. In between, you can enjoy fine dining or lodging with indescribable views of Denali at **Mary's McKinley View Lodge** at mile 134.5 (907–733–1555). This is the same Mary whose fiddlehead farm you passed a few miles back. Or you can pitch a camp in the stellar lake, stream, and forest country at **Beyer Lake Campground** at mile 147. The overnight fee is $12. *Caution:* Especially if you go hiking in the woods there, make noise. Grizzlies roamed the area last time we camped at this site.

At roughly mile 210 on the Parks Highway you arrive at **Cantwell** and the junction of the Parks and Denali Highways. Before hurrying on to Denali National Park, spend a little time around this small community, which many pass by. (For details see the section on the Denali Highway in the chapter on Interior Alaska.)

The entrance to **Denali National Park and Preserve** lies just past mile 237. For information about exploring and enjoying this grand national parkland, see the following chapter on Interior Alaska.

Glenn Highway:
Anchorage to Glennallen

The Glenn Highway is one of the most traveled routes in Alaska. It's also one of the most scenic. The sky-piercing Mentasta and Wrangell Mountains abut this route. It dissects long, wide valleys of spruce, alder, and birch forests, and in the Matanuska and Susitna Valleys it courses through Alaska's principal agricultural districts. The Glenn provides the principal access between Anchorage and Tok on the Alaska Highway.

Alaskans often talk about the Anchorage–Tok link as if it were one road. (And, indeed, the state Department of Highways designates it, plus part of the Seward Highway and all of the Sterling, as Alaska Route 1.) To be accurate, however, we should note that the 328-mile route actually consists of two separate highways and part of a third—the Glenn itself, which extends 189 miles from Anchorage to Glennallen; a 14-mile portion of the Richardson Highway, from Glennallen to Gakona; and the 125-mile Tok Cutoff, extending from Gakona to Tok, where it connects with the Alaska Highway.

We'll explore the Glenn and Richardson sections of the highway in this Southcentral Alaska section of the book; you'll find the Tok Cutoff portion in the following chapter on Interior Alaska.

Leaving Anchorage on the Glenn, you pass access roads to Elmendorf Air Force Base and Fort Richardson, and about 13 miles out, you come to a community called **Eagle River,** most of whose residents work in Anchorage. (By the way, if you happen to like Thai food, skip all the choices in Anchorage and make the drive out to Eagle River. A great little place, called **Thai Siam,** at 907–694–7246, has excellent noodle dishes and garlic broccoli.) From downtown Eagle River, drive 12.5 miles easterly on the Eagle River Road to the **Chugach State Park** and the nonprofit **Eagle River Nature Center.** There's lots of good information to be picked up here, including hiking maps and updates on recreation sites in one of Alaska's and America's largest state parks. Take a short hike on nearby trails, and check out nature walks and other get-togethers offered by area naturalists. The center also rents out a public-use cabin or yurt for $45 a night each; it's the perfect overnight getaway if you're not prepared for a long trek. The cabin, just built in 1998, is only a little more than a mile down the trail behind the nature center. The yurt, completed this year, is only a few minutes away from the cabin. Both have wood stove, firewood, and sleeping platforms. Just bring yourself and a taste for the wilderness. *A bit of a warning:* Bears are sighted here often, so be on the lookout and give way to the bruins at all times. Also, make your reservations early. The sites are popular and book up fast. Parking at the center is $3.00, unless you're staying at the cabin or yurt, in which case it is complimentary. For more information call (907) 694–2108.

Eklutna Village and *Eklutna Historical Park,* 26 miles from Anchorage, is another of those priceless little places that many pass by in their rush to get from Anchorage to some other, more publicized travel attraction. Through historical records, oral history, and archaeology, the Athabascan village can trace its occupancy of this area back an astonishing 350 years. To get to the park, exit left off the Glenn Highway at Eklutna. The road leads to the nearby park. A half-hour tour starts with an orientation in the Heritage House, which has art displays and lifestyle exhibits. The tour then leads, on a guided gentle walk, to a tiny little Russian Orthodox church built in the 1830s. Visitors then move on to a more modern church and, finally to the village cemetery, where the dead lie buried beneath small, colorfully painted "spirit houses." Admission is $3.50. Phone (907) 696–2828, e-mail ehp@alaska.net, or visit www.alaskaone. com/eklutna.

A great getaway is just a few miles away at Eklutna Lake, where you can rent a kayak and paddle beneath the vistas of Twin Peaks. Call *Lifetime Adventures* at (907) 746–4644, e-mail adventures@ matnet.com, or visit www.matnet.com/adventures.

Just before mile 30 on the Glenn, you have the opportunity to turn right onto the Old Glenn Highway. Both the Glenn and the Old Glenn

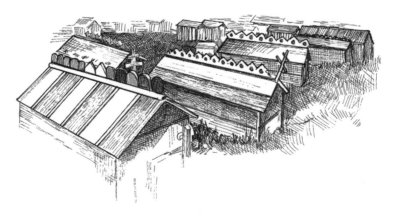

Spirit Houses at Eklutna Historical Park

end up in Palmer, but the older route offers options such as a view of **Bodenburg Butte,** access to a nice view of **Knik Glacier,** and the opportunity to see original Matanuska Valley colony farms. At the **Williams Reindeer Farm** on Bodenburg Loop Road (which begins at mile 11.5 on the Old Glenn) you can see, pet, and even feed reindeer. The farm also now boasts two moose, two elk, and a Sitka black-tailed deer. Admission charge is $5.00. Call (907) 745–4000, or point your Web browser to www.corcom. net/~reindeer/tours.

At the end of the Old Glenn Highway, and at mile 42 on the Glenn, lies **Palmer,** borough seat for the Matanuska Susitna Borough and a major hub for trade and agriculture in the Mat Valley. It's also the site during the eleven days preceding Labor Day each year of the **Alaska State Fair.** (Actually, other celebrations in the state share that designation, but none other is so large and well attended.) It's here, incidentally, that you can see and photograph the valley's huge and famous vegetables, including cabbages that sometimes reach close to one hundred pounds. There are lots of other food and animal exhibits as well as carnival-type rides and—perhaps most fun of all—political booths filled with Alaskan activists gathering petition signatures and giving out information about whatever is politically hot at the moment.

Just beyond Palmer, the partly paved, partly gravel **Fishhook Road** at mile 49.5 on the Glenn Highway offers a delightful side trip to wide-open spaces and vistas. The main attraction along the road, however, is fascinating **Independence Mine State Historical Park,** about 17 miles from the Glenn Highway junction. Here during the summer months you can take escorted tours through old mining structures that date back to the '30s. The cost is $3.00. Call (907) 745–2827. There's no charge for gold panning in the park, and rangers at the visitor center (the old mine manager's house) will direct you to the best prospects. Located on a private inholding within the 761-acre park is the A-framed **Hatcher Pass Lodge,** perched at a 3,000-foot elevation and offering cabins, rooms, and meals. The rate is $70 per night for a room, $115 for the cabins. Call (907) 745–5897, or visit www.hatcherpasslodge.com. Eventually the 49-mile road joins with the George Parks Highway.

Just off the Glenn Highway at about mile 50, a former farm from the old colony days now houses the **Palmer musk ox farm,** the only one of its kind in the country. About seventy of the animals (sort of a scaled-down water buffalo with long hair) live there. Their highly prized qiviut wool is knitted (only by Alaska Natives) into hats, scarves, and other items. An ounce of qiviut is eight times warmer than an equal amount of sheep's wool. The farm is open to the public from 10:00 A.M. to 6:00 P.M., May through September. Admission is $8.00. For information call (907) 745–4151 or visit www.muskoxfarm.org. E-mail is moxfarm@alaska.net.

If you'd like to walk on a glacier—minus the expense of a high-priced helicopter tour—the *Matanuska Glacier* offers a rare opportunity to do so. Turn off the Glenn Highway at mile 102 and take the gravel road to *Glacier Park Resort* (907–745–2534), which is perhaps a rather grand description for a pretty basic camping and tenting area plus gift shop, laundry, showers, liquor store, and snack foods. It nonetheless merits its $6.50 admission fee for adults ($3.50 for children) because from the parking lot you can stroll right up onto the glacier. If you use common sense, it's safe, but be cautious on the ice. It can be slick. And be on the lookout for crevasses that can run deep and cold. Other ways and places to view the glacier include the *Matanuska Glacier State Recreation Site* and camping area at mile 101, the state highway pull-out just past mile 101.5, and *Long Rifle Lodge,* beyond mile 102, where you can dine with a view of the ice river. The interior view at the lodge, incidentally, includes twenty-five wildlife mounts. Overnight rates start at $60 for a double. For dining or lodging reservations, call (800) 770–5151.

B&B usually means "bed-and-breakfast," but at mile 111.5 you'll find *Bunk 'n' Breakfast,* operated by Dee Larson. Rustic cabins sleep six guests (bring your own sleeping bag) at $15 a night. Farther along the highway, at mile 113.5, lies *Sheep Mountain Lodge* (907–745–5121; sheepmtl@alaska.net; www.alaska.net/~sheepmtl), established nearly a half century ago. If you can tear yourself away from the lodge's hot tub and sauna, there's great sheep viewing by telescope as well as excellent hiking in the area. Rates start at $95 for a room. Hostel bunks are available for $15 a night.

Another worthwhile side trip, just short of 20 miles each way, takes you to *Lake Louise* via the Lake Louise Road, which begins just before mile 160 on the Glenn Highway. Several fine fishing and outdoor lodges as well as a state recreation area and campgrounds are located on this lake in one of the North Country's premier water/mountain/glacier settings.

Evergreen Lodge is located on beautiful Lake Louise and provides lodging and B&B accommodations starting at $85 per night. The long-established lodge (907–822–3250, egl@alaska.net) also operates flight-seeing tours, guided fly-out fishing, and rental of a remote wilderness cabin. A five-day vacation package of an innovative safari includes daily fly-outs for fishing, scenery and wildlife photography, hiking, glacier-viewing, and sauna time. Your experience is wrapped up in an edited video souvenir complete with music, voice, and titles. The cost is $1,925.

If you're tenting or driving an RV, *Tolsona Wilderness Campground* lies ¾ mile north of the noise and traffic of the highway at mile 173 and is set in the forest beside Tolsona Creek. One of its newer attractions is a primitive 1-mile hiking trail to an active mud spring, where gases bubbling up from lower Cretaceous and upper Jurassic formations carry fine particles of silt to the surface to form a 2,075-foot hill from which the springs emerge. The spring itself flows year-round and is a source of water for wildlife, especially in the cold and frozen months of the year. Also, be sure to check out the proprietor's varied collection of turn-of-the-century artifacts. It's a museum tour—for free! The fee for tenters is $12, for RV hook-up campsites $18. Call (907) 822–3865, e-mail twcg@alaska.net, or visit www.alaskaoutdoors.com/Tolsona.

The Glenn and Richardson Highways meet and blend at Glennallen. Beyond this community, for 14 miles you're really traveling on the Richardson Highway and therefore the mileposts indicate miles from its start at Valdez. Then, at Gakona Junction, the Richardson continues north to Delta Junction and Fairbanks, while the *Tok Cutoff,* on the Anchorage–Tok route we're discussing here, courses northeasterly. You're right, it can be a little confusing, so be alert.

And . . . not to confuse you further, beyond Glennallen you're really traveling in Interior Alaska, so for information about the more northerly portions of this route, refer to the chapter on Interior Alaska.

The Richardson Highway– Southern Section: Valdez to Gakona Junction

When you drive on the 368-mile Richardson Highway, you're traveling along a historic gold rush route first pioneered in 1898 as the Valdez–Eagle Trail. The trail at that time, however, began with a treacherous start literally over the ice of Valdez Glacier, a fact that devastated or turned back many a would-be prospector before he ever started his trek to the gold fields. The following year Captain W. R. Abercrombie created an alternate route through Keystone Canyon and across Thompson Pass, bypassing the glacier. The route—first a sled dog and horse trail, now paved and fully modern—has been a major Alaskan land link between Prince William Sound and the Interior ever since. Today the Richardson connects Valdez with Delta Junction and Fairbanks. As the road approaches its second century, a few of its pioneer (but now renovated) roadhouses remain along the way, reminders of the era when warm, welcome accommodations were spaced a day's horse or dog team travel apart.

The canyon drive into or out of Valdez is one of Alaska's most spectacular, with high, steep walls and no small number of breathtaking waterfalls. The surrounding mountains are likewise high, rugged, and

I Before E, Unless You're a Miner

*I*s it Kennecott with an "e" or Kennicott with an "i"? The river and glacier, deep in the Wrangell Mountains, are Kennicott, named for Robert Kennicott. The much-photographed mine, with its deep red buildings, is known today as Kennecott due to a misspelling made in 1906.

The Kennecott Mines Co. established a camp and offices on the bank of National Creek, meaning to take its name from the Kennicott Glacier 3 miles to the north. But inadvertently its owners dropped the "i" and added an "e." It stuck. In 1908 the U.S. Postal Service established the post office of Kennecott. The town, which grew to a population of 494 by 1920, took its name from the mining company. During its heyday the Kennecott mined more than 590,000 tons of copper ore, making it the richest copper mine in the world. By 1938 copper prices had crashed and the company closed the mine.

To visit the mine you must make a sometimes harrowing drive to the town of McCarthy. From Glennallen follow the Edgerton Highway 66 miles to the hamlet of Chitina, population 49. After crossing the steel-span bridge over the Copper River, you're on the McCarthy Road, which follows the old Copper River and Northwestern Railway built between 1907 and 1911 to carry copper to the town of Cordova on Prince William Sound.

The 60-mile-long McCarthy Road is unpaved and often bumpy. In dry weather, it's dusty. In rainy weather, it's muddy. Top speed on the road is 20 mph.

For years the final stage of the journey to McCarthy and Kennecott was the hand-pulled cable car used by locals and visitors alike to cross the braided Kennicott River. In 1997 safety concerns finally forced the construction of a railed footbridge to replace the cable car.

spectacular. It's in this area and on these death-defying near-vertical mountain slopes each winter that the community hosts the *World Extreme Skiing Championships.* The event attracts practitioners of the daredevil sport from all over the world, and it's fast becoming a favorite spectator sport (with surprisingly good binocular views from the highway) among Southcentral Alaskans. For more information call the Valdez Visitors and Convention Bureau at (800) 770–5954.

It sounds pleasurable and it is: *Blueberry Lake State Recreation Site,* with loop entrances at both mile 23 and mile 24 along the Richardson, is a visual delight and a favorite campground for Alaskans. An alpine area situated above timberline, the site offers a sweeping sight of Keystone Canyon as well as close-up views of dwarf plants and other flora usually associated with northern tundra. It's also the natural habitat for Alaska's state bird, the willow ptarmigan. Flocks of dozens are not uncommon. The state camping fee is $12 per night.

At mile 26 you come to 2,678-foot *Thompson Pass,* where winter snowfall totaling nearly 1,000 inches has been recorded. The long, tall poles alongside the road guide snowplows and snowblowers in the snowy season. About 2 1/2 miles beyond the pass is *Worthington Glacier State Recreation Site,* where you'll find displays and exhibits explaining the huge river of ice. You can, if you'd like, drive up practically to the glacier.

At about mile 83 you come to the paved 35-mile *Edgerton Highway* to *Chitina* (pronounced CHIT-na; the second "i" is silent), which connects at the highway's end with the 60-mile gravel *McCarthy Road.* This road, in turn, leads over a former railroad bed to the near–ghost towns of *McCarthy* and *Kennecott,* within Wrangell–St. Elias National Park. Take the time to drive at least to Chitina, stopping en route perhaps at *Kenny Lake Mercantile and RV Park* (at mile 7.5) to top off your gas tank or, if you're pulling a rig, to drop off your RV and proceed unencumbered. In fact, you can even leave your car and RV here if you wish. This is a pickup point for scheduled van service to McCarthy and Kennecott. Call (907) 822–3313, e-mail knnylake@alaska.net, or visit www. alaskaoutdoors.com/kennylake/index.htm for details. If you enjoy collecting nature scenics, stop at mile 23.5 at bubbling, forested Liberty Creek and thunderous Liberty Falls in *Liberty Falls State Recreation Site*. The highway itself bisects rolling hills and takes in views of wide, forested valleys, grand lakes, and the imposing peaks of the Wrangells. If you're really lucky, you may even see bison herds across the Copper River.

The **National Park Service** has a ranger office in Chitina, and the staff there can tell you about park and local attractions as well as conditions on the McCarthy Road, which begins where the Edgerton ends. Picturesque Chitina is almost a ghost town—just ask the locals, who have painted humorous, ghostly pictures on a few of the town's abandoned turn-of-the-century structures. Hand-hewn log cabins, western-style stores, and rusting old cars, trucks, and wagons give testimony to the town's gold rush past.

If you're game, by all means continue beyond Chitina on the **McCarthy Road,** but be advised that it can be a slow, bumpy, and narrow. It can also be pretty muddy in the rain. Still, the rewards are many when you make it to the road's end at the Kennicott River. **McCarthy,** the town for which the road is named, lies across the river and you can access it easily by a footbridge across the water.

About two dozen hardy souls call McCarthy home, including lifelong Alaskans Gary and Betty Hickling, who operate **McCarthy Lodge restaurant and saloon** as well as the **Ma Johnson Hotel** (circa 1916). Visitor rooms, all of which are located in the hotel, are in the early twentieth–century tradition, long and slender and furnished in Victorian decor. The hotel does, however, offer modern shared baths. The $180 rate for two includes three meals daily for each person. The Hicklings also operate a hostel called the **Bunkhouse.** The nightly cost is $25; bring your own sleeping bag. Call (907) 554–4402 for more information.

The **McCarthy Museum,** housed in the old railway depot, displays items and photographs from the community's mining glory days. Five miles down the road (van pickup is available) lies the abandoned town and copper mine of **Kennecott** and **Kennicott Glacier Lodge,** a thoroughly modern, thoroughly elegant twenty-six-room lodge built in the style and decor of the surrounding old structures. Rates for the Kennicott Glacier Lodge, including transport from McCarthy, a guided tour of the ghost town, and three meals a day, begin at $127.50 per person per night, double occupancy. Call (800) 582–5128, or visit www.kennicottlodge.com for details. There's lots of exploring and poking around to be done in this National Historic Landmark community.

Two bush flight services based in McCarthy offer a wide variety of flight-seeing, hiker drop-off, and transportation services, including flights to Kennecott and Kennicott Glacier Lodge. **Wrangell Mountain Air** (800–478–1160; flywma@aol.com; www.wrangellmountainair.com) and **McCarthy Air** (907–554–4440) can serve you from McCarthy or from Chitina as well as from Glennallen or even Anchorage. Sample rates: ***Wrangell Mountain Air*** will ferry you from Chitina to McCarthy (thus relieving you of a long bumpy ride) for $130 round-trip; McCarthy Air prices thirty minutes of flight-seeing from McCarthy over valleys, glaciers, and historic mining sites at $100 per person per hour. Wrangell Mountain Air offers flight-seeing tours from $50 and hiking, rafting, and glacier-trek fly-ins from $60.

St. Elias Alpine Guides (907–554–4445 or 888–933–5427; stelias44@aol. com; www.steliasguides.com) offers a wide selection of options, including a Root Glacier Hike for $50 per person. This four- to six-hour trek allows you, while wearing crampons of course, to explore the ice formations, waterfalls, and blue-water pools that make glaciers so exotic. A Root Glacier fly-in is $150 per person. Alpine hikes are in the $35 to $95 range, for those who want their feet to stay planted firmly on the ground. Owner Bob Jacobs also guides travelers on a fly-in river rafting trek down the Kennicott and Nizina Rivers for $285 per person.

Abandoned Kennecott Copper Mine

Another well-regarded guide service is Howard Mozen's *Copper Oar,* which has been offering river rafting trips since 1985. A popular day trip is the Nizina Canyon full-day package, a seven-hour experience beginning with a river float and ending with a flight-see back to McCarthy. The $225 trip includes the flight and a gourmet lunch. Other trips range from two hours on the Kennicott River ($45) to nine days going all the way to the ocean near Cordova. For more information call (800) 523–4453, e-mail howmoz@aol.com, or visit www. alaskan.com/ copper_oar.

Back on the Richardson Highway, you come to the turnoff for *Copper Center* just beyond mile 100. The highway officially bypasses this community which grew out of a nineteenth-century trading post, but *you* shouldn't. Turn right onto the *Old* Richardson just past mile 100. The historic old *Copper Center Lodge,* still serving travelers as it has since 1897, is today fully modern, but well preserved. Rates start at $84 for rooms with shared bath, $94 for rooms with private facilities. Call (907) 822–3245 or (800) 822–3245. The lodge's restaurant serves sourdough pancakes made with a starter that can be traced back more than a century. Next door, in a small log cabin, you'll find one of two small but worthwhile stops for history buffs. The *George Ashby Memorial Museum* houses mining, trapping, Indian, and pioneer relics and displays. Half the cabin is an authentic old log bunkhouse. And within the museum you can walk through the actual iron doors of the old Copper Center Jailhouse. There is no charge, but donations are accepted. The other (relatively recent) historical stop is the log *Chapel on the Hill,* at mile 101 on the *Old* Richardson Highway, constructed in the early forties by U.S. Army servicemen. Daily free slide shows give visitors a visual look at Copper Valley and its features.

The park headquarters and visitor center for the *Wrangell–St. Elias National Park and Preserve* (the nation's largest, at 13.2 million acres) is located at mile 105.5 on the *Old* Richardson Highway, just north of Copper Center. The park, which is the size of six Yellowstones, contains nine of the sixteen highest peaks in the nation—not to mention countless glaciers, forested valleys, and many species of wildlife. The headquarters is your source of information about park hiking, camping, road access (extremely limited), and attractions. Call (907) 822–5235.

Driving north from Copper Center, the old segment of the Richardson Highway connects with the north end of the bypass at mile 106, and you're officially back on the Richardson. At mile 115 the highway meets at *Glennallen* with the Glenn Highway from Anchorage. For the next 14 miles, the Richardson Highway and the Glenn Highway–Tok Cutoff route are the same. Near mile 129 and Gakona Junction, the Tok Cutoff heads northeast, while the Richardson continues north to Delta Junction and Fairbanks.

And now, although there's no official boundary between Southcentral Alaska and the Interior, this is probably a good place to separate the two regions. For information about the northern portion of the Richardson Highway, see the next chapter on Interior Alaska.

PLACES TO STAY IN SOUTHCENTRAL ALASKA

ANCHORAGE
Hotel Captain Cook, Fourth Avenue and K Street; (907) 276–6000.

Anchorage Hotel, 330 E Street; (907) 272–4553.

GIRDWOOD
Alyeska Prince Hotel, 1000 Arlberg Avenue; (907) 754–1111. Luxury in the heart of the Girdwood skiing community.

HOMER
Land's End, 4786 Homer Spit Road; (907) 235–2500. At the end of the Homer Spit.

SEWARD
Seward Windsong Lodge, Mile 1/2, Exit Glacier Road; (800) 208–0200 or www.sewardlodging.com. On the road to Exit Glacier, just outside Seward.

SOLDOTNA
Goodnight Inn Lodge, 44715 Sterling Highway; (907) 262–4584. Right by the Kenai River.

PLACES TO EAT IN SOUTHCENTRAL ALASKA

ANCHORAGE
Glacier BrewHouse, 737 West Fifth Avenue; (907) 274–2739. Great Alaska seafood and freshly prepared side dishes that are both artful and tasty.

Moose's Tooth Pub & Pizzeria, 3300 Old Seward Highway; (907) 258–2537. Gourmet pizza and microbrew.

EAGLE RIVER
Thai Siam, 11823 Old Glenn Highway; (907) 694–7246. Extensive menu of authentic Thai cuisine.

HOMER
Cafe Cups, 162 West Pioneer Avenue; (907) 235–8330. Eclectic combination of vegetarian, prime seafood, and meat in an artistic, relaxed setting.

The Saltry, on the dock at Halibut Cove, across from Homer on Kachemak Bay; (907) 296–2223. Fresh-caught Alaska seafood.

SEWARD
Resurrection Bay Roadhouse, Mile 1/2, Exit Glacier Road: (800) 208–0200, www.sewardlodging.com. Just outside of Seward. Broad menu, but the pizza is the best.

Interior Alaska

From one point in Alaska's Interior region—the summit of Denali (Mt. McKinley)—climbers can literally look down on every other mountaintop, hill, ridge, valley, and plain in North America. (Although McKinley is the name the federal government officially recognizes for the continent's highest peak, Alaskans, noting that President William McKinley, of Ohio, never once laid eyes on even a little mountain in Alaska, greatly prefer to use the beautiful Athabascan Indian name for the peak, *Denali*, which means "the high one." Entreaties from the Alaska Legislature and Alaska's delegation in Congress to officially change the name, however, have fallen on deaf ears. The Ohio Congressional delegation seems always to succeed in blocking the change.) The view from Denali may explain why Interior Alaskans speak in such expansive terms about their region of sky-piercing mountains, rolling hills, long and mighty rivers, sub-Arctic tundra lands, and vast taiga

Denali's Wife

Traveling through Alaska, you'll notice reference to a mountain called Foraker, a 17,400-foot peak at the head of Foraker Glacier in Denali National Park and Preserve. It was named in 1899 for Joseph Benson Foraker, a U.S. Senator from Ohio. It wasn't uncommon at the time to name mountains, valleys, and towns after political officials, even if they had never stepped foot on Alaska soil.

But Foraker wasn't always singled out. When Russian explorers first discovered North America's highest peak, officially called Mount McKinley after President William McKinley, *they saw Foraker in its shadow and thought it to be part of the same mountain. They called the two, collectively,* Bolshaya Gora, *or "Big Mountain." Likewise, before the Russians, the Tanaina Indians of the Susitna River Valley also considered Foraker and McKinley one mountain, calling the massif Denali, meaning "the great one" or "the high one."*

However, the Tanana Indians in the Lake Minchumena area had a broadside view of the massif and could differentiate the two peaks. They referred to Foraker as Sultana, *the "woman," or* Menlale, *meaning "Denali's wife."*

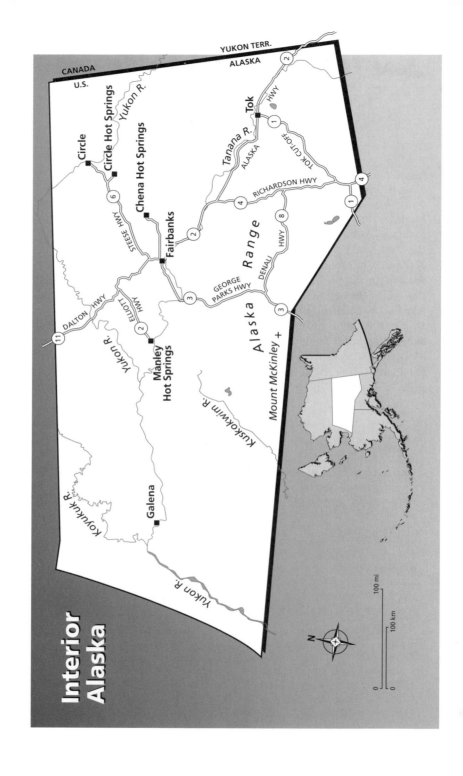

Interior Alaska

TOP 10 PLACES IN INTERIOR ALASKA

*Denali National Park
   and Preserve*

*Husky Homestead at
   Goose Lake Kennels*

*Denali National Park
   Wilderness Center—
   Camp Denali*

*The Resort at Chena
   Hot Springs*

The End Game Enterprise

*Cleft of the Rock Bed and
   Breakfast/Alaska Biking
   Adventures*

Arctic Circle Hot Springs

*Huck Hobbit's Homestead
   Campground and Retreat*

Tangle Lakes Lodge

Fairbanks Exploration Inn

forests. This is gold mining country and has been since Felix Pedro's 1902 strike near present-day Fairbanks. It's oil country as well, at least in the sense that a large share of the 800-mile Trans-Alaska Pipeline passes through the Interior on its way from Prudhoe Bay to the coast at Valdez.

And the Interior is grand traveling country. It's a land of long roads and riverways and remote fly-in lodges and cabins. It is also a place with a rich Athabascan Native culture, and a place of grizzlies, moose, caribou, wolves, and scores of smaller species. It's a warm and balmy region in the summer (though temperatures can plummet to sixty *below* in the winter).

Fairbanks, about 300 miles from the border and the second-largest community in Alaska, serves as transportation and travel hub for the region, and for that reason we describe the many facets of Fairbanks at the beginning of this chapter. We then deal with pleasurable things to see and do along Interior Alaska's roads and highways, most of which (but not all) lead to or from Fairbanks. We will examine the Interior portions of the state's four multiregion highways in the same order in which they appeared in earlier chapters. Specifically we'll describe the Alaska Highway from the border (where we left off in the Yukon chapter) to the highway's end at Delta Junction. We'll examine the northern portions of the George Parks Highway connecting Anchorage and Fairbanks and the Glenn Highway–Tok Cutoff route, which runs from Anchorage to Tok. And of course we will cover the northern portion of the Richardson Highway that begins at Valdez and ends in Fairbanks. We'll look, too, at the Steese Highway from Fairbanks to Circle City on the Yukon River. Not to be overlooked in these pages are the smaller and often-overlooked Denali Highway and the Elliott Highway; they're noted, too.

Fairbanks

A bustling, busy, dynamic city is **Fairbanks,** on the banks of the Chena River. Fairbanksans call it the Golden Heart of Alaska, and it was indeed gold in the early years of the century that brought about the founding of the town.

When, in 1901, Captain E.T. Barnette set out from St. Michael, at the mouth of the Yukon River, aboard the stern-wheeler *Lavelle Young,* he intended to establish a trading post in the gold prospecting area at Tanana Crossing, about halfway between Valdez and Eagle. He didn't get that far, however. The ship couldn't navigate the shallow Chena River beyond present-day Fairbanks, so he established his post there. And a fortunate choice it turned out to be. Felix Pedro, an Italian prospector, discovered gold in the area a year later, and a "rush" to Fairbanks soon followed.

The **Fairbanks Convention and Visitor Bureau Information Center** (800–327–5774; www.fairbanks.polarnet.com; info4fbk@eagle.ptialaska. net), right downtown on the banks of the Chena River at 550 First Avenue, provides lots of up-to-date information on things to see and do, places to go, restaurants, and overnight options. For the traveler seeking off-the-beaten-path options, an even more important resource is, once again, the **Alaska Public Lands Information Center,** which you'll find on the lower level of Courthouse Square, at Cushman Street and Third Avenue. Here you'll see displays, wildlife mounts, cultural artifacts, and basic information about the Interior's outdoor touring, camping, and recreational opportunities. There is no admission charge. Call (907) 456–0527, e-mail betsy-rossini@nps.gov, or visit www.nps. gov/aplic/center.

Interior Alaska Trivia

Between 1926 and 1957 the Fairbanks Exploration Company mined approximately $70 million worth of gold from the Fairbanks area.

Captain Jim Binkley's **stern-wheeler** Discovery III *cruise* is Fairbanks's most popular tour; it's also very much an off-the-beaten-path and educational experience. Twice daily, at 8:45 A.M. and 2:00 P.M., the vessel departs from its docks at 1975 Discovery Drive (southwest of downtown) for a cruise down the Chena and Tanana Rivers. En route, as the hustle and hurry of Fairbanks fades further and further behind, passengers learn about the Native Athabascan peoples of this area—some of whom are onboard as guides—as well as the history of gold rushes and oil booms and homesteading hereabouts. They watch as huge fish wheels, powered by stream currents, scoop fish into large holding baskets from the rivers they're cruising. If they're lucky, they even see moose in the woods along the shore. Finally, the vessel stops at a river island for a visit at **Old Chena Indian Village.** There, musher David Munson (whose wife Susan Butcher has won the grueling 1,000-mile Iditarod sled dog classic four times) demonstrates sled dog mushing. There, too, as visitors wander from site to site on the island, they see how Athabascan Indians and Eskimos from farther north smoke fish, tan wildlife hides, sew leather, bead garments, and live in a harsh but bountiful environment. The cost is $39.95. Call (907) 479–6673, e-mail discovery@ARTTinc. com, or visit www.ptialaska.net/~discovry.

If you're interested at all in birds, *Creamer's Field Migratory Waterfowl Refuge,* only 1 mile from downtown, provides great viewing of huge flocks of ducks and geese in the spring and fall and sandhill cranes during the summer months. You can walk along a 2-mile self-guided nature trail and visit the restored farmhouse that now serves as visitor center. The start of the trail is located at 1300 College Road. College Road is one of Fairbanks's principal east-west thoroughfares. It is located about 1 mile north of downtown. Donations are accepted. Call (907) 452–5162.

Close by Creamer's Field, on College Road at the *Tanana Valley Fairgrounds,* you can shop at the *Tanana Valley Farmer's Market* for fresh veggies, meats, bakery items, flowers, and craft goods on Wednesday from noon to 5:00 P.M.; Saturday from 9:00 A.M. until 4:00 P.M. It's the only market of its kind in Interior Alaska.

At the *University of Alaska Museum,* on the UA Fairbanks campus, northwest of downtown, you can view natural and historical exhibits, such as an incredible 36,000-year-old Steppe bison that was almost perfectly preserved in Alaska's permafrost until its discovery in this century. Also on display are contemporary wildlife mounts (including a really humungous brown bear), the state's largest exhibit of gold, Native art, plus an exhibit on the aurora borealis (northern lights). Admission is $5.00 for adults; the museum is open daily. Call (907) 474–7505, e-mail fyuamvs@aurora.alaska.edu, or visit zorba.uafadm. alaska.edu: 80/museum for details.

For your photo collection of strange beasties of the Arctic, tour the university's considerably less visited *Large Animal Research Station*

Chatanika Days Outhouse Races: *Here's something different in the Interior community of Chatanika off the Steese Highway. Held each March, this winter festival also includes a long-johns contest and snow-machine tug-of-war. (907) 389–2164.*

Ice Art Competition: *Held each March in Fairbanks, this competition pits the world's best ice carvers, who make intricate ice sculptures. (800) 327–5774; info4fbk@eagle.ptialaska.net; www.fairbanks.polarnet.com.*

Buffalo Wallow Square Dance Jamboree: *Held in May in Delta Junction, home to the state's largest buffalo herd. (907) 895–9941.*

World Eskimo-Indian Olympics: *Held every July in Fairbanks. (800) 327–5774; info4fbk@eagle.ptialaska.net; www.fairbanks.polarnet.com.*

Mainstreet Alaska Sourdough Potlach: *In Tok each August. (907) 883–5775; info@TokAlaskaInfo.com; www.TokAlaskaInfo.com.*

(907–474–7945; fnweh@uaf.edu), off Yankovich Road north of the main campus. There, among other animals, you'll find the shaggy, horned musk ox, once hunted to extinction within Alaska. With the help of imported animals from Canada, the species is making a comeback. UAF also offers tours of the **Geophysical Institute,** where scholars ferret out knowledge of the earth's deepest regions and the heaven's northern lights. And for the botanically inclined, the university will give you a guided visit to the Agricultural and Forestry Experiment

This Is Sled Dog Country

The yapping of dogs on a usually busy downtown street in Fairbanks drew me to the crowd of spectators. I am a dog lover, an animal lover actually, so it was only natural that I check out what was going on. I was greeted with the North American Sled Dog races, one of the most competitive sprint sled dog races in the world. I watched in awe as teams of twenty or more dogs were hooked up to one little wooden sled with one musher standing at the runners, and I wondered how in the world these people can control so many excited, yanking, lunging dogs.

When I first moved to Alaska and got into the sport of mushing, I'm sure I was like most novices. I thought it would be fun, like taking a ride on a snow machine and having complete control. Well, it's not that way at all. I ran eight dogs the first time I took to the runners of a sled, and in retrospect I realize that was about six too many for a beginner. But my mushing buddy was confident in my ability (or he just wanted get a good laugh!) and he told me this: "No matter what, don't let go of the sled."

We took off out of the dog yard, and I immediately felt out of control. The sled whipped and bumped, and the

dogs were absolutely intent on running as fast as they possibly could. Within a half mile, the sled slid out from under me on a turn, and I was being dragged and bounced along behind it—but still holding on. The dogs never looked back. I somehow righted the sled as we continued, and I brushed myself off. Five minutes later, I repeated my antics, still clinging desperately to the handlebow, and righted myself just in time to see Gus, with his team ahead of me, looking back watching my progress.

In Fairbanks, I watched the teams cross the finish line. It took more than a simple snow hook to brake these dogs. Groups of men and women would come from the finish-line crowd and lunge at the sled as it crossed, helping to slow the dogs, while the musher stood with all his weight on the brake. The dogs looked no slower coming in than they had leaving the starting chute.

Today, with my own small team, I can truly appreciate what I saw that day in Fairbanks, which serves as a sort of hub for Interior mushers. I never underestimate a dog's power, I never assume a run will go perfectly, and, no matter what, I never let go of the sled.

Station's **Georgeson Botanical Garden.** Call (907) 474–1944, visit www.lter.alaska.edu, or e-mail ffpsh@aurora.alaska.edu.

In 1967, wanting to commemorate the one hundredth anniversary of Alaska's purchase from Russia in a lasting way, the people of Fairbanks and the State of Alaska created a forty-four-acre pioneer theme park called Alaska 67. Renamed **Alaskaland** (907–459–1087) after the official year of celebration ended, the park continues in business on Airport Way, with a wide variety of things to see and do. There's no admission charge to enter Alaskaland, but there are fees to visit some portions of the park. Among various things to see and do, you'll find a genuine stern-wheeler riverboat (the **S.S. Nenana,** a national historic landmark), a **Gold Rush Town** of relocated and restored homes and stores from Fairbanks's early days, the frontier **Palace Theatre and Saloon,** a miniature mining valley, a newly created pioneer air museum of early aircraft, plus one of the two best salmon bakes/barbecues in Alaska. (The other is in Juneau.) Circling it all is the **Crooked Creek & Whiskey Island Railroad,** not terribly authentic, perhaps, but it is fun and a good way to get the lay of the land before you start wandering around the acreage.

For the culturally curious, one of Alaskaland's most interesting locales is the **Native Village,** where Athabascan Indian young people proudly entertain and educate visitors with stories and ancient dances. In the village museum, where you'll note a pleasant faint scent of cottonwood-smoked animal skins, you'll see a wide variety of artifacts, tools, weapons (such as a bear-killing spear), and art, including masterful beadwork. The young people share legends, history, and their techniques of survival in one of the harshest environments on earth. There's also an Athabascan *kashim,* a log house with sod roof, as well as a traditional underground sod home of the type once used by Alaska's Eskimo peoples. There is a modest admission fee to the village.

Here's a chance to collect another Alaska superlative. If you're a golfer and want to play some really far out golf, be aware that two courses in Fairbanks lay claim to being the farthest north golf course in the world. Friends in the city tell me that the **North Star Golf Club** is actually a tad more northerly (though on the opposite side of the city) than the **Fairbanks Golf and Country Club**—but who's measuring? The thing to do is play them both. You'll find North Star northeast of town off Old Steese Highway on Golf Club Drive. Call (907) 457–4653 for tee times. The

Fairbanks Golf and Country Club is located northwest, near the intersection of Farmers Loop Road and Ballaine Road. Phone (907) 479–6555.

You can relive some of Fairbanks's gold heritage at a working gold mine and visitor operation called **El Dorado Gold Camp,** about 9 miles northwest of Fairbanks on the Elliott Highway. You'll be treated to a short train ride on a tour of old and new "diggin's" at the mine, then a demonstration of how sluicing and panning for gold works. Once you're ready, they turn you loose with a pan of your own and some ore that's guaranteed to contain "color." You can keep all you find. The experience runs $24.95. Call (907) 479–7613, or e-mail discovery@ARIInc.com.

Historic **Gold Dredge Number 8,** at mile 9 on the Old Steese Highway, is a restored relic from an important mining era in Alaska's gold country. Between 1928 and 1959 this huge, floating hulk, five decks high and 250 feet long, scooped $3 billion worth of gold from creeks near Fairbanks. You can take a guided tour of the now-inoperative dredge for $20, which includes the tour, a video presentation of the dredge in action, and gold panning—manager Gideon Garcia says you're guaranteed to find some gold. Five tours are operated daily. Time your visit between 11:00 A.M. and 3:00 P.M., and lunch is served in the dining hall for $8.00 for adults. Call (907) 457–6058, or e-mail gidg@alaska.net.

Lots of people arrive in Alaska and regret that they left their camping equipment, bicycles, or canoe at home. **Independent Rental, Inc.,** at 2020 South Cushman in the heart of Fairbanks, will rent not only these items but also inflatable rafts and boats, fishing gear, tools, even video cameras. Call (907) 456–6595 or e-mail ilcoinfo@mosquitonet.com.

Among the smaller Alaska-based tour companies operating out of Fairbanks is Terry McGhee's **Trans-Arctic Circle Treks Ltd.** (800–336–8735, for reservations only; 907–479–5451; arctictk@ptialaska.net; www.arctictreks.com or www.glacierblue.com). Trans-Arctic Circle Treks offers one-, two-, three- and ten/fourteen-day adventures across the northern portion of the state. An Arctic Circle Weekend Special will take you from either Fairbanks or Anchorage to the Arctic Circle in the comfort of a fifteen-passenger van. From Fairbanks the cost is $99; from Anchorage, $275. The other end of the spectrum is the ten- to fourteen-day sun-filled summer tour that takes you from Anchorage to the Arctic Circle and beyond. This summertime trip has unlimited possibilities, and Terry will customize each trip to your liking.

Alaska is one of those places where, even if you don't imbibe, you really ought to visit a few of the more colorful frontier saloons. In Fairbanks, at least three watering holes match that description: the

Palace Theatre and Saloon at Alaskaland; the *Dog Sled Saloon* (907–452–1888; cbi@ptialaska. net) in the Captain Bartlett Inn, itself rather a colorful log motel, at 1411 Airport Way; and the *Malemute Saloon,* at the Ester Gold Camp just off mile 351.7 on the George Parks Highway. The last is one of those atmospheric places frequented by locals as well as visitors where patrons throw peanut shells on the sawdust floor and gawk at the artifacts and the art junk on the walls. In the glow of a single lantern each evening an Alaska sourdough recites Robert Service's epic poems of the Yukon.

It's not cheap, but you can book one of Alaska's highest rated backcountry flight tours from Fairbanks via *Frontier Flying Service* (907–474–0014; www.frontierflying.com; info@frontier-flying.com). It's the company's full-day excursion to *Anaktuvuk Pass* north of the Arctic Circle on the northern edge of the Brooks Range. The pass is both a geographic location and a Nunamiut ("People of the Land") Eskimo village. Your surroundings are the majestic peaks encompassed in Gates of the Arctic National Park. During the course of your flight-seeing and four-hour ground tour in the village, you'll meet the hardy, friendly people who still live largely a subsistence caribou-hunting and fishing lifestyle. You'll walk through the village with a local resident, tour the Simon Paneak Museum, and visit Gates of the Arctic U.S. Park Service headquarters. The cost is $299 round-trip and is booked through Northern Alaska Tours (907) 474–8600).

Larry's Flying Service (907–474–9169) offers an interesting idea if you want to see Anaktuvuk Pass, but not necessarily be led on a guided tour. It will save you some money, and you're likely to meet one of the locals on the plane. For $175 at 1:00 P.M. Tuesday and Friday, the mail plane heads to the pass, and you can jump aboard for the flight. You'll land in the village long enough to toodle around for a bit on your own, then fly back with the pilot and outgoing mail. If you'd rather charter a plane, the rate is $225 per hour for a five-passenger plane, which can be split among your traveling companions. The flight to and from Anaktuvuk, incidentally, is about three hours.

The geographic center of Alaska lies 60 miles northwest of Mount McKinley (Denali), at 63 degrees-50 north, 152 degrees west.

The Yukon River is Alaska's longest river. It runs 1,400 miles from Canada to the Bering Sea.

The first oil pumped through the 800-mile trans-Alaska oil pipeline took thirty-eight days, twelve hours and fifty-four minutes to arrive in Valdez.

Anaktuvuk Pass is the last remaining settlement of Nunamiut Eskimos, an inland Inupiat whose ancestors date to 500 B.C.

The Brooks Range includes nine groups of mountains, but not Mount McKinley, which is in the Alaska Range.

Another flight-seeing service, the **Fairbanks Flight Train** (907–474–0757), takes you on a sixty- to ninety-minute excursion with an onboard narrator-naturalist, flying over the pipeline, the small community of Fox, gold mines, and Gold Dredge Number 8, plus Tanana and Minto flats, where you may see moose, geese, and bears. Fares vary from $79 to $89. The company will pick you up at your hotel.

Athabasca Cultural Journeys is the name of a bush adventure that begins with a small plane flight from Fairbanks to the Native village of Huslia and continues by boat up the Koyukuk River to an authentic Athabascan fish camp in the *Koyukuk National Wildlife Refuge.* An Indian family will serve as your hosts during a four-day visit, during which you may well see moose, caribou, bear, otter, and beaver plus eagles, hawks, owls, and other birds. Accommodations are clean, roomy canvas tents with extra wide cots. Generous meals may include moose-meat stew. There's time for recreational fishing and visits to archaeological sites as well. For details, call (800) 423–0094.

If you're looking for a classic, woodsy Alaska wilderness-type lodge located within a fifteen- to twenty-minute drive from downtown, Tom Ridner's **North Woods Lodge,** on Chena Hills Drive, is the answer to your quest. The main lodge is constructed from massive logs and can handle a group of any size, from a couple to several families traveling together. Guests can relax on a large deck running the full length of the building or soak up some "midnight sun" at the end of a day in a

Malemute Saloon, Fairbanks

twelve-person Jacuzzi hot tub. Bedrooms average about $65, but accommodations in the hostel sleeping loft can run as low as $15. A separate 10-by-12-foot cabin with two twin bunks rents for $45 for two.

The newest additions to Tom's lodge include three one-room log cabins that are $45 for a single or $55 for two or more. This still leaves room, if you like, for tent spaces, which are $12 for a single and $15 for two or more people. This price includes use of a kitchenette and showers, a welcome amenity if you're returning to town after a trek in the wilderness. Call (907) 478–5305 or (907) 479–5300, or visit www.Alaska.One.com/northlodge.

Also set on Chena Ridge among towering spruce with panoramic views of the Tanana Valley, the Alaska Range, and Fairbanks is **Forget-Me-Not Lodge-Aurora Express** (800–221–0073; www.aurora-express.com). Owners Mike and Susan Wilson have made a business of renovating rail cars to use as attractive rooms for guests. Among their lodging options aboard their Aurora Express are the National Emblem, which has two bathrooms and sleeps up to five people—a good choice for families; the Arlene, a private car with two bedrooms; the National Domain, four rooms, each with private entries and private baths; and the Golden Nelly, a special room in the caboose (the locomotive is there just for looks). Rooms range from $85 to $200. For those who prefer an equally elegant but traditional setting, the Wilsons' 5,000-square-foot lodge home offers a variety of choices, including the 650-square-foot Lilac and Lace Suite with cathedral ceilings, a king-size bed, and private bath. Breakfasts are beyond the description of "full," and are more like a Sunday brunch every day. Don't be surprised to find king crab Muenster crepes, fruit tortes, and any number of elegant offerings. Breakfasts are buffet style in a comfortable setting.

For tasteful and attractive lodging in town, don't miss a visit to the historic **Fairbanks Exploration Inn** at 505 Illinois Street. Originally built in 1926 for the employees of the Fairbanks Exploration gold mining company, this inn now is on the National Register of Historic Places. Today, it is in a parklike setting with extensive gardens and lots of trees. There are sixteen rooms, fourteen of which have private baths. The

Interior Alaska Trivia

The town of Glennallen derives its name from the combined last names of Captain Edwin Forbes Glenn and Lieutenant Henry T. Allen, who explored the Copper River region in the late 1800s.

rooms are situated in separate houses, each of which has a common room with fireplace and a place to relax. Breakfasts are extensive continental, with fresh bagels or muffins, a fruit plate, smoked salmon or whitefish, cereal, juice, and coffee or tea. Call (907) 451–1920 or (888) 452–1920, e-mail FEInn@polarnet.com, or visit www2. polarnet. com/~FEInn.

G.O. Shuttle Service, in Fairbanks, offers shuttles from the airport or rail or bus depot to any of the B&Bs in town. Fares run about $7.00 per person. It also provides tours and transfers to other points of interest in Fairbanks. Phone (907) 474–3847, or e-mail goalaska@aol.com.

For standard Alaska fare that is prepared nicely, try **The Pumphouse Restaurant,** at 796 Chena Pump Road. The seafood is particularly good. Phone (907) 479–8452, e-mail pumphse@polarnet.com, or visit www.ptialaska.net/~pumphse. **Pikes Landing,** on the Chena riverbanks, at 4438 Airport Way, is another favorite. We usually choose the casual outdoor setting, on the large deck (907–479–7113; duffy@ mosquitonet.com). Or try the **Two Rivers Lodge** (907–488–6815), at mile 16 on the Chena Hot Springs Road, where your choices range from seafood to steaks and Cajun cuisine.

The Alaska Highway: U.S. Border to Delta Junction

Now, back to the Alaska Highway, where, in the Yukon chapter, we left off at the U.S. and Canada border. Your first stop in Interior Alaska, mandatory if you're coming in from Canada on the Alaska Highway, is the **U.S. Customs and Immigration Station** at mile 1,221.8, right at the international boundary. The station sits sort of out in the middle of nowhere, with no large community nearby.

At mile 1,229, similarly situated, the **U.S. Fish and Wildlife Service** maintains a log cabin visitor center with an observation deck and outdoor exhibits about Alaska's wildlife. There's more of the same indoors, along with animal mounts and lots of good information about Alaska's fish, birds, and other wild critters.

The **Naabia Niign Athabascan Indian Crafts** store (907–778–2297) is located at the junction of the Alaska Highway and the Northway

Road, at mile 1,264. If you'd like to examine intricately and colorfully beaded moccasins, mukluks (boots), mitts, vests, and other apparel, this is an excellent place to do so. There's also a campground with full services at the site.

At mile 1,302 you come to the Tetlin Junction, a meeting of the Alaska Highway and the *Taylor Highway,* which extends north to Eagle. The Taylor, in turn, provides access to the Canadian Yukon Territory's *Top of the World Highway* to Dawson City, Yukon. For information about these roads, see the sections after Dawson City in the chapter Canada's Yukon.

You'll come to the next major highway junction at mile 1,314, right in the middle of *Tok* (rhymes with poke), where the Alaska Highway, heading sort of west, meets the Tok Cutoff–Glenn Highway from southwesterly Anchorage. Just before the junction, you'll see the *Alaska Public Lands Information Center* (907–883–5667), where you can get tons of information about state and federal lands, waters, and outdoor recreation. Audiovisual aids, wildlife mounts, and helpful staff will provide you with the latest about places and things to do both on and off the beaten path. Also worth a visit is *Alaska's Mainstreet Visitor Center* (907–883–5775; www.TokAlaskaInfo.com; info@TokAlaskaInfo.com), operated by Tok's chamber of commerce. The center, also at the above-mentioned junction, is located in the largest log structure in the state. It features a number of mounted wildlife and birdlife dioramas. A real treat at the visitor center is "Sourdough Sunday," in which old-time Alaskans share their stories of life in the Last Frontier. One of those people likely will be the "Tent Lady," Donna Blasor-Bernhardt, who will tell you about the year she and her family lived in a wall tent, sometimes shivering through temperatures as low as 69 degrees below zero. Blasor-Bernhardt is also the town's "poet laureate" and owner/operator of *A Winter Cabin Bed and Breakfast,* 3 blocks off the Alaska Highway at mile 1,316.5. She offers three newly built log cabins with a shared bathhouse and cozy, comfortable "Alaska-style" rooms. Breakfasts are continental style, with all the makings right in your room for an eat-at-your-leisure pace. The rates are $60 to $80, depending on which cabin you chose. Phone (907) 883–5655, e-mail wntrcabn@ptialaska.net, or visit www2.polarnet. com/~wntrcabn/Donna.html.

> ### Interior Alaska Trivia
>
> *The lowest body temperature recorded in a living mammal is minus 2.9 degrees Celsius in hibernating arctic ground squirrels. A high sugar condition may keep the animals' blood from freezing.*

Here in Tok the locals take sled dog racing, Alaska's official state sport, very seriously. You can see mushing demonstrations at the *Burnt Paw* gift shop (907–883–4121), beyond mile 1,314 on the Alaska Highway, nightly except Sunday at 7:30 P.M. and at the **Westmark Hotel** (907–883–5174 or 800–544–0970), near the Alaska Highway–Tok Cutoff junction. (Check at the desk for times.) You can also take a sled ride at **Mukluk Land** theme park, at mile 1,317. Sleds, of course, are on wheels in the summer, since the snow is long gone. Incidentally, Donna Blasor-Bernhardt's original tent is on display at the park.

Speaking of sled dog racing, winter visitors can see mushers and their dogs almost any weekend working out or racing on the Tok Dog Mushers Association trail, which starts at their log headquarters building at mile 1,312.8 on the Alaska Highway. Spectators can view the 20-mile course from many points along the highway.

If you'd like to start your day and your visit in a thoroughly Alaskan way, try the **sourdough pancake breakfast with Alaska reindeer sausage** at the Sourdough Campground, 1 1/2 miles south of the junction on the Tok Cutoff. The cost is $6.25. Phone (907) 883–5543.

For a tasty end to your day, try **Tok Gateway Salmon Bake**, at about mile 1,313, which features outdoor grilled king salmon, halibut, ribs, and reindeer sausage. It's open 11:00 A.M. to 9:00 P.M. every day except Sunday, when it opens at 4:00 P.M. Phone (907) 883–5555, or visit www.tokalaska. com/toksamon.shtml.

Perhaps your best lodging option in Tok is John and Jill Rusyniak's **Cleft of the Rock Bed and Breakfast,** 1 1/2 miles down Sundog Trail and 3 miles northwest of Tok. The Rusyniaks have guest rooms and suites as well as Alaska log cabins, with rates ranging from $55 to $115 year-round. A hot breakfast is served each morning. The B&B is situated in a black spruce forest with bike trails nearby, which is convenient since the Rusyniaks also own **Alaska Biking Adventures**. They offer bike rentals and guided wilderness tours ranging from two hours to all day. Guided trips are $25 to $65. Bike rentals start at $5.00 an hour, but guests get a nice discount. To access either business call (800) 478–5646, or e-mail cleftrck@ptialaska.net. The Web sites for the two businesses are http://tokalaska.com/cleftroc.shtml (B&B) and www.ptialaska.net/~cleftrck/ABA.html.

If you're traveling by RV or roughing it in a tent, **Rita's Campground and RV Park** (907–883–4342) at mile 1,315 is a good choice, with electric hookups, showers, and picnic spots. The rates start at $15 and up for RVs, and $12 for two for a campsite.

Flight-seeing can be had through **40-Mile Air,** which will take you over the Alaska Range to see glistening glaciers. The fifty-minute flights offer you a chance to see moose, bears, and Dall sheep as well. Call (907) 883–5191.

North Pole was named by a development company that hoped to attract a toy manufacturer that could advertise its toys were made at the North Pole, Santa's home.

When you get to **Delta Junction,** at mile 1,422, you've come to the end of the Alaska Highway. From that point on north, the road to Fairbanks is the **Richardson Highway,** and the mileposts beside the road indicate distance from Valdez. Delta Junction's Richardson Highway milepost is 266. For information about the Richardson from Delta Junction north, see the section in this chapter on the Richardson Highway.

The George Parks Highway— Northern Section: Denali to Fairbanks

The George Parks Highway, you'll recall, runs for nearly 360 miles from near Anchorage on the shores of Cook Inlet, to Fairbanks. In our Southcentral chapter, we followed the course of this excellent highway to Denali National Park and Preserve, where this section picks up this road once more.

For many, **Denali National Park** is the high point of an Alaska vacation. (No pun was intended, but as a matter of fact, the top of Denali Mountain, at 20,320 feet, is the highest point in North America.) And in the surrounding parklands, visitors may well see more game— moose, grizzly bears, caribou, Dall mountain sheep, perhaps even wolves plus any number of smaller creatures and birds—than anywhere else they travel in the state.

It should be noted, however, that much of the park and its environs are by no means off the beaten path. In particular, the strip along the George Parks Highway near the mile 237 park entrance overwhelms with hotels, lodges, motels, cabins, RV parks, and varied visitor services. Most of the overnight accommodations there are roomy, nice, and comfortable, like **Denali Sourdough Cabins,** at mile 238.8 (907–683–2773 or 800–354–6020; www.denalisourdoughcabins.com). Some of them, such as the **Denali Princess** (800–426–0500) and **Denali Parks Resorts** (800–276–7234; www.denalinationalpark.com) properties, are quite superior. But the sheer numbers of such places provide ample evidence that many thousands of visitors beat down this path every summer. So where, if you're a dedicated offbeat traveler, can you stay? And what can you do away from the crowds?

Actually you have options, not the least of which is to pitch a tent or park your RV at one of seven National Park Service campgrounds within the park itself, then hike in the backcountry hills, valleys, mountain slopes, and open spaces in splendid isolation. Isolation, that is, from the human sort. During the nine-day backcountry trek I went on with a friend a few years back, we were greeted face to face by a curious grizzly bear just moments after making a short river crossing. Needless to say, when you're this far off the beaten path, you can expect something like that to

"Bearly" Escaped

The big brown bear walked deliberately toward me, and I hustled to hoist my pack on my shoulders and start backing away. The instructions of the Denali National Park and Preserve rangers rushed through my mind in a jumble, and I couldn't keep the order straight—drop and play dead or wait until the big bruin charges, stand my ground and shout the thing off (yeah, right . . .), or, despite their warnings, follow my own instincts and turn tail and run as fast as I can with the fifty-pound pack on my back? My hiking partner shouldered her pack and we stood side by side. In a collective but unspoken agreement we began shouting "Go away bear! Hey, bear! Get out of here, bear!" We waved our walking sticks and tried to make ourselves look ominous, too big of a problem for the bear to mess with.

Still, it walked toward us. At about 7 feet, I turned to Michele. "Do we drop now?" I asked. Michele didn't answer and just kept shouting at the bear. It wasn't being aggressive, no need to play dead. We stayed put, two 125-pound women versus a 450-pound
grizzly bear. It came even closer—6 feet, 5 feet, now 4 feet. I could hear my heart pounding and willed it to quiet down for fear of aggravating the bear.

I've been scared before, so scared that the rush of adrenaline set my hands to quivering and my heart to beating extra-fast. It's happened during near misses of a head-on collision, when I almost fell down the steps with my newborn in my arms, when my husband jumped from behind a door to "startle" me. But never have I been more frightened than I was that day in Denali National Park during a nine-day backcountry trek into trailless wilderness.

The bear seemed more curious than aggressive. It stuck its dark, pointed nose in the air and stuck out a cotton-candy-pink tongue. It licked the air, tasting our scent. It herded us a few more feet backward. And it turned and walked away. We stood motionless on the river bar, our sticks still in the air, our mouths set tight with tension. The bear ambled into the brush and was gone.

happen. Be aware, however, that overnight backcountry hikes require a permit, and the number of backcountry users permitted in a given area is limited. *Another caution:* Campsites within the park are often hard to come by, so it's wise to reserve months ahead if you can by calling the reservations line, (800) 622–7275 (in Anchorage call 907–272–7275). If all advance-reservation camping slots have been assigned for the days you plan to visit, you may be able to reserve space up to two days in advance on a first-come first-served basis at the *Park Service visitor center* on the main park road, 1/2 mile inside the park boundary.

If you enjoy day hikes, check the bulletin boards and with the ranger on duty at the information center for the times, location, and degree of hiking skills required for various ranger-escorted treks not only in the park entrance area but at bus-accessible points along the single road that bisects the park and at the *Eielson Visitor Center* and *Wonder Lake,* near the road's end.

If you're not a camper, consider spending a few days at award-winning *Denali National Park Wilderness Center–Camp Denali,* at the western end of the park road, just outside the National Park Service boundary. This is one of Alaska's best-loved backcountry ecotourism lodges and has been since its founding nearly a half century ago. Guests enjoy breathtaking views of Denali and other peaks of the Alaska Range from hillside log cabins. Meals are served family style in the main lodge building. Short walks and wildlife-viewing hikes, guided by experienced wilderness interpreters, provide fascinating insight into the nature of things. Canoeing, biking, rafting, flight-seeing, gold panning, and evening natural history talks provide further options. Call (907) 683–2290, e-mail dnpwild@alaska.net, or visit www.gorp.com/dnpwild.

Also at the far western end of the road lies *Kantishna Roadhouse* and the former gold mining town of Kantishna, now a wilderness resort. The accommodations are in a new log lodge and cabins. Attractions include the Smokey Joe Saloon, escorted nature walks, wagon tours, and horseback rides plus mountain biking, gold panning, and fishing. Rates, including round-trip bus transportation from Denali train depot, all meals, and most activities, start at $280 per person per night in a twin room. Call (800) 942–7420, e-mail kantishna@polarnet.com, or visit www.kantishnaroadhouse.com.

Another option, this one a remote lodge accessible only by a twenty-minute bush flight from Denali Airport, also lies outside the park boundary. *Denali Wilderness Lodge,* in pristine Wood River Valley, contains twenty-eight hand-hewn log buildings set in a tiny enclave among 2,000 square miles of wilderness. Structures include a rustic but luxurious main lodge and wildlife museum (one hundred game mounts from around the world), more than a dozen cabins, each with private bath, and various support cabins. Guests hike and ride horseback on guided and unguided sight-seeing and photography treks. Meals are bountiful and of gourmet quality. Lodging is $290 per night, which includes meals, naturalist hikes, and horseback riding. The flight in is separate and costs $50 one-way. Day adventures vary from a $190 three- to four-hour guided tour to a $300 full-day horseback trek. Contact (800) 541–9779, e-mail denwild@alaska.net, or visit www.AlaskaOne.com/dwlodge.

Within Denali Park itself, you'll spot most wildlife during bus or motor-coach tours that run daily on the single park road. Although the Park Service no longer offers free shuttles on the road as it once did, a new program of low-cost bus rides represents a "best buy" option for frugal travelers. The price now for a trip on the road ranges from $12.50 to $27.00 per adult, depending on a visitor's destination in the park. Discounts are available for three- and six-day passes. Note that travelers can now book shuttle reservations and buy tickets through the same toll-free number they can use to reserve campsites, (800) 622–PARK or visit www.nps.gov/dena/. Narrated tours in roomier coaches are offered by Denali Park Resorts (800–276–7234; www. denalinationalpark.com). The six- to eight-hour *Tundra Wildlife Tour,* priced at $64, travels to the Toklat River in the park and includes a naturalist guide and a boxed lunch. The shorter, $35 *Natural History Tour* is three hours.

Denali National Park is one of my favorite places, and I've been there at least half a dozen times. I often wish I lived there, especially if it could be somewhere like Denali musher Jeff King's home. Three-time Iditarod Sled Dog Race champion King, his wife, Donna, their three daughters, and 80-plus dogs live on a ridge just south of the park, and a tour of this world-class musher's dog yard is a must-see on your itinerary. Called *Husky Homestead at Goose Lake Kennels,* this ninety-minute narrated kennel tour offers an in-depth look at dog mushing with one of Alaska's best mushers. King knows how to get to you. As you step out of the van that will take you to his home, you'll be greeted by fluffy, soft-eared, gentle-eyed sled dog puppies—known as Alaskan huskies to those in the sport—that you can cuddle to your heart's content. You'll see summer training in action and learn about what it takes to mush dogs 1,000 miles from Anchorage to Nome. Jeff has lots of interesting stories to tell from his twenty years of mushing—don't be shy, just ask him. Tours are held three times a day in the summer and cost $30 for adults. Phone (907) 683–2904, or e-mail king@mail. denali.k12.ak.us. By the way, Donna Gates King's wildlife art also ranks as one of the "best," in this author's opinion. Check out her work at the kennels, or visit her Goose Lake Studio just outside the park boundaries.

Also worth a visit at mile 238 on the Park Highway, north of the park entrance, is **Denali Raft Adventures'** two-hour Canyon Run raft trip through such exotic-sounding rapids as Cable Car, Coffee Grinder, and Ice Worm. Two- and four-hour trips are $50 and $70, respectively. If you want to get a little more daring and wield the paddle as part of the crew, try a four-hour float for $75. Call (888) 683–2234, e-mail denraft@ mtaonline.net, or visit www.denaliraft.com.

Who Really Climbed Denali First?

The debate rages on. Who climbed North America's highest peak, Denali, first—adventurer Frederick Cook in 1906 (not to be confused with Captain James Cook, who explored much of Alaska's coastline and named its prominent features in the late 1700s) or Hudson Stuck in 1913. Cook attempted to climb the mountain twice in 1906. He acknowledged defeat on the first attempt but claimed that he made it to the mountain's summit on the second attempt. Many people doubted him, but not having climbed the mountain themselves, they had no way to prove it.

In 1910 a group of Alaskan sourdoughs, during a discussion in a bar, decided they, too, doubted the truth of Cook's story. They decided to climb the mountain themselves and maybe make a rightful claim to fame. So off went Tom Lloyd, Charles McGonagall, Pete Anderson, and Billy Taylor, who, with little climbing experience but lots of Alaska hardscrabble toughness, reached the north peak summit—not realizing that it was actually lower than the south peak—and planted a

spruce pole there to prove they had made it. So their ascent wasn't acknowledged either, but it sure gained them lots of respect.

Three years later, along comes the Reverend Hudson Stuck, Episcopal archdeacon of the Yukon, who decided he, too, would get a little closer to God and make his way up the 20,320-foot Denali. He and three other men began the ascent— Harry Karstens, Robert Tatum, and Walter Harper—and reached the summit in June 1913. Their photographs were deemed authentic, and Hudson, for the most part, has claimed this spot in history. As far as being the first man in that group to reach the summit, though, it was Harper who first stood atop the summit. And perhaps rightly so. The name Denali is an Athabascan Indian word for "the high one" or "the great one"—and Harper was an Athabascan Indian.

Today, as many as 1,000 people a year attempt to climb Denali each spring between April and June, but only a small percentage succeed.

This kind of raft trip will work up your appetite, and if it does, skip the hungry crowds at the park entry eateries and drive south on the Parks Highway to mile 224 to **The Perch,** a local favorite that offers great seafood and steaks in a wooded surrounding. Call (907) 683–2523.

The best and most peaceful lodging, just north of the park entrance, can be had at the **Earth Song Lodge,** run by Jon and Karin Nierenberg. You can stay in one of ten tastefully built log cabins with private baths. There is a naturalist on staff and evening programs in the central lodge. Call (907) 683–2863, e-mail earthsong@mail.denali.k12.ak.us, or visit www.earthsonglodge.com.

The **Denali Hostel** sits about a dozen miles north of the park entrance and provides bunks at $24 per guest. The fee includes coffee and muffins each morning, Visitors come here from all over the world. If you arrive by train, look for the hostel van. With only seventeen beds, reservations are a must. Call (907) 683–1295.

There are, in addition to park ranger–escorted hikes, several quality commercial firms that offer treks and climbs that vary from tender to tough. Whether you want to climb all the way to North America's highest peak—a rigorous, dangerous climb only strong and experienced mountaineers should attempt—or you want a less-demanding but equally adventurous backcountry wilderness trek, **Alaska-Denali Guiding, Inc.,** provides an ample variety of hiking and climbing opportunities. The Talkeetna-based company specializes in guiding small groups to remote areas in the Denali National Park area. Prices range from a four-day, $740 off-trail backpacking experience, to the most challenging of all trips—an attempt to reach Denali's summit—for $3,300 to $3,500. Call (907) 733–2649, e-mail adg@alaska.net, or visit www.alaska.net/~adg.

Mountain Trip, Inc., with headquarters in Anchorage, is another professional guiding firm, this one with a record of fifteen years of leading climbers up Denali as well as other mountains. They also package mountain biking excursions on the Denali Highway and other such roads. Their sixteen- to twenty-four-day Mt. McKinley West Buttress and Traverse expedition is their specialty. Call (907) 345–6499.

Back on the George Parks Highway, roughly 300 miles north of Anchorage, you come to **Nenana,** on the Tanana River. (Nenana is pronounced nee-NAN-a; Tanana is TA-naw-naw.) Don't breeze through without stopping at least to see the **Alaska Railroad Museum,** in the old (1923) railroad depot building alongside the tracks on Front Street. The old-fashioned pressed-tin ceiling is a particular curiosity, and if you happen to be a pin collector, you can pick up lapel pins commemorating not only the Alaska Railroad but various other U.S. and Canadian rail systems as well.

Also worth a look-see is the 1905 log **St. Mark's Episcopal Church,** whose altar is adorned with elaborate Athabascan beadwork. It's located at Front and A Streets, east of the depot. At Nenana's sod-roof log **visitor center** on A Street, just off the Parks Highway, volunteers will tell you about Alaska's most popular annual statewide guessing game—The Nenana Ice Classic, in which the winner can earn more than $300,000 by predicting when the ice will break up on the Tanana River. For information call (907) 832–9953. From Nenana, **Alaska Tolovana Adventures** will rent you a canoe for $25 a day, guide you on two- to seven-day canoe tours, or take you by riverboat to the restored and historic (1923) **Tolovana Lodge** in the Minto Wildlife Range. Call (907) 832–5285 for details. If you want to overnight in Nenana, consider **Bed and Maybe Breakfast** in the old railroad depot. This structure was built specially in 1923 for then-President Harding's visit to Alaska (incidentally, he died soon after that trip). You can see the Native cemetery and the historic railroad bridge from your window. Phone (907) 832–5272 or (907) 832–5556.

The first land and sea grant university in Alaska was in Fairbanks, and it was called the Alaska Agricultural College and School of Mines. It opened in 1917 and in 1935 was renamed the University of Alaska. Today there is the University of Alaska Fairbanks, University of Alaska Anchorage, and University of Alaska Southeast, as well as feeder campuses spread across the state.

New to this village is the **Alfred Starr Nenana Cultural Center**. Here you can learn about Native life and get details on that exciting Nenana Ice Classic guessing game. You can also book river and dog mushing tours here. A salmon bake is scheduled to open during the summers.

Past mile 325 the Parks Highway enters the Fairbanks North Star Borough (county). The old (1936) **Ester Gold Camp,** (800–676–6925; intrasea@polarnet.com; www.alaskasbest.com/ester), which has a hotel, saloon, and dining facilities, lies about ½ mile off the highway, beyond mile 351. At mile 358 you arrive at the exit to the city of **Fairbanks.**

Glenn Highway–Tok Cutoff—Northern Section: Glennallen to Tok

A word of review about the Glenn Highway–Tok Cutoff from Anchorage to Tok. The route, you'll recall, is actually three segments: 189 miles of the Glenn from Anchorage to Glennallen, 14 miles on the Richardson, and a final 125 miles on the Tok Cutoff. This section begins where the section in the Southcentral Alaska chapter left off, at **Glennallen,** where the Copper Valley Chamber of Commerce operates a log cabin **visitor center.** The center itself is worth a stop and a picture, since plants actually grow from the cabin's sod roof. This is authentic Alaskana. Many a sourdough used this same material for insulation on log cabins in the remote bush country.

Fourteen miles farther, at the Richardson Highway's mile 128.6, the Tok Cutoff begins. **Gakona Junction** is mile 0. Tok, our destination, is located at milepost 125. At mile 2, stop at least for an evening meal (no lunches) at the **Carriage House** dining room of the **Gakona Lodge & Trading Post.** The lodge, built in 1905, originally served travelers on the old Richardson Trail and is now on the National Register of Historic Places. The dinner menu ranges from roughly $6.00 to $15.00.

At mile 53 on the Tok Cutoff, the **Grizzly Lake Ranch** offers B&B accommodations plus **Knight Riders Horse and Buggy Rides** along back roads and forested trails. B&B rates start at $45, and the buggy rides cost $60 an hour for two. Call (907) 822–5214.

Just past mile 65 you come to the 45-mile **Nabesna Road** and one of your few opportunities to actually drive into **Wrangell–St. Elias National Park,** one of the wildest, most mountainous and least developed in the U.S. park system. Just beyond the junction, at Slana, you'll see the Slana **National Park Service Ranger Station.** Inquire about road conditions, especially the last dozen miles or so, which can be quite rough. Just before mile 4, you enter the park itself. For the dedicated backwoods aficionado **Huck Hobbit's Homestead Campground and Retreat** has two 12-by-12-foot log cabins to rent. To get to the homestead, turn left on the side road at mile 4, drive 3 miles to the signed parking place for your vehicle, then walk an additional ½ mile of trail to Huck Hobbit's place. He'll meet you at the trailhead if you feel nervous about the hike or if you have lots of gear to haul. He will also rent you camping space and a tent if you need one, has canoes available, and will point you in the direction of the best fishing and berry picking. The rates are $20.00 for a bed or $2.50 for a camping spot. Breakfast is $5.00. Call for reservations at (907) 822–3196. There are several other lodges and overnight accommodations toward the end of the road, including **End of the Road Bed and Breakfast** (907–822–5312) at mile 42. The rates are $65 to $75, depending on which room or cabin you choose. These are "plumbing-free" cabins, but a shower room is available. Driving beyond this point is usually OK in any vehicle—unless it's been raining a lot, in which case creeks can flood the road.

The Glenn–Richardson–Tok Cutoff route from Anchorage to Tok ends at mile 125. (For information about Tok, see the section in this chapter on the Alaska Highway.)

The Richardson Highway— Northern Section: Gakona Junction to Fairbanks

In this section we take a look at the northern portion of the historic Valdez-to-Fairbanks Richardson Highway, commencing at the Gakona Junction where the Richardson meets the Tok Cutoff at mile 128.5.

The terrain along the Richardson continues to reveal tall, majestic mountains, countless big and little lakes, and thick forests. You stand a good chance of seeing moose alongside the road (pay special attention to small ponds, where a huge animal may rise up and break the surface after having scoured the pond's bottom for succulent plantlife) as well as caribou and perhaps grizzly bears. The Trans-Alaska Pipeline shows itself at various times.

If you missed out on king salmon fishing either in Southeast or South-central Alaska, you can, surprisingly, make up for it here on the Gulkana River. *Gulkana Fish Guides* offer jet boat and raft trips June through July from their headquarters at mile 128.5. Also at the headquarters is *Gakona Fish Camp Bed and Breakfast,* which offers clean rooms starting at $59.95. Call (907) 822–3664, or or e-mail gakona@alaska.net.

If it's time to stop for the evening, a good place to overnight is the historic *Paxson Inn & Lodge,* built in 1903. Call (907) 822–3330.

The Richardson Highway connects with the *Denali Highway* at *Paxson* at mile 185.5. If you don't plan to drive all 135 miles to Cantwell and Denali National Park, at least consider round-tripping some of the first 21 paved miles of the road. The panoramic views—of glaciers, lakes, and majestic, snow-covered peaks—from the tops of hills, rises, and turnoff viewing areas are just breathtaking.

At mile 266 the Richardson Highway and the *Alaska Highway* meet at *Delta Junction.* Actually, this is where the Alaska Highway ends. The

Richardson continues north to Fairbanks and mileposts beside the road continue to measure distance from Valdez.

The *Delta Junction Information Center* (907–895–9941), at the junction of the two highways, is a good place to stop for visitor information and road condition updates. Especially if you had your picture taken at the Alaska Highway milepost 0 monument in Dawson Creek, British Columbia, you'll want to do the same at the highway's end monument at the information center.

Interior Alaska Trivia

Caribou—also called reindeer—populate the whole of Interior Alaska. They are the only type of deer in which both sexes grow antlers. One of their characteristics is wide hooves, which enable the animal to cross snow, ice, and slippery slopes.

For campers or RV travelers, there are private and state-owned campgrounds just north and south of town. *Delta State Campground,* at mile 267, is a good, convenient choice that offers twenty-four sites on the banks of the Delta River with views of the Alaska Range. The campground has the basics—water, toilets, and a covered shelter with tables. And at $8.00 per night, it's more than affordable.

Peggy's Alaskan Cabbage Patch Bed and Breakfast offers accommodations in a modern Alaska home and serves up old-fashioned full breakfasts. To get there from the visitors center, drive 2 miles toward Fairbanks on the Richardson Highway. Turn right at Jack Warren Road and go about 6³/₁₀ miles to a dirt road called Arctic Grayling. Peggy's is the second driveway on the right. Says Peggy Christopherson: "Look for the cabbage patch and the pigs." Phone (907) 895–4200.

Among Alaskans, at least, Delta Junction is probably best known for its herd of 500 or so bison (American buffalo). They're the outgrowth of small numbers of the animals established there in the 1920s and roam freely over the 70,000-acre *Delta Bison Range.* Occasionally the bison spill over into adjacent barley farm fields, and farmers are not amused. If you want to see the herd, you stand a pretty good chance at the visitor viewpoint just past mile 241 on the Richardson. If you'd like to tour the workings of a *Trans-Alaska Pipeline pumping station,* you can do so at mile 258. Call (907) 869–3270 or (907) 456–9391 for times and details. Soon after, at mile 275, a terrific photo op awaits where the pipeline crosses over the Tanana River.

Not to be missed is *Rika's Roadhouse* at *Big Delta State Historical Park,* just upstream from the pipeline river crossing. The roadhouse is right out of Alaska's history. Built in 1910 and purchased by Rika Wallen in 1923, it served for decades as a major overnight stop on the Richardson wagon road and highway for travelers between Valdez and Fairbanks. Today the roadhouse has been restored, as have a sod-roofed museum building, an old U.S. Army Signal Corps station, and other historic structures. Staff in 1920s garb will guide you around the park for an informative tour that includes live farm animals. The *Packhouse Restaurant* is one of the best you'll find along Alaska's road system and features breads from the Alaska Baking Company on-site and home-made soups. There is no admission charge to visit the roadhouse, but tent or RV sites at the state campground run $8.00 per night. Phone (907) 895–4201.

Harding Lake, 1½ miles off the Richardson Highway from mile 321.5, is a great place to swim, have a beach picnic, or camp overnight. Avoid it Friday night through Sunday, however. Lots of Fairbanksans drive down for the weekend, and it gets pretty crowded. The camping fee is $8.00 per night.

As you approach Fairbanks, don't let your desire to get there lead you to bypass the *Chena Lakes Recreation Area,* accessible from a 2-mile side road at mile 346.7. Whether you're RV camping or simply looking for a superb picnic spot, this place is definitely worth a look-see. (It's not to be confused, incidentally, with the Chena River State Recreation Site in Fairbanks, nor with the Chena River State Recreation Area on the Chena Hot Springs Road.) The Chena Lakes Rec Area is a sprawling, lake-oriented, 2,178-acre site with scores of campsites, lots of picnic areas, swimming beaches, even a children's playground. There's at least one island with camping and picnic facilities. Again, local Alaskans tend to use it most heavily on weekends and holidays.

Also worth a stop before you arrive in Fairbanks is *Santa Claus House* in (where else?) *North Pole,* Alaska. The large shop, located at mile 349, is packed with Christmas-type gifts, including Santa Claus letters for kids that Santa will mail and postmark from North Pole in December.

The Richardson ends at mile 364. If you started your Alaska Highway–Richardson trip in Dawson Creek, British Columbia, you've traveled 1,520 miles.

The Steese Highway: Fairbanks to Circle City

Although it's paved for only 44 of its 162 miles from Fairbanks, the Steese Highway is one of the most satisfying among the backroads in Alaska. Along the way you see the sites of old mining camps and new ones, hot springs spas, gorgeous rolling hills and mountains, small authentic Alaska communities, some of the most intensely colorful wildflower viewing to be found anywhere, and the Chatanika and Chena River Recreation Areas. We've found midweek travel easier, with less gravel dust in the air than on weekends, when many Alaskans head for hot springs spas and good fishing along the route.

You've barely been traveling northwest along Steese Highway from its beginning at the junction of the Richardson and Parks Highways when, at mile 4.9, you come to the *Chena Hot Springs Road.* The road is paved and generally well maintained but drive carefully; it can be bumpy. For a good portion of its nearly 57 miles, the road travels through the *Chena River Recreation Area,* with lots of scenic spots for camping, picnics, fishing, and wildlife viewing.

About 20 miles or so down the road, you'll approach the Two Rivers area, which can be accurately described as sled dog country. Some of the state's most dedicated mushers come from this area. Among them is Rick Armstrong, who runs *The End Game Enterprise,* which offers daylong to two-week winter dog sledding adventures for the true outdoorsperson. Armstrong's trips are custom-made, and he specializes in trips to the Brooks Range and the Arctic National Wildlife Refuge. Included in his tours are use of his sled dogs for your own team, all the necessary equipment and clothing for cold-weather camping, and catered food, including belly-pleasing moose stews to keep you warm at night. Guided overnight trips are $400 per person; the cost of two-week trips depends on the number of people and the destination. Call (907) 488–4060.

If you want to stock up on groceries or other supplies along the way, stop at mile 23.5 on the hot springs road at *Tacks' General Store and Greenhouse Cafe,* a genuine, old-fashioned general store and an institution in these parts. The greenhouse is full of flowers and colorful hanging baskets. Generous breakfasts, incidentally, are served until 8:00 P.M. The home-baked pies are arguably the best in Alaska.

At road's end you'll find lodging, a restaurant, bar, and other facilities at *The Resort at Chena Hot Springs,* with its spring-fed pool, hot tub, and 2,800-square-foot redwood deck with ten-person spa. Accommodations range from luxury hotel rooms (starting at $105 in summer; $175 in winter) to rustic cabins that rent for $65 to $125 year-round. Activities, besides soaking, include horseback riding, canoeing, hiking, mountain biking, and hayrides. Phone (907) 452–7867, e-mail chenahs@polarnet.com, or visit www.chenahotsprings.com.

Back on the Steese Highway, one of the best places to see the **Trans-Alaska Pipeline** up close is about 10 miles north of downtown Fairbanks, just off the highway. The pipe, in fact, is elevated, so you can stand right under it and have your picture taken while countless gallons of crude oil flow over your head.

Also at the site is an Alyeska Pipeline Service Company information center with interpretive displays, which is open daily, May to September. Phone (907) 456–9391.

The **Old F.E. Gold Camp,** at mile 27.5 at **Chatanika,** is right out of Alaska's glory mining days. The F. E. (for Fairbanks Exploration) Company operated from 1926 to 1957 and is today on the National Register of Historic Places. On-site you'll see lots of vintage mining gear from the

> ### Interior Alaska Trivia
>
> *Vast portions of the Interior were not glaciated during the last Ice Age. Therefore they remain in a state similar to that which they were during the Pleistocene era.*

forties, thirties, and even earlier. In the buildings you'll come across Alaska artifacts and antiques, including a 200-year-old brass bed. The camp offers overnight accommodations as well as items of Alaskana. Rooms in the bunkhouse or cabins start at $20, depending on the time of year. The restaurant features fresh Alaskan fish dinners and giant steaks (we're talking forty-eight-ounce top sirlions!) on Saturday and Sunday mornings, sourdough pancake buffets. Call (907) 389–2414.

If you happen to be traveling on the Steese Highway about the time of the Summer Solstice (June 20 or 21), plan to celebrate the change of seasons the way many Fairbanksans do—by driving to **Eagle Summit** (mile 108) for a midnight picnic and a view of the sun dipping close to the horizon *but not quite setting,* then rising again to start a new day and a new summer season. The summit lies south of the Arctic Circle, but this phenomena is possible because of its 3,624-foot elevation.

Arctic Circle Hot Springs (907–520–5113), near Central on the Steese Highway, is a don't-miss-it experience. This is one of Alaska's oldest (1930) visitor destinations and an Alaskan favorite. Today, though thoroughly modern, rooms at the resort continue to reflect the style and furnishings of the early 1900s. If you prefer something more rustic, you can rent a log cabin.

The warm waters of the Olympic-size swimming pool are, of course, the resort's best known feature, but the spa also offers Jacuzzzis, hot tubs, a colorful log saloon, an RV park, and hillside campsites. As if that's not enough, the owners recently added an exercise room and massage therapy. Meals are home-cooked and delicious. You can bunk in the fourth-floor hostel dorm for as little as $20 per person or rent bare-bones cabins for $85 (no running water, bathrooms, or kitchens). Deluxe cabins and apartments start at $110. Suite rooms in the resort are $125, and double rooms are $100. Camping also is an option for $15. To get to Circle Hot Springs, take the turnoff at mile 127.8 on the Steese and drive to mile 8.3 on the Circle Hot Springs Road. Or fly in. There is an airstrip in Circle.

The Steese Highway dead ends at mile 162, at the picturesque community of *Circle,* a community of mostly Native Alaskan residents. The town got its name when early prospectors thought it straddled the Arctic Circle. It doesn't—the circle lies 50 miles north—but the town does sit on the banks of the Yukon River, which made it a busy transportation and trading hub during the early and middle years of the century.

Camping can be had at the end of the road on the banks of the Yukon River. There are tables, toilets, and a parking area there.

An interesting spot to visit in Circle is the old *Pioneer Cemetery,* with markers dating to the 1800s. To get there walk upriver past some old machinery on a gravel road, until you reach a barricade to private property. It's OK to cross through the front yard (using good manners, obviously) to the trailhead. After about ten minutes—and a million mosquitos—you'll see the graves on the left.

Elliott Highway: Fairbanks to Manley Hot Springs

Most of the travelers you'll meet on the *Elliott Highway,* especially beyond the road's mile 73.1 junction with the Dalton Highway to Deadhorse, will be Alaskans. And chances are they'll be heading to or coming from one of Fairbanks's favorite getaway destinations, *Manley Hot Springs.* It's one of three popular hot springs spas in the region, the others being Chena Hot Springs and Arctic Circle Hot Springs, at the ends of access roads off the Steese Highway.

The Elliott Highway takes off from the Steese about 11 miles north of Fairbanks, and for the first 30 miles it's paved. Beyond that it's gravel, but not a bad road at all, although it gets slick in places when it rains. There are, as well, some roller coaster rises and falls, but if you keep your speed at a reasonable rate, it's no problem.

At mile 1.2 on the Elliott, you come to *El Dorado Gold Mine,* a worthwhile stop that's both a commercial operation and a visitor attraction. (For a description, see the Fairbanks section.)

At mile 49.5 you can visit **Arctic Circle Trading Post**, which includes the **Wildwood General Store**. To be had here, for those of you who like interesting collectibles, are Arctic Circle Certificates and the official Arctic Circle registry. Put your name down in history as someone who's been to the Arctic Circle. The certificates are proof! The owners of the trading post encourage you to talk with the employees, who will tell you what it's like to live so far from "citified civilization." Call (907) 474–4565.

Roughly 21 miles later you come to a junction with a 2-mile access road to **Livengood** (pronounced LYV-en-good). It was a major gold camp at times in the first half of the century, but now only one hundred or so people live in the area. Just past mile 73, the Elliott meets with the Dalton Highway supply road to the North Slope, Deadhorse, and Prudhoe Bay.

At mile 94.5 you come to a generous double pullout on the south side of the road. From here you have a good view of Minto Flats, the Tanana River, and the foothills of the Alaska Range. After mile 97 keep your eyes peeled northerly for great views of Sawtooth, Wolverine, and Elephant Mountains. At mile 110 the highway joins an 11-mile access road to the Native village of **Minto** (there's a lodge that provides meals and a general store, if you're looking for a place to eat or buy snacks), and 40 miles farther down the Elliott, you come to **Manley Hot Springs.**

Very Alaskan, this place. **Manley Roadhouse** is one of a vanishing breed of accommodations that once were common along the sled dog and horse trails of the north. This one was built in 1906, when the community served as a trading center for mining districts in the area. The roadhouse accommodated riverboat crews, miners, and commercial travelers. Today owner Robert E. Lee offers visitors the chance to revisit those days in his roadhouse with single and double sleeping accommodations, a rustic, antiques-filled sitting room, and the Roadhouse Bar, with Alaska's largest back bar. Rooms start at $90 for a double, $75 for a cabin with no plumbing. The rate is $65 for a single. For reservations call (907) 672–3161.

Denali Highway: Paxson to Cantwell

They used to call the **Denali Highway** one of the worst roads in Alaska. It's still bumpy in places, a washboard in others, and you do have to watch for potholes. But if you keep your speed down and your eyes open, you can drive its 136 miles from Paxson on the Richardson Highway to Cantwell on the George Parks Highway without fear or foreboding. At its Cantwell end, it's only a few minutes to the entrance of Denali National Park. Because of the road's relatively high elevation, right at timberline or a bit above, you can enjoy lots of high tundra views. Sights of Alaska Range peaks are frequent and fabulous.

Perhaps because the Denali's old and unsavory reputation won't quite die, the road receives surprisingly less traffic than you would expect, considering its location. And because of its sparse traffic, the highway today is much appreciated by stream and lake anglers who don't care for bumper-to-bumper "combat fishing" crowds. There are several state and private RV campgrounds along the way as well as private lodges.

Off-road vehicle enthusiasts enjoy its designated routes, and mountain bikers and hikers also regard highly its marked and unmarked trails. *A caution, though:* If you're heading far off the road, be sure to carry a compass. It's distressingly easy to get turned around in the woods, or even in open tundra, if clouds close in. From your first entry onto the road at Paxson (mile 0), keep your eye out for brown (grizzly) bears, moose, and other wild critters. They're often spotted.

The Denali is paved at its start, but the asphalt ends at mile 21. (Paving is planned for some sections, beginning in 1999.) **Tangle Lakes Lodge** is located at mile 22. A fire destroyed the original lodge and bar in 1998, so the present structure is newly built and ready to greet guests in beautiful surroundings—not to mention one of the best Arctic grayling fisheries in the state. Owners Rich and Linda Holmstrom will make your stay memorable. If you're a birder, be sure to talk to Rich, who can convey some of the most accurate birding information on the highway, including the whereabouts of ptarmigan (which is Alaska's state bird, not the eagle as many people assume), Arctic warblers, gyrfalcons, wandering tattlers, and many other oft-sighted species. The Holmstroms offer cabin, canoe, and three meals for two persons for $150. If you just want a canoe, they rent for $3.00 an hour or $10.00 for three hours. For more information call (907) 259–7302 in the summer or (907) 688–9173 in the winter, e-mail tanglelakeslodge@corcom.net, or visit www.alaskan.com/tanglelakes.

Comes mile 135.5, and you've arrived in **Cantwell,** which began life as a rail line flag stop and continues to be served by the Alaska Railroad on its run between Anchorage and Fairbanks. Newer businesses have located near the intersection of the Denali and George Parks Highways, but if you'd like to peek into Alaska's yesteryear, stop by for a meal, lodging, or beverage at the *Cantwell Lodge* (907–768–2300) in the older section of town, 2 miles west of the junction. Meals (summer only) range from $7.00 for a hamburger and fries to $17.00 for a steak.

PLACES TO STAY IN INTERIOR ALASKA

CANTWELL
Cantwell Lodge, western end of Denali Highway; (907) 768–2300.

CHENA HOT SPRINGS
The Resort at Chena Hot Springs, Chena Hot Springs Road; (907) 452–7867, www.chenahotsprings.com.

DELTA JUNCTION
Delta State Campground, mile 267 Richardson–Alaska Highway.

Peggy's Alaskan Cabbage Patch Bed and Breakfast, Arctic Grayling Road; (907) 895–4200.

DENALI HIGHWAY
Tangle Lakes Lodge, mile 22 Denali Highway; (907) 259–7302, www.alaskan. com/tanglelakes.

DENALI NATIONAL PARK
Denali National Park Wilderness Center–Camp Denali, western end of Park Road. (907) 683–2290, www.gorp.com/dnpwild.

Denali Parks Resorts; (800) 276–7234, www.denalinationalpark. com. Three locations in and around the park.

Denali Wilderness Lodge; (800) 541–9779, www.AlaskaOne.com/ dwlodge. In Wood River Valley, accessible only by a twenty–minute bush flight from Denali Airport.

Earth Song Lodge; (907) 683–2863, www.earthsonglodge.com. Just north of Denali National Park in Healy.

Kantishna Roadhouse, western end of Park Road; (800) 942–7420, www kantishnaroadhouse.com.

National Park Service campgrounds; (800) 622–7275, in Anchorage (907) 272–7275. Seven locations in the park.

Sourdough Cabins, mile 238.8 George Parks High-way; (907) 683–2773, (800) 354–6020, www.denalisourdoughcab-ins.com.

FAIRBANKS
Forget–Me–Not Lodge–Aurora Express: Overlooking Chena Ridge and Fairbanks. (800) 221–0073, www.aurora–express.com.

Fairbanks Exploration Inn, 505 Illinois Street; (907) 451–1920, (888) 452–1920, www2.polarnet. com/~FEInn.

North Woods Lodge, Chena Hills Drive; (907) 478–5305, (907) 479–5300, www.AlaskaOne.com/ northlodge.

GAKONA
Gakona Fish Camp Bed and Breakfast; (907) 822–3664.

Grizzly Lake Ranch Bed & Breakfast, mile 53 Tok Cutoff; (907) 822–5214.

MANLEY HOT SPRINGS
Manley Roadhouse, mile 152 Elliot Highway; (907) 672–3161.

NENANA
Bed and Maybe Breakfast; (907) 832–5272, (907) 832–5556. In the old railroad depot.

PAXSON
Paxson Inn & Lodge, mile 185.5 Richardson Highway; (907) 822–3330.

SLANA
End of the Road Bed and Breakfast, mile 42 Nabesna Road; (907) 822–5312. "Plumbing–free" cabins, showers available.

Huck Hobbit's Homestead Campground and Retreat, mile 4 Nabesna Road; (907) 822–3196. Log cabins for rent.

TOK

Cleft of the Rock Bed & Breakfast, 1½ miles down Sundog Trail; (800) 478–5646, www.ptialaska.net/~cleft-rck/ABA.html. Three miles northwest of Tok.

Rita's Campground and RV Park, mile 1,315 Alaska Highway; (907) 883–4342.

A Winter Cabin Bed and Breakfast, 3 blocks off the Alaska Highway at mile 1,316.5; (907) 883–5655, www2.polarnet.com/~wntrcabn/Donna.html.

PLACES TO EAT IN INTERIOR ALASKA

CANTWELL

Cantwell Lodge, western terminus of Denali Highway; (907) 768–2300.

CENTRAL

Arctic Circle Hot Springs, 8.3 miles from Steese Highway on Circle Hot Springs Road; (907) 520–5113.

CHENA HOT SPRINGS

Tacks' General Store and Greenhouse Cafe, mile 23.5 Chena Hot Springs Road; (907) 488–3242.

DELTA JUNCTION

Packhouse Restaurant, mile 275 Richardson–Alaska Highway near Delta Junction; (907) 895–4201. Fresh bread and home-made soup.

DENALI HIGHWAY

Tangle Lakes Lodge, mile 22 Denali Highway; (907) 259–7302, www.alaskan.com/tangle-lakes.

DENALI NATIONAL PARK

The Perch, mile 224 George Parks Highway; (907) 683–2523. Just south of Denali National Park and Preserve, away from the park crowds. Tasty fish, pasta, and steaks.

FAIRBANKS

Pikes Landing, 4438 Airport Way; (907) 479–7113, duffy@mosquitonet.com. Delicious Sunday buffet. Overlooking the Chena River.

The Pumphouse Restaurant, 796 Chena Pump Road; (907) 479–8452, www.ptialaska. net/~pumphse. Good seafood.

GAKONA

Carriage House, mile 2 Tok Cutoff; (907) 822–3482. Part of the Gakona Lodge & Trading Post, a 1905 lodge now on the National Register of Historic Places.

TOK

Tok Gateway Salmon Bake, mile 1,313 Alaska Highway; (907) 883–5555, www.tokalaska. com/toksamon.shtml. Outdoor grilled king salmon, halibut, ribs, and reindeer sausage.

Alaska's Far North

laska's Far North, more than any other region, is a land of extremes. As its name implies, this region lies farther north than any other in the state or nation. It's the only part of the United States lapped by the Arctic Ocean's summer waters and barricaded by its winter pack ice. At its northernmost reaches, the region enjoys the country's longest period of daylight—eighty-four continuous days of constant daylight from May 10 to August 2. In contrast, during the dark days of winter, the sun literally does not rise for sixty-seven days. At least one of the region's wildlife species, the polar bear, can be found nowhere else in the nation. And, of course, Alaska's Far North is home to North America's largest oil field, Prudhoe Bay.

Although some may imagine the Far North as drab and lifeless, the tundra country, especially in summer, can turn virtually ablaze with wildflowers, berries, and other colorful plantlife. Millions of birds migrate to the northern tundra from North and even South America each spring. Especially during flight-seeing tours, but during road trips as well, you stand a good chance of seeing grizzly bears, caribou, and moose.

A Place to Celebrate

Shaped like a giant Ulu knife, the new Inupiat Heritage Center in Barrow is a place for young and old Inupiat Eskimos to share their culture and pass on traditions. It cost almost $12 million to build. The building has four rooms: a 20,000-plus volume consortium library, a room where Inupiat artists can work on their art, an exhibit room to show off some of the results of their labor, and a multipurpose room for demonstrations and lectures. The creations that can be seen at the center include umiaks (kayak) and dog sleds, ivory carving, and skin sewing.

In building such a monument to their way of life, the Inupiats are showing they are a culture steeped in tradition. In fact, during the building's dedication, a ceremony in which strips of baleen were placed at the corners of the building symbolized the passage of the cultural traditions of the elders to the young people in the community.

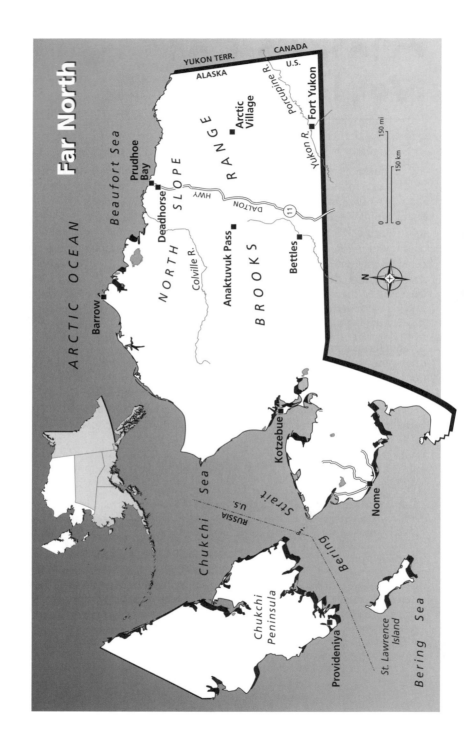

TOP 10 PLACES IN THE FAR NORTH

*Northernmost tip
    of Point Barrow*

Great Kobuk Sand Dunes

Serpentine Hot Springs

*Gates of the Arctic
    National Park*

*Arctic National
    Wildlife Refuge*

*Iditarod Trail (of the
    Sled Dog Race)*

The beaches of Nome

*Museum of the Arctic,
    Kotzebue*

Sunlight North Expeditions

Pilgrim Hot Springs

Among Native peoples of the region, there are two groups of Eskimos: the Inupiat on the shores of the Alaska mainland and the Yu'pik Eskimos, who reside in Gambell and Savoonga on St. Lawrence Island, a large island in the Bering Sea only 40 miles from Russian Siberia. A small number of Nunamiut inland Eskimos live at Anaktuvuk Pass, about 260 miles north-northwest of Fairbanks, while Athabascan Indian communities may be found as far north as Arctic Village in the Brooks Range, 290 miles north of Fairbanks and roughly 100 miles north of Fort Yukon.

Major Communities of the Far North

Barrow is just about as far off the beaten path as you can get and still have your feet planted on North American soil. Located 330 miles north of the Arctic Circle, the mostly Eskimo town is, in fact, the northernmost community in the Western Hemisphere. That's only one of the superlatives you can collect during a visit here. Barrow is also the seat of government for the North Slope Borough, which, at 88,000 square miles, ranks as the largest municipality in the world. (A borough, in Alaska, is rather like a county in the Lower Forty-eight, but not really. . . . It gets kind of complicated.)

In spite of its remoteness, you can get to Barrow easily. Alaska Airlines provides daily jet service from Anchorage and Fairbanks, and once you've arrived, you'll find several ground tour organizations with one- and two-day excursions designed to maximize your time at the Top of the World. Biggest of these is **Tundra Tours,** which also operates the fully modern **Top of the World Hotel.** On Tundra's tours you'll travel beside the Arctic Ocean, pass through an old U.S. Navy research site, visit a Distant Early Warning System installation, take a short trek on the tundra for a look at an old-time traditional hunting camp, and finally reach the northernmost point your bus can take you. From there you can disembark and go beachcombing and maybe even stick your toe in the chilly Arctic Ocean waters. Contact Tundra Tours or the Top of the World Hotel at (907) 852–3900. Rates at the hotel start at $179 for a double.

A tour of Barrow can be arranged by **Alaska Airlines Vacations** (800–468–2248 or www.alaskaair.com). One-day tours, including airfare, are

$395 from Fairbanks and $565 from Anchorage. Overnight tours, which include airfare, a tour, and lodging, are $438 from Fairbanks and $608 from Anchorage.

Northern Alaska Tour Company offers village tours as well, emphasizing the Inupiat Eskimo culture with a program of traditional dance and song plus demonstrations of skin sewing, Native games, and the Eskimo blanket toss. The tours also explore Arctic shores. One-day tours run $395 per person, and overnight tours are $438. Prices are slightly higher in the winter, when fewer flights leave for this far-flung community. Call (907) 474–8600, or visit www.alaskasarctic.com.

Once in Barrow, you may want to get around on your own for some even more off-the-beaten-path destinations, and you'll need wheels to do that. Two places come highly recommended: *North Slope General Auto* (907–852–7325) and *UIC Auto Rental* (907–852–2700). Prices are on the high side—in the $75 per day range—but, hey, how else are you going to get wheels this far north?

Far North Alaska Trivia

The oldest frame building north of Arctic Circle is the Cape Smythe Whaling and Trading Station, built in 1893 in Browerville, a whaling community near Barrow.

You could put that daily car rental fee toward a good guide instead, who will do all the driving for you. Try *Arctic Tour Company* at (907) 852–4512, which will take you to the northernmost point in Alaska, literally. In the military style Hummer vehicles, you'll go where the tour buses can't to the original Point Barrow. Most of the time you'll even see polar bears, says Arctic Tours' owner and operator. The two-hour tour is $55 per person; no reservations are accepted. Just call when you get there.

By far the best hotel choice in Barrow is the newly built *King Eider Inn,* with rooms in the $130 to $190 range. Call (888) 303–4337 or e-mail eider@barrow.com.

One final superlative for Barrow: *Pepe's North of the Border* is indisputably the farthest north Mexican restaurant in North America. By Lower Forty-eight standards it's expensive (everything has to be flown in from "down south"), but the food is good and you can meet the locals there. Phone (907) 852–8200.

The best food, however, can be had at *Artic Pizza,* which besides pizza serves seafood, Mexican, and American fare. Call (907) 852–4222.

Alaska's largest Eskimo community, *Kotzebue,* lies 26 miles north of the Arctic Circle, 550 air miles from Anchorage, and 200 miles from the

TOP ANNUAL EVENT IN THE FAR NORTH

shores of the Russian Far East. This fascinating Eskimo community, truth to tell, is probably easiest seen as part of a package tour. You can, if you want, put all the elements together yourself, but there's really only one hotel, the principal transportation option is a tour bus, and the sights you probably want to see are covered in regular bus tours. The principal tour operator is **Tour Arctic** (907–442–3301 in the summer or 800–478–2000 in the winter. Or visit www.tour-arctic.com.)

The easiest way to book one-day or overnight visits is through **Alaska Airlines Vacations** (800–468–2248 or www.alaskaair.com), whose airfare-inclusive tours from Anchorage start at $365 for one day and $494 for two days, including an overnight at the fully modern **Nullagvik Hotel.** The carrier also packages combination tours of Kotzebue and Nome from $494. Tour Arctic offers several add-on package tours of Kotzebue and Nome. Among the more interesting are the **Native Village Life** tour, which will take you even farther out by plane from Kotzebue for a Native village tour, lunch, and an additional night in Kotzebue. You'll be guided by Inupiat Eskimo hosts, enjoy lunch in the village, and enjoy a sight-seeing flight back to Kotzebue that takes you over the **Selawik Wildlife Refuge,** the **Great Kobuk Sand Dunes,** and **Kobuk Valley National Park**. The tour is $350 per person, double occupancy; $435 for singles.

The Northwest Alaska Native Association (NANA) regional Native corporation's **Museum of the Arctic** is certainly a must-see on anyone's Kotzebue itinerary. Here, in a two-hour program set within a huge, world-class **wildlife diorama** containing scores of mounted Alaskan animals, your Eskimo hosts put on a panoramic slide show and introduce you to Eskimo dancing, sewing, leathercraft, ivory carving, and the culture of the hardy people who live in these climes. Afterward the action moves to the attached **jade factory,** where you can see products made from the precious gem available in these parts. Finally, outdoors, you get to witness the famed **Eskimo blanket toss.** Jumpers are propelled 20 or 30 feet into the air by pullers, including visitors, around a large, walrus hide blanket. The museum hours are 9:15 A.M. to 3:00 P.M. The admission charge, if you're not on an inclusive package tour, is $20. For more information, call (907) 442–3747, or visit www.tour-arctic.com.

More adventurous than the standard airline tour is LaVonne Hendricks' **Arctic Circle Adventures,** whose options range from one-day area

Iditarod Trail Sled Dog Race: The main event in a monthlong celebration in Nome. During the first two weeks in March, mushers begin arriving anytime after the ninth day in Nome. A Mushers and Miners Ball, a statewide basketball tournament, and the Bering Sea Ice Golf Classic are all held during March. (907–443–5535; tourinfo@ci.nome.ak.us.; www.alaska.net/~nome.

tours to five-day customized all-in-one packages. Each trip is an adventure in itself, but here's a sampling of what you might experience with LaVonne: tundra hiking, bird-watching, ethnic and Inupiat cultural tours, a tour of a beachfront commercial salmon fish camp about 5 miles from Kotzebue via a four-wheel-drive road, and lodging at rustic cabins nestled beneath 250-foot bluffs. Food includes family-style dinners of fish, meat, and greens harvested from the tundra—with local folks as dinner guests—and breakfasts of sourdough pancakes, reindeer sausage, fresh trout, and salmon. The rates vary depending on your length of stay and what you want to see, but plan on somewhere between $150 to $300 per person, per day. Call (907) 442–3509 in the summer to leave a message or (907) 442–6013 at LaVonne's camp between June 15 and August 15. In the winter call (907) 276–0976. The Arctic Circle Adventures Web site is fishcamp.org and e-mail is lavonne@fishcamp.org.

Far North Alaska Trivia

If you're outside of the village of Kivalina, north of Kotzebue, and want to go camping, don't pitch your tent at Siniktagnelik on the right bank of the Wulik River. The Eskimo word "Siniktagnelik" means "no camping place because one cannot sleep because many years ago some people mysteriously died here."

In addition to having its own worthwhile attractions, Kotzebue serves as a major jumping-off place for expeditions to the surrounding bush. From the community, you can fly **Baker Aviation** (907–442–3108) to the nearby village of **Kiana** (the round-trip is $120) for modern lodgings and riverboat trips via **Kobuk River Jets,** hosted by Inupiat Eskimos Lorry and Nellie Schuerch. On their trips you can tour **Kobuk Valley National Park,** see incredible sand dunes in the Arctic, view wildlife, sample traditional foods, and experience the unique Inupiat culture. Guided fishing is available, and the Schuerchs also rent kayaks and inflatables for do-it-yourselfers. Call (907) 475–2149 for more information.

Lower Forty-eight residents seem to know at least three things about **Nome.** First, it was the site of a lively gold stampede from 1898 through the early years of this century. Second, each year in March, the 1,000-mile Iditarod Trail Sled Dog Race finishes there under a massive timber-burled winner's arch, having started some nine days to two weeks earlier in Anchorage. And, third, Nome lies in the far, far north, well above the Arctic Circle.

Well, two out of three's not bad.

Although virtually everyone thinks of Nome as an Arctic community, it's actually a bit south of the Arctic Circle. The town does, however, experience Arctic-like weather, especially in the wintertime. Seas freeze solid off its shores well into late spring. Each year in March, in fact, the Nome Lions Club sponsors a ***Bering Sea Ice Golf Classic,*** during which shivering duffers play a six-hole, par 41 course consisting of fairways on frozen sea ice with flagged holes made from coffee cans sunk into the ice.

Nome, with a population of 4,000, more than half of them Alaska Native Eskimos, is a fair-sized city by Alaska standards, but except for an occasional "far out" cruise ship, you can get there only by air. The air service, however, is excellent. Alaska Airlines jets fly to the city several times daily. And here's one of Alaska's best kept secrets: Once you've arrived here on the shores of the Bering Sea, there are hundreds of miles of good roads to explore. Places to visit and things to see include former gold mining sites, Native villages, impressive scenic vistas, even a hot springs. Nome is also one of the few places in North America where you can take a side trip to Russia.

The Red Dog Mine in the Northwest Arctic Borough is the world's largest producer of zinc.

The sun does not set in Barrow between May 10 and August 2 each summer, and it does not rise between November 18 and January 24 each winter.

Cape Prince of Wales, at the tip of the Seward Peninsula, is the westernmost point of mainland Alaska. Cape Mountain (2,289 feet), which rises above the Eskimo village of Wales, is the terminus of the Continental Divide.

A little history: One unconfirmed account records that Nome got its start in 1897, when John Hummel, an aging prospector suffering from scurvy, arrived in the area to search for gold, which many had predicted would be found there. But unlike others, Hummel did his panning on the beach, more hopeful of curing his ailments in the sun and salt air than of anything else. Incredibly, while sifting the beach sands he found gold. More incredible still, as he tested up and down the shoreline, he continued to see precious metal in every pan. In no time the rush was on! Another, more substantiated, version of Nome's beginning states that "three lucky Swedes"—Jafet Lindberg, Erik Lindblom, and John Brynteson—started the rush by finding gold in Anvil Creek in 1898 and that the beach finds came a year or so later.

However the rush began, it hasn't stopped yet. Mining remains a big part of Nome's economy. These days the rush consists of tourists eager to see where all the excitement took place. When you arrive in town, your first stop should be the Nome Convention and Visitor Bureau's ***Visitor Information Center*** (907–443–5535, www.alaska.net/~nome, and tour-info@ci.nome.ak.us), located downtown on Front Street, across from City Hall. Lots of free brochures, walking maps, restaurant menus, antiques, and historic photos are available or on display Monday through Friday. Also on Front Street, in the basement of the library building, you'll find the **Carrie McLain Museum** (907–443–2566), with its wide variety of Alaskan artifacts and historical memorabilia. At the **XYZ Center** (907–443–5238), located in the north end of the City Hall building, fall, winter, and spring visitors can join Nome's elders for lunch and interesting conversation. (Please make a donation, even if you're a senior yourself.) The menu might include reindeer, blueberries, or other foods from the area. Any time of the year your most vivid memories of Nome may well be the **gold dredges.** One old and abandoned dredge is within walking distance of town. The huge lumbering behemoths once created their own ponds as they crept and floated across the tundra, scooping up ore and extracting gold. And, of course, what could be more fitting for a visit to Nome than to buy a gold pan at one of the local stores and pan for some "color" of your own on the beaches where thousands once labored for nuggets and fortunes?

About those highways: For a place you can't drive to, Nome has lots of miles to tour by auto. Three major roads offer access to wildlife viewing, rivers to fish, mining ruins to examine, plus awesome seascapes and landscapes to photograph. You have three choices for rentals—Alaska

Life on the Beach

I lay on my sleeping bag with my head propped up, reading a book and relaxing. It's bedtime, but I can still feel the warmth of the sun through the tent fly. Of course, this is to be expected when you're camping just below the Arctic Circle in the middle of the summer. The sun barely sets this time of year. I am in Nome, Alaska, on the Bering Sea coast, and I'm camped on the beach. All I hear are the waves lapping tamely along the shore or an occasional bird that still hasn't settled for the evening.

Then I hear something different, a soft swoosh every now and then, like a stocking-footed child padding into a room. I peek outside my tent and am amazed to be surrounded by what must be at least a hundred reindeer making their way to the water's edge. These animals are part of several reindeer herds owned by Native Alaskans living in the region. The locals have told me not to be surprised to see them. They'll often visit the beaches, not for fun in the sun, but to seek refuge from the hordes of mosquitoes that plague them inland.

I'm a bit daunted by the sight of these big creatures encircling my little blue tent, but there's not much else I can do but get back in my tent and hope they don't decide to stampede. In the morning I awake and they are gone, only fading impressions of their hooves left in the sand are evidence that it wasn't a dream.

Cab Garage (907–443–2939), Stampede Rent-A-Car (907–443–3838), and, if you can believe such a service exists this far out, Chauffer de Anvil City limo service (907–443–2083).

The *Nome–Council Road,* which extends 72 miles east from Nome's main thoroughfare, Front Street, follows the coast for about 30 miles, then moves inland past rivers and sloping hills to the village of Council. About halfway out you'll come to the former community of Solomon, with its picturesque graveyard of old abandoned railroad engines and cars. Locals call this the Last Train to Nowhere. The 73-mile *Nome–Teller Road* leads to the village of Teller (population 200). You reach this highway from the west end of Front Street by turning north on Bering Street, which leads into the northwest-heading Teller Road.

A shorter driving option (about 3 miles one way) takes you to the top of *Anvil Mountain,* near an inoperative communications site. The rewarding view takes in the city of Nome, the Bering Sea, Sledge Island, and a colorful expanse of Arctic tundra.

Perhaps most rewarding, you can drive to *Pilgrim Hot Springs* on the Kougarok Road, which is accessible about 2 miles north of town by turning north off Bering Street. The experience offers a lot of natural history, mining history, and vast fields of tiny colorful flowers growing wild on the tundra. The 36-mile drive will take about forty-five minutes one way. Pack a snack to enjoy on the shores of Salmon Lake at the Bureau of Land Management campground. Farther down the road comes historic Pilgrim Hot Springs—once the site of a Catholic mission orphanage—and experimental gardens where tons of beets, carrots, turnips, cabbage, kale, rutabagas, rhubarb, onions, and potatoes were harvested from the hot springs–heated ground. Visitors are welcome to soak up the local

An Arctic Desert

*A*bove the Arctic Circle, northwest of Kotzebue, lie the shifting sands of the Great Kobuk Sand Dunes. This, the largest active dune field in the Arctic, is composed mainly of glacial silt. Some of the dunes reach heights of 100 feet, and summer temperatures there can reach 90 degrees Fahrenheit.

The dunes are part of the Kobuk Valley

National Park, a 1.7-million-acre area set aside in 1980 to protect them. During the Ice Age the Kobuk Valley remained ice free, providing a corridor adjoining the Bering Sea land bridge, which once linked Alaska and Siberia. Little has changed in this valley since then. The cold, dry climate remains, and plant life resembles the flora of the late Pleistocene era.

atmosphere by spending quality time in a *Pilgrim Hot Springs hot tub.* (Bring your own towel.) There's time, as well, for bird-watching, trail hiking, and angling for trout or grayling in the Pilgrim River. During a drive north on the Kougarok Road, you'll pass through the Nome River Valley, where it's not uncommon to spot musk ox, moose, and reindeer.

If you'd prefer to have a local expert along to show you the sights, contact Richard Beneville, owner of *Nome Discovery Tours.* From beach gold panning to traveling Nome's road system to learning about the area's history, Beneville will customize a trip to suit your needs. Prices vary depending on the adventure you choose. Phone (907) 443–2814, e-mail discover@dwarf.nome.net, or visit www.nome.net/~discover/.

Nome Tour & Marketing (907–443–2651; www.nome.net/~nuggetin/) has a $52 tour that takes visitors along Nome's "golden beaches" to Iditarod musher Howard Farley's camp. There, in the summer, they can watch him mushing his team. Also on the schedule is Little Creek Mine, where Kitty Scott, a gold miner's daughter, will walk you back in time through slides and stories from Nome's past. You can also pan for gold on the trip and pet a reindeer.

If you think Nome is fascinating by foot or vehicle, try seeing it from a few thousand feet in the air. Area air services can take you so far off the beaten path, there is no trail at all. *Olson Air Service* is a good place to start. If you want to say you've been overseas, that can be arranged, as Olson flies you over two islands belonging to two different nations—Little Diomede, USA, and Big Diomede, Russia—which, incidentally, will take you into "tomorrow" as you cross the international date line. The cost is $500 a flying hour, which can be divided among as many as nine passengers on the twin-engine craft that will fly you. That's an odd-enough adventure, but here's one that I find even more unique. How about a flight to one of the country's least known national parks, where you can overnight in a bunkhouse and reinvigorate your soul in a naturally occurring hot springs? This flight to the *Bering Land Bridge National Park* takes you to *Serpentine Hot Springs* for $275 per flying hour (count on a two-hour flight or double that if you plan to spend the night). Stranger still is a flight-see over ancient lava beds—yup, you can find just about anything if you look hard enough in Alaska—between Nome and the Native village of *Golovin.* It's about 60 miles from Nome. For more charter options call Olson at (907) 443–2229.

Other air tours include *Cape Smythe Air* flights to *Gambell* and *Savoonga* villages on *St. Lawrence Island,* off the coast of Siberia. Call

(907) 443–2414, or visit http://csas-ome.capes-mythe.com/ for more information. Various carriers also offer trips to the villages of **St. Michael,** known for its grass baskets; **Shaktoolik,** where you'll find Eskimo dolls, parkas, and mukluks; and **White Mountain,** which has excellent earrings of porcupine quills, beads, and ivory.

Don't be surprised if you see Pacific walrus during a visit to Nome. They migrate between the Chukchi and Bering seas. A bull walrus can weigh up to two tons.

When you're standing at the Arctic Circle on the summer solstice, the sun never sets. And if you're standing there on the winter solstice, the sun will not rise above the horizon.

Arranging flights from Nome to **Provideniya, Russia,** isn't quite as simple as booking a sightseeing tour, but flights to the former Soviet Union are possible, and hundreds of Nome visitors book them every year. **Bering Air** (907–443–5464; www.beringair.com; info@beringair.com) helped lift the "Iron Curtain" when the carrier transported American visitors across the international border in May 1988. The company has flown more than 600 such charter flights since and now operates regularly scheduled flights each week. Upon request the airline will send literature explaining how to arrange permission from the Russians to enter the country. Passengers traveling individually and with flexible schedules may be able to travel on a seat-fare basis for as little as $250 each way.

Lori Egge's **Sky Trekking Alaska** (800–770–4966; skytrek@alaska.net; www.skytrekkingalaska.com) is based in Wasilla, but she flies clients pretty much anywhere they want to go. Her custom-designed, one- to twelve-day adventures range from $450 to $11,000 for something really out there. From Nome, for instance, she'll fly-trek you on an eight-day trip to St. Lawrence Island in the Bering Sea. Trips can include dogsledding, backpacking, fishing, and bush country photography hikes. There's nothing bushy, however, about the meals. They're planned by chef Duncan Boyd of Nora's Restaurant in Washington, D.C. Lori prides herself on taking her customers to "places where there are no tourists at all," other than yourself, of course.

Several hotels offer lodging and dining accommodations in Nome, including the **Nome Nugget Inn** (907–443–2323; www.nome.net/~nuggetin/), where most of the airline tourists stay. If you like more informal surroundings, consider Shirley Bronston's **Ocean View Manor,** a spacious home with a spectacular view of the Bering Sea. Room options include private or shared baths. Breakfasts are continental style, available anytime. Doubles cost $50; call (907) 443–2133. And who says there's no such thing as a real igloo in Alaska? **Betty's Igloo Bed and Breakfast** is situated in Betty and Michael Hannigan's home, with attractive, comfortable rooms, and a beautiful ocean view. The rate of $70 for a double and $55 for a single includes an extensive continental breakfast. Call (907) 443–2419.

While these places offer more creature comforts, I've got to tell you that the best way to stay in Nome—especially if you're as lucky as I've been and have crystal-clear weather—is on the beach on the east side of town. Believe it or not, it's free and convenient to town. When I was there for a mountain biking trip a few years ago, I'd simply ride the half mile or so into town for breakfast (*Fat Freddie's,* 907–443–5899, has the best diner breakfasts in town and offers a view of the Bering Sea) and, once my belly was full, begin the day's adventures. And if I didn't feel like cooking my dinners on a camp stove, I could ride down to the *Fort Davis Roadhouse* (907–443–2660) on the edge of town for a delicious meal. To get information on camping call the convention and visitors bureau at (907) 443–5535.

The Bush

Since 1973, the small Brooks Range bush outpost called *Bettles* has been the base of operations for *Sourdough Outfitters,* one of the unquestioned pioneers in North Country guiding and outfitting. The outfitters' menu of more than two dozen choices range from easy, *Alatna River Canoeing,* for instance, to demanding, like the *Gates of the Arctic Winter Dogsledding* trip. They also offer rental cabins in the Brooks Mountains wilderness, float trips on the storied *Kobuk River,* camping on the *Arctic Divide* to witness herds of caribou in migration, and exploring the environmentally controversial *Arctic National Wildlife Refuge* (where developers want to drill the coastal plains for oil and environmentalists want protection for the area's rich storehouse of wildlife). Sourdough Outfitters trips range from $1,250 per person for eight days of hiking to $3,200 for twenty days of canoeing. Call (907) 692–5252, e-mail info@sourdoughoutfitters.com, or visit www.sourdoughoutfitters.com.

There are more options in the Brooks Range. *Alaska Discovery,* of Juneau, offers two hiking/boating adventures on the seldom-traveled

Far North Alaska Trivia

Continuous permafrost reaches depths of 2,000 feet in the Far North and can wreak havoc on buildings whose heat causes partial thawing. To remedy the problem, many buildings in the Far North are built on ground that is kept frozen during the summer with refrigeration coils. It is easier to cool the ground for a few months each year than deal with the repairs caused by shifting ice and sagging structures.

ALASKA'S FAR NORTH

Kongakut and Noatak Rivers. Both trips are ten days and originate with bush flights from Fairbanks. The Kongakut River trip, which combines rafting and hiking, is $2,980. The Noatak River float trip is by hiking and canoe in the ***Gates of the Arctic National Park.*** This is a great late-summer trip and a perfect time to view the fall colors and perhaps see the migrating Western Arctic caribou herd. You'll be just above the Arctic Circle for this adventure, which costs $2,750. Phone (800) 586–1911, e-mail akdisco@alaska.net, or visit www.akdiscovery. com.

Another Gates of the Arctic option well worth visiting is ***Peace of Selby*** on Selby/Narvak Lake in the Brooks Range. Fully furnished, comfortable lodge accommodations, with meals included, are $300 a night per person. Rustic cabins (bring your own food and sleeping bag) are $300 per group per night. Tent camps are available on request. Guided float trips, canoeing, day or overnight hikes, and fishing expeditions also are available. This is a photographer's or bird-watcher's heaven. Also popular at Peace of Selby are winter adventures, ranging from cross-country skiing, to snowshoeing to watching the caribou migration. Access, of course, is by air from Fairbanks or Bettles. For more details phone (907) 672–3206, e-mail peaceofselby@compuserve.com or visit www.gorp. com/selby/.

For those who enjoy bird-watching, not just to check off another species on their list but to see birds in their most natural environment, ***Wilderness Birding Adventures*** offers an exciting assortment of possibilities in Prince William Sound in Southcentral Alaska to the far north Arctic. Among the latter are float trips of the Colville River as well as floats or base-camp adventures on a small island of mountains protruding from the Arctic coastal plain in the ***Arctic National Wildlife Refuge.*** A float down the Marsh Fork/Canning River on the western edge of the refuge offers a chance to see many species of birds. The company also packages tours of Gambell on St. Lawrence Island, and of Nome, where rare species fly over from Siberia. Tours are priced as low as $395 for a two-day ***Owls of the North*** excursion from Anchorage to $2,990 for a ten-day trip of ***Kongakut River Rafting*** through perhaps some of the most remote wilderness in the United States. Call (907) 694–7442, or e-mail wildbird@alaska.net.

Perhaps one of the best options for Far North trekking is ***Sunlight North Expeditions,*** run by Clancy Crawford, who not only is an excellent outdoorsman, but a responsible steward of the land. He's been guiding for almost thirty years and offers trips from sea kayaking to Noatak River raft treks to canoeing to treks in the Arctic National Wildlife Refuge. A former school teacher, Clancy now guides full time. Be sure to ask him about his daughter, who is a world-class skier. For details call (907) 346–2027, e-mail sunlight@alaska.net, or visit www. alaskan.com/sunlight.

Jim Campbell and Carol Kasza, husband and wife, have hiked and climbed mountains around the world, but to establish their own guiding business—*Arctic Treks*—they selected the Brooks Range. They offer a wide selection of wilderness hiking, backpacking, and rafting options from eight days to twenty-one. Prices range from $2,050 to $3,875, including air from Fairbanks. They take only six to nine clients per trip. Call (907) 455–6502, e-mail arctreks@polarnet.com, or visit www.gorp.com/arctreks.

Established in 1847 by the Hudson's Bay Company, *Fort Yukon* is today one of Alaska's oldest settlements and the largest Athabascan Indian village in the state. Actually, the Gwich'in Athabascans have lived in this area for literally thousands of years. The town, which the people call *Gwichyaa Zhee* (meaning "house on the flats") lies 8 miles north of the Arctic Circle, and about 140 miles northeast of Fairbanks. You can get there by air via three scheduled carriers and four charter outfits or by boat. No roads lead to Fort Yukon.

If you enjoy buying souvenirs at the source, check out the Alaska Commercial Company store for beaded moose skin accessories. Most visitor services are available. One of the principal visitor attractions is a *replica of the original Fort Yukon.* Nearby is the old Hudson's Bay cemetery. Interestingly, Hudson's Bay built the fort not for protection from the Indians, but as a safeguard against the Russians who "owned" Alaska until 1867. Be sure also to see the *Old Mission School,* which is on the National Register of Historic Places. Ask to visit *St. Stephen's Territorial Episcopal Church,* where you can view exquisite and colorful Athabascan beaded embroidery on the altar cloth there. The Athabascans are renowned for their beadwork designs, which decorate boots, moccasins, jackets, and gloves.

Richard and Kathy Carroll's *Alaska Yukon Tours* (907–662–2727) range from a one-hour $20 tour of Fort Yukon to an overnight $240 to $290 riverboat tour, which includes meals, riverboat ride, tent camping, and fishing. Richard offers a variety of specialized trips that allow for hiking, canoeing, wildlife-watching, fishing, and camping. Prices vary from a modest $180 overnight lake tour on his family's land to a $3,000 weeklong getaway to the only resort lodge in the Arctic National Wildlife Refuge, *Porcupine River Lodge.* The Carrolls were born and raised in Fort Yukon and serve as excellent guides to the land's natural history and the people's way of life. Fairbanks air carriers that serve Fort Yukon include Frontier Flying Service (907–474–0014), Larry's Flying Service (907–474–9169), and Warbelow's Air Ventures (907–474–0518).

Arctic Village

The northernmost Indian village in the world, *Arctic Village,* in the foothills of the Brooks Range, is home to about 140 Gwich'in Athabascan Indians, who are doggedly determined to preserve their hunting/fishing/subsistence way of life. They're nonetheless willing to share their culture with a restricted number of visitors each year. Visits can be as brief as a fly-in, one-day excursion from Fairbanks to tour the village, sample traditional Native foods, and enjoy cultural presentations (including fiddling, borrowed from early Caucasian explorers), or trips can span several days with guided excursions into the wilderness to view caribou, moose, Dall sheep, and bears. Tours, which include a necessary visitor's entry permit, can be arranged by calling *Arctic Village Tours* at (907) 479–4648 or e-mailing ftmk@uaf.edu.

A one-day summer tour, including round-trip flight, village tour, and lunch, is $320. Two overnight tours are offered, one of Arctic Village and another of the nearby *Venetie* (pronounce Veen-I-ty). Airfare to Arctic Village is $260; the tour, food, lodging, and ground transportation are $180 per night. The Venetie trip is $220 and $180, respectively.

The Dalton Highway

This road—the only overland route into the Arctic from Alaska's highway network—is not for the timid or the unprepared. But the *Dalton Highway* is one of the great, last adventure roads in the United States. If you have the right vehicle and plan ahead, it can be one of the most satisfying drives of a lifetime. *A little history:* Alaska began construction of the 414-mile road in April 1974 and had it operational that fall in order to expedite construction of the 800-mile pipeline from Prudhoe Bay to Valdez.

The Dalton is gravel, two lanes, hilly in places, bumpy in many more, lonely (you may not see another car for hours), and has few service

Far North Alaska Trivia

Don't be surprised if you hear locals call the Dalton Highway the "haul" road. This 414-mile scenic but often rough road was built in 1974 as a transport road during the construction of the trans-Alaska oil pipeline, and it is still used to "haul" materials to keep the pipeline in operation.

facilities along the way. If you break down, you may not get help until an Alaska state trooper comes by on patrol. That's the bad news. The good news is that it is safely negotiable if you use common sense, and it opens up some of the most awesome northern mountain and tundra country in the world.

If you want to experience the highway but you don't want the hassle of planning, preparing, or driving the Dalton on your own, there's an easy option: Book reservations with one of several large or little tour companies that schedule motor-coach or van trips all summer long. Several of these offer drive-fly three-day itineraries during which you cruise the highway in one direction and fly between Fairbanks and Prudhoe Bay in the other. Among the companies that offer this and other options are *Princess Tours* (800–835–8907), *Gray Line of Alaska* (800–544–2206), *Northern Alaska Tour Company* (907–474–8600), and *Trans-Arctic Circle Treks, Ltd.* (907–479–5451). Prices vary with the different companies, points of origin, and whether you're traveling in a high or "shoulder" season. Princess Tours, which offers the trip only as part of several package options, is a less off the beaten path option. Trans-Arctic Circle Treks, Ltd., is more personalized, and suited to the independent traveler.

If you decide to drive the road yourself, make sure your car is in top mechanical condition. It's a good idea to call the Alaska Department of Transportation (907–451–2210) before you leave to find out the current road conditions. To be safe, carry an extra tire and two mounted spares. Chances are, you'll need at least one. Especially if you're camping out along the way (in fact, even if you're not), bring lots of bug dope. And by all means, pack plenty of film. It's a long, long drive to the nearest photo shop. If you don't plan to camp, make sure you've called ahead and reserved motel space in Coldfoot and Deadhorse. Be aware that gasoline is available along the way only at the Yukon River (mile 56), at Coldfoot (mile 175), and at Deadhorse at road's end (mile 414).

Whether you're in the family vehicle or an air-conditioned motor coach, the adventure begins when you leave the Elliott Highway past mile 73 and head north on the Dalton. Four miles later you're descending a steep incline into Lost Creek Valley, with the pipeline visible (as it frequently will be) to your right. From time to time, the pipe will crisscross under the road. Sometimes the line will be buried for many miles, and you won't see it at all.

About 48 miles out you begin your descent to the Yukon River, and at mile 55.6, there it is, the storied Yukon and an impressive 2,290-foot wood-decked bridge that rises (or falls, depending on which way you're driving) at a 6 percent grade.

Across the river on its northern bank, you can top off your fuel tank at **Yukon Ventures Alaska** (907–655–9001) as well as eat a restaurant meal and overnight in a motel. You can also take one of **Yukon River Tours'** daily 10-mile boat trips aboard the forty-nine-passenger cabin vessel *Yookene Spirit* to an Athabascan Indian fish camp. The boat trip costs $25; with an overnight tenting experience, the cost is $45. Bring your own sleeping bag and food. For information, call (907) 452–7162, e-mail dlacey@mosquitonet.com, or visit www.mosquitonet.com/~dlacey/yrt.html.

At mile 115.3 you can expose a photo you'll be proud to hang on your living room wall. Here you will officially cross the **Arctic Circle** at 66 degrees, 33 minutes north latitude, and there's a big sign there to prove it.

At mile 175 you'll come to **Coldfoot,** which started life as an old-time mining camp and exists today as the major overnight spot for truckers and visitors on the Dalton Highway. The name, according to local legend, came about when early gold stampeders got this far north, then got "cold feet" and retreated south.

If you want to overnight in Coldfoot, try **Arctic Circle Bed and Breakfast,** which not only has rooms, but canoe rentals and fishing as well. Phone (907) 452–0081.

The services provided by **Coldfoot Services and Arctic Acres Inn** include gas, phone, tire and mechanical repair, RV hookups, motel, lounge, and lots of good contact with authentic bush-country Alaskans. Call (907) 678–5201. The National Park Service maintains a **visitor center** at Coldfoot, offering road and travel updates as well as programs each night about the Arctic.

Approaching mile 189 along the highway, you join a short access road to **Wiseman.** Like many others of its kind, this community once thrived as a trading center for prospectors and miners. These days, about two dozen determined souls still live there year-round, joined by others in the summer. The **Wiseman Museum** is a good place to stop and check out old mining artifacts and photos. And if you don't want to tent out, call **Arctic Getaway Bed & Breakfast** at (907) 796–9001. It's not fancy, but hosts Berni and Uta Hicker will make you feel at home.

At mile 235.3, just south of a highway turn-off, you'll see the northernmost spruce tree in Alaska. No others grow beyond this point. This is also the start of a long and very steep grade—10 percent. Be sure to give any downhill-traveling trucks you meet their full half of the road.

Another steep ascent begins just beyond mile 242 and ends at Atigun Pass, which at 4,800 feet is the highest in Alaska. Watch for Dall sheep, especially on Slope Mountain.

About 75 miles later you'll see a pingo 5 miles west of the road. These curious circular mounds, more common the closer you get to the Arctic Ocean's shores, rise dramatically from surrounding table-top smooth terrain. They're caused by frozen water beneath the surface.

At mile 414 you've arrived at **Deadhorse,** the gathering point where crude oil from Prudhoe Bay, Kuparuk River, and other lesser oil fields is brought in by a network of smaller pipelines and directed into the 48-inch Trans-Alaska Pipeline for transport to Valdez, 800 miles to the south.

The Trans-Alaska Pipeline along the Dalton Highway

Truth to tell, you'll probably judge Deadhorse a pretty bleak and dreary place. Some of the Arco and BP oil company buildings (with self-contained dorms, cafeterias, libraries, and recreation centers) are modern and bright, even cheerful, and some of the subcontractor structures and quarters are on a par with counterparts in industrial parks in the Lower Forty-eight. But a considerable number of Deadhorse's buildings and lots are unkempt, junky, littered, and strewn with unused or abandoned pipe, equipment, and building material. No one really seems to care, since almost no one lives here year-round. Virtually the entire population consists of crews and individuals who arrive or depart on periodic shift assignments. There are no church buildings, schools, movie theaters, or any of the other trappings of a bona fide community. Few if any of the workers bring wives or family. They claim residence in Anchorage, Fairbanks, and even far-flung points like Dallas and Fort Worth.

So what's the attraction? Well, it may be drab, dreary, and desolate, but in a strange sort of way, it's dramatic and absorbing. There's a lot of coming-going-moving-shaking activity, and if you take one of the organized tours available, you'll learn a lot about the place and the process from which the United States gets a whopping 1.8 million barrels of crude oil a day. You can have your picture taken at **Pipeline Mile Zero.** You'll likely see wild caribou grazing virtually in the shadow of oil rigs and pipelines just outside of town, and any number of waterfowl bird species resting or nesting on the tundra. And if you don't happen to have Point Barrow on your itinerary, where else will you be able to skip a stone on the **Arctic Ocean?** (Or, if you're a winter or very early summer visitor, actually take a few steps out onto the Arctic ice pack.)

You can't, by the way, just mosey around Deadhorse in your car on your own as you would back home. Much of this community, including many roads, is private property, and you need permission to visit many sites, including the shores of the Arctic Ocean. This is the reason many visitors choose all-inclusive van or motor-coach drive-fly tours from Fairbanks or Anchorage. If you plan to drive here in your own vehicle, you should definitely make housing reservations ahead of time. The **Prudhoe Bay Hotel** (907–659–2449) is open year-round and accommodates visitors as well as petroleum workers. The management offers tours of the area as well. **Arctic Caribou Inn** (907–659–2368, summer; 907–659–2840, winter) provides rooms, tours, breakfasts, dinners, and a gas station.

If you feel you still haven't gone far north enough, go to the **Tesoro Gas Station** (907–659–3198) and book a **White Nights Arctic Ocean Tours** flight-seeing tour over the Polar Sea. You'll see the floating ice pack, Inupiat whaling camps, the Prudhoe oil fields, and, probably, lots of wildlife. The Deadhorse Airport also offers flight-seeing tours.

Prudhoe Bay Fleet Shop or the *Veco Light Vehicle Shop* will repair your car if need be, and gas can be had at either *NANA* or the Tesoro station, which is open twenty-four hours. Incidentally, no one uses street addresses here. To find something, just look for signs or ask someone.

The Dalton Highway, of course, is a north-south, single road. There are no loops or alternate routes back. If you're driving, when your visit ends, you simply retrace your path to the Elliott Highway, to Fairbanks, or wherever.

PLACES TO STAY IN THE FAR NORTH

BARROW
Top of the World Hotel, 1204 Agvik; (907) 852–3900. Fully modern and in town.

COLDFOOT
Arctic Circle Bed and Breakfast; (907) 452–0081.

DEADHORSE
Arctic Caribou Inn; (907) 659–2368.

Prudhoe Bay Hotel; (907) 659–2449.

KOTZEBUE
Nullagvik Hotel; (907) 442–3331.

NOME
Betty's Igloo Bed and Breakfast; (907) 443–2419.

Nome Nugget Inn, Building 2, Front Street; (907) 443–2323, www.nome.net/~nuggetin

Ocean View Manor; (907) 443–2133.

SELBY/NARVAK LAKE
Peace of Selby, within Gates of the Arctic National Park and Noatak National Preserve; (907) 672–3206, www.gorp.com/selby. It's out there, but certainly peaceful.

WISEMAN
Arctic Getaway Bed and Breakfast, mile 189 Dalton Highway; (907) 796–9001.

PLACES TO EAT IN THE FAR NORTH

NOME
Fat Freddie's, 563 Front Street; (907) 443–5899. Not fancy, but tasty and filling diner food.

Fort Davis Roadhouse; (907) 443–2660. On the edge of town; delicious food.

BARROW
Pepe's North of the Border, 1204 Agvik; (907) 852–8200. Mexican cuisine.

KOTZEBUE
Nullagvik Restaurant; (907) 442–3331. Reindeer stew and sausage, fresh local fish, and other tasty fare.

Southwestern Alaska

S trange opportunity you have in Southwestern Alaska. If you really want to, you can travel farther off the beaten path in this region than in any other in the nation. Farther west and—here's the strange part—farther *east*.

The Aleutian Islands, as you probably know, stretch from the end of the Alaska Peninsula almost to Japan. The westernmost point in the United States lies on one of those islands, Amatignak at 179 degrees, 10 minutes west.

Now about the easternmost point. Just across the 180th meridian that separates the earth's Western Hemisphere from the Eastern Hemisphere (and exactly halfway around the world from the prime meridian at Greenwich, England) is Semisopochnoi Island's Pochnoi Point, at 179 degrees, 46 minutes east. Thus the nation's most northern (at Point Barrow), western, and eastern real estate is located in Alaska. (The most southern, if you're curious, is on the southern side of the Big Island of Hawaii.)

Here are some other Alaska-sized statistics about this region: You can visit Alaska's largest island, Kodiak, and in the process see the nation's biggest land omnivore, the Kodiak brown bear. You can photograph the biggest moose in Alaska on the Alaska Peninsula. Some of North America's most volatile volcanoes have blown their tops in this area—one of the most awesome, Novarupta, is part of Katmai National Park and Preserve. Through the region flow some of the nation's wildest rivers. And way, way, *way* out in the Bering Sea you'll find two tiny islands on which you'll see more birds of more species than you ever thought possible. Every visitor comes home from the Pribilof Islands a confirmed bird-watcher.

Among Native residents in the region, you'll meet Yu'pik Eskimos on

> ## Southwest Alaska Trivia
>
> *Mishap Creek, also known as Big Loss Creek, on Unimak Island in the Aleutians, derived its name from an incident. A lightkeeper, attempting to cross the creek after finding the bridge washed out, bundled up his clothes and tried to throw them across. Misjudging the distance, his clothes fell short of the far bank and were washed away.*
>
> *—Source: US Coast and Geodetic Survey*

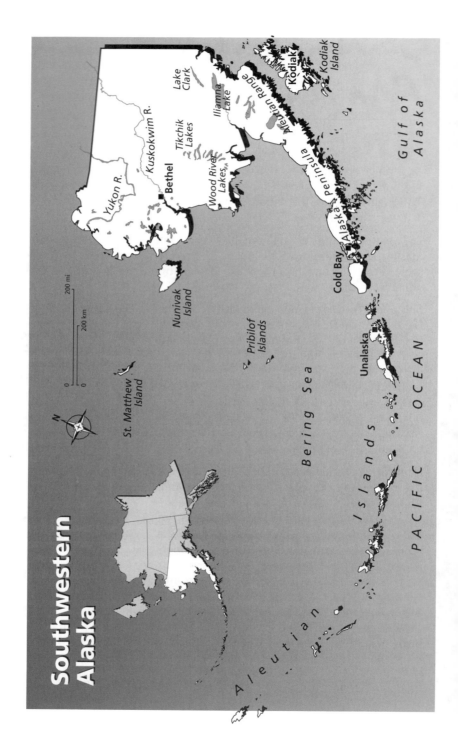

Top 10 Places in Southwest Alaska

Kodiak Cattle Company,
Kodiak

Fort Abercrombie State
Park, Kodiak

Harborside Coffee
and Goods, Kodiak

Margaret Bay, Unalaska

Dimitri's Greek restaurant,
Bethel

Raspberry Island Remote
Camps

Shahafka Bed and
Breakfast, Kodiak

Shuyak Island

Lake Clark National Park
and Preserve

Aniakchak National
Monument and Preserve

the western mainland, Aleuts on the Aleutian and Pribilof Islands, and Alutiiq Natives on Kodiak Island.

Kodiak Island, in fact, is a good place to start an exploration of the region. The island ranks not only as the largest in Alaska, with a population of about 14,100, it also contains Alaska's earliest continuing European settlement, the *city of Kodiak.*

No roads or bridges connect Kodiak Island to the Alaska mainland, but the Alaska Marine Highway System (800–526–6731; akferry@ptialaska.net; www.ak-biz.com/alaskamarine/) offers regular, dependable passenger and vehicle ferry service from Homer and Seward on the Kenai Peninsula several times each week. Alaska Airlines and ERA Aviation provide daily flights from Anchorage. There are visitor accommodations and services aplenty in the community. For information contact the **Kodiak Island Convention and Visitors Bureau,** at (907–486–4782) at 100 Marine Way, or e-mail kicvb@ptia laska.net.

Tourism as a major industry has not yet discovered Kodiak. It's clearly still off the beaten path. The result is, you can come away from a visit with a genuine feel for the way Alaskans live and work and play in this part of the "Last Frontier." It's fun simply to wander along the boat docks and cannery sites, watching the frantic, frenzied busyness of salmon, crab, halibut, shrimp, and other fisheries landings. More than 3,000 commercial vessels—some quite large—utilize Kodiak's two harbors, St. Paul and St. Herman, each year, making the area one of the busiest in the world. While you're at St. Paul harbor downtown checking out the fleet, make sure to stop in at **Harborside Coffee and Goods** (907–486–5862), a friendly, comfortable coffeehouse with a water view. My husband and I once passed an entire afternoon there, just watching the boats come and go, the fishermen tend to their chores, and the seabirds ride the wind.

A great deal of Alaska's early European history resides in Kodiak. The first Russian settlement, established in 1784, was at Three Saints Bay, but the Russian trader and manager Alexander Baranov relocated his headquarters to present Kodiak in 1792. Originally Baranov's warehouse for precious sea otter pelts, and now the **Baranov Museum,** it was constructed about 1808 and is the oldest Russian building in Alaska. It's at 101 Marine

Way and contains antiques and artifacts of the Russian and pre-Russian era, including grand samovars, handcrafted silver jewelry, and fine-woven Alutiiq basketry. Admission is $2.00. Phone (907) 486–5920 for information.

Kodiak's *Holy Resurrection Russian Orthodox Church,* the oldest parish in Alaska, stands in the city's downtown district at Kashaveroff Street and Mission Avenue. Tour hours are 1:00 to 3:00 P.M., daily except Sunday in the summer. At other times, call (907) 486–3854 (www.oca.org). You'll see colorful religious trappings of the Orthodox faith, including icons that date back to Russia's czarist period. Additional icons, artifacts, and reminders of the area's Christian spiritual beginnings can be found at the *Saint Innocent Veniaminov Research Institute Museum* at Saint Herman Theological Seminary, on Mission Road north of the church. Father Herman was one of the early Orthodox monks who arrived to evangelize, educate, and provide medical attention to Alaska Natives. On August 9, 1970, he became the first North American religious to be canonized by the Russian Orthodox Church. For museum hours, check with the visitor center downtown.

Celebrating a Saint's Life

*I*f you're in Kodiak in early August, you can take part in a unique celebration of a unique man. On August 9, pilgrims from around the world gather in Kodiak to celebrate the canonization of Saint Herman by the Russian Orthodox Church.

Father Herman came to Kodiak in 1794 to convert the Natives of Alaska to Christianity and protect them from abuse by the fur traders of the Russian American Co. He helped build the first church in Kodiak and eventually moved to a nearby island, which he named New Valaam, now called Spruce Island.

There, at Monk's Lagoon, he started an orphanage and school for Native children and developed what was probably the first experimental agri-culture station. Father Herman is credited with miraculous powers, including healings, averting a tsunami, and befriending Kodiak brown bears. He died on the island in 1837.

Father Herman was canonized Saint Herman on August 9, 1970, and each year on that date a flotilla of boats, all volunteer, line up at St. Paul Harbor in Kodiak to ferry pilgrims to Monk's Lagoon for a short service commemorating Herman's elevation to sainthood. The trip takes most of the day, so bring a lunch. There is no charge, and all who want to visit this holy place are welcomed.

For information on the pilgrimage call the Holy Resurrection Russian Orthodox Church at (907) 486–5532.

Holy Resurrection Orthodox Church, Kodiak

Of course, before the Americans and before the Russians, there were the Native residents of Kodiak, the Alutiiq (pronounced Al-LOO-tig) people. In Kodiak you can learn a lot of indigenous history simply by attending the dances performed by a talented group called the **Kodiak Alutiiq Dancers.** And these Alutiiq performers are truly one of a kind in their stories and music and in their unique "snow falling" attire, with tassels of brilliant white Arctic fox descending over black parkas. Three dozen or so dancers perform daily, Monday through Saturday, at their *barabara,* or traditional Alutiiq dwelling, at 713 Rezanof Street near downtown. Performers range from small children to elders, and their dances run the gamut from an ancestral "kayaking" dance to more contemporary, enacted stories of rich humor, such as the tale of a little boy who eats pudding as fast as his frantic parents can make it. For information call (907) 486–4449.

New on the Kodiak scene is the **Alutiiq Museum and Archaeological Repository,** which opened in 1995 at 215 Mission Road. Housed there are artifacts from numerous archaeological sites around the Kodiak Island Archipelago, and plans are under way to repatriate additional artifacts and artwork that are now scattered in museums around the world. The new facility features a display gallery, state-of-the-art storage for sensitive artifacts, and a research laboratory. There's also a museum store, which showcases the work of local artists. Hours are 10:00 A.M. to 4:00 P.M., Monday through Friday and noon until 3:00 P.M. on Saturday and Sunday. Admission is $2.00 (907–486–7004; alutiiq@ptialaska.net).

For some close-to-town hiking or exploring, walk across the bridge to **Near Island.** An easy walking path that circles the north end of the island starts on the north side of the road, just beyond the end of the bridge. Continue on down the hill and you'll find **St. Herman's Harbor,** where during the summer you'll see the island's salmon fleet, if they aren't out fishing.

To view recent history, visitors can take a 4-mile drive out the Rezanof-Monashka Road to **Fort Abercrombie State Park** to see the remains of World War II gun emplacements, restored bunkers, and other such artifacts. It's a toss-up which you'll find the more interesting—the massive concrete bunkers and fortifications that once protected Kodiak from a Japanese invasion or the breathtaking, panoramic view from rugged cliffsides and gentle shores. The area is thickly forested

Kodiak's Waterfront

I walked with my husband along the docks of Kodiak's St. Paul Harbor on an unusually sunny morning in the middle of the week. Everyone was hard at work, doing their day-to-day thing. For us, it was a vacation, a weekend getaway from our Kenai Peninsula home. My husband lived here once, before we met, and he was serving as something of a tour guide. As we neared the ferry dock at the Near Island channel, I saw nothing out of the ordinary. A commercial fishing boat was tied up, and a fisherman hosed off the decks. The Near Island bridge loomed above, a sharp concrete contrast to the beauty of this mostly green place.

"Why are we stopping here?" I asked. I was anxious to check out the historic looking church I had seen earlier in the morning.

"You'll see," Andy replied, and he led me closer to the edge of the dock.

I peered into the inky blue water and looked. Nothing.

"Just give it a minute," Andy said, and he continued to stare into the water.

In a moment I saw a brown blur appear from the depths of the water, then, just as quickly, disappear again. Within seconds it returned, and then, as my eyes adjusted to this maritime setting, I saw them: sea lions. Not just one, or two, or even a handful, but more than a dozen of them—diving low, surfacing, racing one another around the fishing boat vying for the scraps of fish being hosed off the deck. They swarmed the place like so many ants on a picnic blanket.

Take advantage of this close-up—and free—glimpse of the North Pacific's wildlife. These thousand-pound-plus sea mammals may seem plentiful here, but elsewhere in Southwest Alaska their numbers are on the decline. Scientists are currently trying to figure out why they are disappearing.

with Sitka spruce, berry plants, and wildflowers. Included in this 183-acre park are thirteen campsites for tenters and RVers, hiking trails, picnicking facilities, and good fishing and swimming spots. Call (907) 486–6339.

Several roads are worth exploring, including the **Chiniak Highway** that runs southwest from town then southeast. Particularly scenic points and beaches can be found from about mile 35 to the end of the 42-mile road. It's great for picnics, photography, and viewing more World War II gun battery emplacements. If you do your beach exploring at low tide, you'll be amazed at the sealife left behind in small pools after the tide has receded—tiny crabs, anemones, starfish, sea dollars, snails, itty-bitty fish, seaweeds, and all manner of other creepy-crawlies.

The **Anton Larsen Bay Road,** which begins about 5 miles from downtown at a junction with the Chiniak Highway, leads to Anton Larsen Bay. Along the way you just may spot a brown bear. They don't call the golf course at mile 3 (from the junction) Bear Valley Golf Course for nothing.

The road to **Pasagshak Bay** and Narrow Cape begins at mile 30.6 on the Chiniak Highway. The 16½-mile road brings you through scenic Pasagshak Pass to **Pasagshak River State Recreation Site,** which has rest room facilities, a picnic area, and camping. Beyond the river's mouth, visit Pasagshak Beach, where diehard, neoprene-clad surfers often can be seen catching the relentless waves. At mile 14.6, you'll pass the entrance to the Kodiak Cattle Company. You may encounter the ranch's buffalo wandering the hillsides, but don't give in to any strange temptation to approach them. They are livestock, yet essentially live as wild animals. The road ends as **Fossil Beach.** Be careful when approaching the cliffs: They're unstable and falling rocks are a hazard.

If Kodiak has been, until recently, a lesser-known visitor destination, it has nonetheless been one of North America's best known hunting areas for decades. The reason is *ursus arctos middendorffi*, the Kodiak brown bear, which can weigh in at 1,500 pounds or more. Around 2,700 or more

Camai Native Dance Festival in Bethel, held each spring to celebrate, well, just to celebrate. Features Native crafts, dance, food, and other activities. For information call (907) 543–2321, or e-mail bcarts@unicom-alaska.com.

Kodiak Crab Festival, held each May in Kodiak to celebrate spring. Lots of rides, crafts, entertainment, and a survival-suit race pitting those brave enough to swim in the cold. Call (907) 486–5557, or e-mail chamber@kodiak.org.

Unalaska World Record Halibut Derby, held each year in Unalaska. See if you can beat Jack Tragis's world-record 459-pound halibut and win $100,000. For information call (907) 581–2612, or e-mail updhcvb@ansi.net.

The Aleuts are known for producing beautiful hand-woven baskets. The baskets come in all shapes but are most often cylindrical with a small knob as a handle. They are made from rye grass and can be ornately woven. The three most common styles of Aleut baskets are named after their islands of origin— Atka, Unalaska, and Attu.

of the big bruins live on Kodiak Island, according to biologists. Most reside in the 2,491-square-mile **Kodiak National Wildlife Refuge** (www.alaskaone.com/nwr/kodi.htm) on Kodiak and nearby Uganik, Ban, and Afognak Islands. Visitors can dwell among these critters if they like by renting one of several backcountry recreation cabins constructed by the U.S. Fish and Wildlife Service. Access, incidentally, is only by float-equipped airplanes or boats. For information contact the Kodiak National Wildlife Refuge Manager, 1390 Buskin Road, Kodiak 99615 (907–487–2600), or stop by the **U.S. Fish and Wildlife Service Visitor Center,** about 4¹/₂ miles from downtown on Chiniak Highway.

If you don't want to arrange your own sight-seeing, fishing, or hiking expeditions, there are several Kodiak outfitters that can get you set up. **Alaska Outback Tours,** with German- and English-speaking hosts, offers salmon fishing packages on any of the several salmon-rich rivers in and around Kodiak, tours that take in all the historic buildings in town, and wildlife-viewing and scenic coastal drives throughout the island. Call (907) 486–5101, or visit www. ptialaska.net/~aktours/.

Kodiak Sports & Tour is operated by Scott and Sonja Phelps in nearby Port Lions. The Phelpses offer sight-seeing and photography trips, fishing charters, and hiking tours. For a really "out-there" experience, try scuba diving or a guided fly-in float trip on the Uganik River. Call (907) 454–2419, or e-mail kstkodiak@aol.com.

Saltery Lake Lodge offers fishing, photography, and (in season) hunting adventures on Saltery Lake, near Ugak Bay on the eastern side of Kodiak Island. The lodge operates a floatplane and fishing vessel to aid guests in their quests for sockeye, pink, chum, and silver salmon as well as Dolly Varden, rainbow, and steelhead. A canoe also is available for exploring the lake. Prices begin at $365 a day and decrease as length of stay increases. Call (800) 770–5037, e-mail info@salterylake.com, or visit www. salterylake.com.

No trip to Kodiak is complete without exploring the many bays, inlets, and coves that are home to Alaska's diverse wildlife. And what a safe place from which to view an occasional Kodiak brown bear! In town, try **Mythos Expeditions Kodiak** (907–486–5536 mythosdk@ptialaska. net; www.ptialaska.net/~mythosdk/mythos/index.html). Operating year-round

SOUTHWESTERN ALASKA

and specializing in small groups, Mythos owners Dave and Jan Kubiak will help plan all sorts of expeditions, from close to town to far-off islands. Local day tours are available for those on a budget at $40 for two hours and $75 for four hours.

A little farther out is *Spirit of Alaska Wilderness Adventures,* a business located on the south end of the already-remote Amook Island in Uyak Bay. This company is designed with the independent traveler in mind. Getting there—usually by float plane then by boat—will cost the most, and it'll cost you $100 per person per day for all the kayaking, wildlife viewing, fishing, beachcombing, or whatever else you choose to do, as well as lodging. Call (800) 677–8641, e-mail steele@spiritofalaska.com, or visit www.members. tripod.com/~spiritofalaska/.

For a completely different experience, try horseback riding at Bill Burton's 21,000-acre *Kodiak Cattle Company,* where you'll see not only ranch cattle but also huge buffalo wandering over the range. Burton's been in Kodiak since the sixties and has tried raising just about every breed of cattle known. But a rather large problem, the Kodiak brown bear, kept killing off the cattle. It wasn't until Burton began raising buffalo that he found success. Even a Kodiak brown won't mess with these big creatures. This is a working ranch, to be sure, but there are enough horses there to borrow one for a few hours. The rate is $45 for two hours. Phone (907) 486–3705.

For whale-watching or charter fishing, try *Three Sons Charters* (907–486–6824; threesns@ptialaska.net; www.ptialaska.net/~threesns). Rates are $100 for a half day with drinks and snacks and $175 for a full day with lunch.

Another option is Eric Stirrup's *MV Ten Bears* (907–486–2200; info@tenbears.com; www.tenbears.com). Stirrup has offered quality fishing charters since 1979.

If by boat and by horse isn't enough, yet another option is by bike, and Kodiak is a great place for cycling. Bike rentals are available at *58 Degrees North,* located at 1231 Mill Bay Road (907–486–6249; thowland@ ptialaska.net). Rates begin at $25 for twenty-four hours for a mountain bike and $35 for twenty-four hours for a tandem bike. Bikes also may be rented hourly for $5.00 per hour.

For oceanfront lodging close to downtown Kodiak, try **Shahafka Cove Bed & Breakfast,** which is somewhat of a town legend, as it once was a "house of ill repute." Today, however, the place is renovated, comfortable, and tastefully decorated; it offers affordable rooms, starting at $65 a night with full breakfast. Perhaps the best feature of all is the place's location— right on the water, with a 90-foot deck and a stairway leading down to the beach. For more information call (907) 486–2409, e-mail rwoitel@ptialaska.net, or visit www.ptialaska.net/~ rwoitel/.

R&R Lodge is a small, personal, backcountry lodge on remote Ugak Bay. Host Robin Reed books only one party at a time and limits the size to four (maybe six by special arrangement). The attractions here are fishing, of course, plus unstructured sight-seeing to observe seals, sea lions, sea otters, orca (killer) whales, grey and other whale species as well as Kodiak brown bears, deer, foxes, and even mountain goats. Rates are $1,280 per person for a five-day vacation, air fare not included. For more information call (907) 486–3704, e-mail ptialaska.net/~rlreed, or visit www. rnrinfo@eagle.ptialaska.net.

A truly remote destination is **Raspberry Island Remote Camps,** operated by Lee and Cilla Robbins. The camp is situated amid an ancient spruce forest that prompts wide-eyed gawking. At the Robbinses' camp, you'll enjoy daily program of fishing, sight-seeing, hiking, boating— you name it. Then, at the end of the day, you're on your own to lounge in the camp's hot spa or sauna, relax on the sundeck, or just retreat to your room to relax. Phone (907) 486-1781, e-mail adventure@raspberryisland.com, or www.ptialaska.net/~rirc.

Katmai National Park

During the morning of June 1, 1912, a volcanic mountain in what is now **Katmai National Park and Preserve** began a series of violent quakes and eruptions, the likes of which had seldom been recorded in earth's history. A full foot of volcanic ash fell on Kodiak, 100 miles distant, and darkened the sky to inky blackness. When the eruptions subsided, a valley at the site lay buried under 700 feet of ash. In 1916 when the first expedition entered the area, thousands of still-steaming fumeroles inspired the name "Valley of 10,000 Smokes." That valley, curiously, remains stark and desolate to this day, though the surrounding area now thrives with lush growth and beautiful lakes and rivers that teem with salmon and other fish. You can visit the park easily, though no roads lead to it. Propeller-equipped aircraft offer daily

Southwest Alaska Facts

access from King Salmon (accessible by jet from Anchorage) and less frequent flights are also available from Kodiak.

If you're a photographer you may want to join an annual **Joseph Van Os Photo Safari** in Katmai. Air transportation from Anchorage, hotel accommodations, meals, tours, and the expertise of a professional wildlife photographer are included in the weeklong tour. Call (206) 463–5383 for more information.

Incidentally, if you want to bring a tent and camp in the Park Service **Brooks Campground** near the Brooks Lodge, be advised there's a lottery system now in effect and a four-day limit for campground reservations. For more details call the superintendent's office at (800) 365– 2267. The phone is often busy, so you can also request information by mail from Katmai National Park, P.O. Box 7, King Salmon 99613.

Lake Iliamna, on the Alaska Peninsula in Southwest Alaska, is the state's largest lake. It covers 1,000 square miles and is 70 miles long, 20 miles wide, and 1,000 feet deep.

Kodiak became the first capital of Russian America in the late 1700s and was a major fur-trading center for many years.

Kayak Island in the Gulf of Alaska was the site of the first landing of Europeans in Alaska, on July 20, 1741.

Katmai Wilderness Lodge, headquartered in Kodiak and located on Kukak Bay on the eastern coast of Katmai National Park, limits its guest list to six visitors a day. The company promises abundant wildlife viewing both ashore and from the water, including brown bears digging for razor clams plus whales and sea otters. There are also glacier treks, nature hikes, and kayak trips. Birders have identified 231 species so far; maybe you'll spot the 232nd. The area is especially rich in archaeological resources. A two-day bear-viewing package from Kodiak costs $1,250; three nights and four days in a comfortable log cabin, with cook and guide, cost $2,000. Prices include a floatplane trip from Kodiak. For details call (800) 488–8767, e-mail katbears@ptialaska.net or visit www.ptialaska.net/~katbears/index2.htm.

Unalaska/Dutch Harbor

If you look just at location, **Unalaska** and its adjacent neighbor, **Dutch Harbor,** would seem the most unlikely of tourist destinations, situated as they are out on the Aleutian chain. The two towns (actually, they're really just one; only a small bridge separates them) lie 800 air miles from Anchorage, about midway along the 1,000-mile Aleutian Islands chain that extends westerly from the Alaska Peninsula almost to Japan.

Don't, if you're a true fan of out-of-the-way travel, overlook this destination. Unalaska/Dutch Harbor offers a surprising number of pleasurable places to see, lots of things to do, and an amazing comfort level. Although no roads or surface highways lead there, the towns enjoy excellent daily air service from Anchorage (via Alaska Airlines, Reeve Aleutian Airways, and PenAir) as well as a monthly schedule of calls by the Alaska Marine Highway System's passenger and auto ferry *Tustumena.* Traveling aboard the stateroom-equipped *Trusty Tusty,* as she's called, is in fact a terrific way to see this part of Alaska. The vessel leaves Homer one Tuesday a month, April through September, en route to Kodiak, Chignik, Sand Point, King Cove, Cold Bay, False Pass, and Unalaska. She leaves Unalaska on a Saturday and arrives back in Homer the following Tuesday. One-way fare costs $242 from Homer, $250 from Seward, meals not included; cabins begin at $208 and $218. Call (800) 382–9229, or visit www.akms.com/ferry.

Now for some geography: Unalaska is located on Unalaska Island and Dutch Harbor is situated on Amaknak Island. The bridge that connects them is called the Bridge to the Other Side.

Rich in Aleut, early Russian, and World War II history, Unalaska/Dutch Harbor has become a major bustling seafood landing and processing center in recent years. It is, in fact, the number-one port in the United States in terms of pounds and value of fish and crab landed. The year-round population totals more than 4,300 residents, and there are thousands of additional commercial fishermen coming and going at all

A Land Rich in History

There's a place in Unalaska that tells much of the story of life in the Aleutians before the white man arrived. The site, in Margaret Bay, is being studied by scientists from around the country. But if you're interested in archeaology yourself, you can study it, too. Excavation of the site has revealed the tools and implements used by the Unangan people who inhabited this village more than 6,000 years ago.

Excavations at the site began in May,

1996. It revealed remains of several stone-walled semisubterranean houses, as well as tools made of chipped stone, blades, stone lamps, bowls, lebrets, grinders, and pendants. The researchers even uncovered some miniature carved masks.

The Grand Aleutian Hotel offers an adventure package that includes digging alongside professional archaeologists by day and relaxing in the comfort of Unalaska's nicest hotel by night. Call (907) 581–2612.

times. Recently the community has enjoyed a small but growing visitor influx, particularly World War II veterans who served in this theater in the 1940s. Many return to see once again the site of Japanese bombing attacks and the defensive fortifications the U.S. troops built and manned along shorelines and on mountainsides.

Birders come from around the world to see the rare whiskered auklet and other species, and anglers journey here to land world-class halibut and three kinds of salmon.

Accommodations here are much more plush than you might imagine. The wonderfully named *Grand Aleutian Hotel,* in fact, offers uncompromising luxury in its 112 rooms, public areas, and gourmet restaurant, the *Chart Room,* where the chefs make innovative use of locally abundant seafood. The hotel offers rooms starting at $135 as well as tour packages for sight-seers, birders, and sportfishers. Call (800) 891–1194, e-mail grand_aleutian@ansi.net, or visit www.ansi.net/~ grand_aleutian/ for information and reservations.

Located downtown is *Carl's Bayview Inn.* Carl's offers a variety of accommodations from standard rooms to suites. Prices range from $90 to $175. Call (800) 581–1230.

Not quite so new, but commendable nonetheless, is the *UniSea Inn,* both a hotel and a short-order sports bar and grill. The pizza, in particular, comes highly recommended. Rooms start at $100 for a double. Phone (907) 581–1325.

With such excellent commercial fishing in this region, it goes without saying that those who enjoy recreational fishing will have a fine time here. *Shuregood Adventures* is one of several outfits offering halibut fishing and sight-seeing excursions out of Dutch Harbor. Phone (907) 581–2378, e-mail shurgood@ansi.net, or visit www.ansi.net/~shurgood.

Surely the most compelling cultural and historical site is *Holy Ascension Russian Orthodox Cathedral,* constructed 1894–96. It contains an astonishing 697 documented icons, artifacts, and significant works of art, one of the largest and richest such collections in Alaska. Within the structure, too, are remnants of even earlier churches and chapels used in 1808, 1826, and 1853. Most ground tours offer a visit to this historic landmark. Call the Convention and Visitor Bureau at (907) 581–2612 for details, or visit www.arctic.net/~updhcvb.

Other possibilities in Unalaska/Dutch Harbor include nature excursions that focus on wildlife and geological features, marine adventures including World War II shipwrecks, gold mining claims, sportfishing aboard

Lake Iliamna, the state's largest lake, is reported to be inhabited by a sea monster. There's speculation that it is either a whale that somehow made its way into the lake in pursuit of salmon (the lake, by the way, supports the world's largest sockeye salmon run) or an oversized sturgeon.

charter vessels, and visits to a state-of-the-art processing plant. Again, contact the Convention and Visitors Bureau.

The community's 30,000-square-foot **recreation center** is open for daily or weekly use. Call the office at (907) 581–1297, or stop by the recreation center at Broadway and Airport Beach Road.

Greg Hawthorne offers an option even farther afield. His **Volcano Bay Adventures** tour starts with a fifteen-minute floatplane ride around the end of Unalaska Island to a lake at the foot of Mt. Makushin. The camp there consists of five large wall tents, complete with kitchen-dining facilities, where a chef prepares hot meals daily. The main attraction, however, is stellar salmon fishing. Call (907) 581–3414 or visit www. ansi.net/~volcanobay.

Much of the land on Unalaska, Amaknak, and Sedanka Islands is privately owned by the **Ounalashka Corporation,** an Alaska Native corporation. It asks visitors who want to hike, ski, bike, or camp on this land to first obtain a permit from the corporate office. Permits may be requested by phone at (907) 581–1276 or from their office between 8:00 A.M. and 5:00 P.M., Monday through Friday. The office is located on Salmon Way.

The Pribilof Islands

I f you think the Aleutians are "far out," wait until you hear about **St. Paul** and **St. George** Islands in the lonesome middle of the Bering Sea. Located about 800 air miles west-southwest of Anchorage and more than 200 miles north of the Aleutian chain, the Pribilof Islands are home to fewer than 1,000 people, but—in the summer at least—the islands provide a hauling out place for an estimated one and a quarter million howling, barking, fighting, breeding, birthing fur seals. In addition, the islands' craggy sea cliffs provide a summer nesting sanctuary for more than two million seabirds (211 species), some of which you'll see nowhere else in this hemisphere. Add to this, domestic reindeer and fascinating Native Aleut cultures and history, and you have a superb, offbeat travel destination.

It's surprisingly easy to visit the Pribilofs. Many hundreds do each year. Reeve Aleutian Airways (800–544–2248; sales@reevecorp.com; www. reeveair.com) offers three- to eight-day tours that include round-trip airfare from Anchorage to *St. Paul,* accommodations at the warm and rustic *King Eider Hotel,* and daily excursions to beaches and cliffs. From behind protective blinds at various beaches, you'll view thousands of fur seals, including bellowing "beachmasters," their "harems," and pups. At numerous cliffs you can easily photograph super-abundant bird species. You'll also visit the ornate *Russian Orthodox Church,* and you'll meet members of the largest population of Aleuts anywhere. The three-day tour costs $938.52. The eight-day option goes for $1,693.77. Meals are extra and average $30 to $36 daily for breakfast, lunch, and dinner.

Dedicated offbeat travelers—especially birders—will want to extend their trips to *St. George,* about 40 air miles south of St. Paul. Travelers (or their travel agents) will have to make more of their own arrangements, but also the opportunity here is to view not only fur seals (250,000 come to the island each year) but the largest seabird colony in the Northern Hemisphere. On its precipitous cliffs, St. George hosts the largest colony of thick-billed murres in the North Pacific as well as 98 percent of the world's population of red-legged kittiwakes. It's also the the largest breeding colony for parakeet auklets . . . and the list goes on.

PenAir (800–448–4226; www.penair.com) operates between St. George and St. Paul (round-trip fare, $120) and also provides regular service between Anchorage, St. George, St. Paul, and back for $620. Tours that include accommodations and meals unfortunately aren't available. The single hotel on St. George is the ten-room *Tanaq Hotel,* which can accommodate a total of eighteen guests, and although the hotel offers no meal service, guests have free use of the kitchen and dining room facilities. A grocery store is located about a block away. The rate is $89 per person per night. Call (907) 859–2255.

Southwest Alaska Trivia

Unimak, the first island in the Aleutian Chain, is home to Shishaldin volcano. Shishaldin has erupted several times over the last two centuries, earning the local name of Smoking Moses and before that "Pogromni," Russian for desolation.

Lake Clark National Park

I t's probably one of the National Park System's least known and visited parks—but that's one of the things that make *Lake Clark National Park and Preserve* across Cook Inlet from the Kenai Peninsula special. Access is only by air (or water, on the shores of Cook Inlet), you certainly won't find Yellowstone- or Yosemite-type roads and trails within the park boundaries. This is some of the wildest and most breathtakingly beautiful country on earth, with saltwater shores, turquoise blue lakes, steaming volcanoes, and cascading waterfalls that drop from towering mountainsides. Three rivers in the park have been designated National Wild Rivers. You travel in this country by foot, by boat, or by air. Accommodations are tents; either you bring your own or book with an outdoor guiding service that provides everything from fly-in charters to shelter, food, and expertise.

Among the companies that offer this expertise is **Alaskan Sojourns, Wilderness Guides,** operated by Rod and Sara Arno since 1974. At times, say the Arnos, campers in the Lake Clark region can witness the migration of hundreds of caribou. A short hike can bring Dall sheep within camera range. Moose forage everywhere. Their Saturday-to-Saturday package tours cost $2,500, including bush flights within the park. For the traveler seeking an even more challenging camping experience,

Food cache at Lake Clark National Park and Preserve

Alaskan Sojourns offers a seven-day trip to *Aniakchak National Monument and Preserve* on the Alaska Peninsula west of Anchorage. The centerpiece of the monument is a massive active volcano caldera containing turquoise lake waters, cinder cones, lava plugs, and steaming hot springs. The caldera is, in fact, one of the largest in the world. This is a trip for strong, fit, and knowledgeable campers only, but for those who qualify it is truly one of earth's great outdoor destinations. The cost is $2,500, including bush flights from and to King Salmon. The Arnos also package fishing excursions, sea kayaking expeditions, and other hiking/camping options on the Kenai Peninsula, in Bristol Bay, Prince William Sound, and Katmai National Park. For brochures or information call (907) 376–2913, e-mail arno@alaska.net.

Eruk's Wilderness Float Tours takes small groups, including families, on floats from lakes in the park down the Chilikidrotna River. Along the way, says Eruk Williamson, "bears and wolves are particularly active and visible." Game trails and dry channels offer frequent opportunities to explore, notes Williamson, a wildlife biologist.

Eruk offers fishing, hunting, and wildlife-watching trips, but he'll admit—fly-fishing is his specialty. A superb choice is the Salmon River. An eight-day summer trip is $2,890; ten-day excursions run $3,400, which includes airfare from Anchorage to this remote Southwest river. Other fishing trips include the Nushagak River and Yukon Tributary. Wildlife-viewing takes place via raft in both Lake Clark and Wood-Tikchik State Park. These trips offer opportunities to see caribou by the thousands, moose, grizzlies, wolves, wolverine, bald eagles, and foxes. An eleven-day Lake Clark adventure is $3,490. The Wood-Tikchik trip starts at $2,690. Another interesting trip, offered in Aniakchak National Monument, is $3,790. Phone (888) 212–2203, e-mail erukwild@alaska.net, or visit www.alaska.net/~erukwild.

> ## Southwest Alaska Trivia
>
> *Bethel is one of the westernmost communities in Alaska. It began as a mission in 1889 when Moravian missionaries came to "tame" the people. In keeping with its Godly ambitions, the community became known as "Bethel," which comes from the biblical passage Genesis 35:1, "Arise, go up to Bethel, and dwell there."*

Bethel

The city of *Bethel* and the surrounding Yukon–Kuskokwim delta country really doesn't come readily to mind when one compiles a list of Alaska's better known visitor destinations. Located 400 air miles from Anchorage on the banks of the mighty Kuskokwim River, this city of 5,000 mostly Yu'pik Eskimo residents is primarily a commercial fishing, trading, and government center. None of the Goliaths of the travel industry have offices here. Fact is, there aren't many Davids either.

But of course that's what attracts a good number of us. That and the community's location about 90 miles inland from the Bering Sea and the mouth of the Kuskokwim River. Bethel sits in the midst of the United States' largest game refuge, the twenty-million-acre **Yukon Delta National Wildlife Range.**

The range, incidentally, is another of those places where you really ought not to venture on your·own—not, at least, without knowledgeable local advice. Fortunately, such information is readily available. **Kuskokwim Wilderness Adventures** (owned by longtime Alaskans John McDonald, Beverly Hoffman, Mike Hoffman, and Jill Hoffman) rents a variety of outdoor equipment, including rafts, life jackets, tents, cooking gear, and Coleman stoves. If you'd rather not venture out on your own, they can arrange custom tours.

Whether you take a package tour or not, don't fail to include the city's **Yugtarvik Regional Museum** in your itinerary. (*Yugtarvik,* in Yu'pik, means "place for peoples' things.") Located in the city's new cultural center, the museum is chock-full of Eskimo art, artifacts, tools, and household items from the past and present. There's a full-size kayak, complete with a realistic paddler in it, paddle, grass mat, ice pick, and other accessories. You also will find a mounted musk ox head and cape on the wall, mounted birds of the region, dolls, grass baskets, ivory work, and beaded items. Many of the craft items are for sale. Call (907) 543–1819.

There are several hotel and B&B accommodations in Bethel, among them **Pacifica Guest House,** operated by Diane Carpenter. Accommodations include a hot tub, van service, and even such electronic niceties as computer and fax capability. All-you-can-eat breakfasts feature home-baked breads and pastries. Summer room rates start at $90 for a single and $100 for doubles. Diane has added another building to her guest house, this one featuring suites with private baths starting at $135. For those staying long term, Diane offers a bunkhouse with kitchenette. Prices vary depending on length of stay. Phone (907) 543–4305.

Speaking of Diane, there are three places worth mentioning for excellent meals, and Diane's is one of them. She's open for dining every day except Sunday. Also try **Sadik's** (907–543–4200), a newly opened Eastern European restaurant with wonderful dinners, and **Dimitri's** (907–543–3434), which features Greek specialties—be sure to try the gyro.

**PLACES TO STAY IN
SOUTHWESTERN ALASKA**

BETHEL
Pacifica Guest House,
1220 State Highway;
(907) 543–4305.

**KATMAI NATIONAL PARK
AND PRESERVE**
Brooks Campground, near
Brooks Lodge;
(800) 365–2267.

Katmai Wilderness Lodge,
eastern coast of Katmai
National Park;
(800) 488–8767,
www.ptialaska.net/~
katbears.

KODIAK
Best Western Kodiak Inn,
236 Rezanof Drive;
(888) 563–4254.

Buskin River Inn,
1395 Airport Way;
(907) 487–2700.

Saltery Lake Lodge,
1516 Larch Street;
(800) 770–5037.

Shahafka Cove Bed
& Breakfast,
(907) 486–2409,
www.ptialaska.net/~
rwoitel. Walking distance
from downtown.

Raspberry Island Remote
Camps;
(907) 486–1781,
www.ptialaska.net/~rirc.
On Raspberry Island out-
side Kodiak.

R&R Lodge;
(907) 486–3704,
www.ptialaska.net/~rlreed.
On Kodiak Island.

UNALASKA
Carl's Bayview Inn,
1 Bayroad Road;
(800) 581–1230.

Grand Aleutian Hotel,
498 Salmon Way;
(800) 891–1194,
www.ansi.net~grand_
aleutian. Upscale
accommodation.

UniSea Inn,
498 Salmon Way;
(907) 581–1325.

**PLACES TO EAT IN
SOUTHWESTERN ALASKA**

BETHEL
Dimitri's, 281 Fourth
Avenue; (907) 543–3434.
Great Greek food, including
superb gyros.

Sadik's,
320 Tundra Street;
(907) 543–4200.
Eastern European food.

KODIAK
Buskin River Inn,
1395 Airport Way;
(907) 487–2700.
Excellent steak and
seafood.

El Chicano, 103 Center
Avenue; (907) 486–6116.
Tasty Mexican food.

Harborside Coffee
and Goods,
216 Shelikof Avenue;
(907) 486–5862.
Friendly, comfortable
coffeehouse.

UNALASKA
Chart Room at the Grand
Aleutian Hotel,
498 Salmon Way;
(800) 891–1194. Freshly
caught, local seafood.

Index

Entries for Museums and State and National Parks appear only in the special indexes on pages 213 and 214.

A

Admiralty Island Kayaking, 29
Adventuress, 32
Adventures Afloat, 32
Adventure Sports, 30
Air Excursions, 52
AirOne, 6
Alaska Airlines' Vacations, 163–64
Alaska Biking Adventures, 142
Alaska Brewing Company, 27
Alaska Cab Garage, 169
Alaska Chilikat Bald Eagle
    Preserve, 37, 38, 60
Alaska Cruises, 4
Alaska-Denali Guiding, Inc., 148
Alaska Discovery, 29, 38, 51, 172
Alaska Discovery Inn, 50
Alaska Fly 'n' Fish Charters, 29
Alaska Highway, 35, 36, 60, 61, 76
    120, 128, 151
Alaska Highway Interpretive Centre, 61
Alaska Indian Arts, 37
Alaska Marine Highway
    ferry LeConte, 33
Alaska Native Arts and Crafts
    Association, 84
Alaska Native Medical Center, 84
Alaska Ocean View Bed
    and Breakfast, 24
Alaska Outback Tours, 188
Alaska Peak and Seas, 15
Alaska Public Lands
    Information Centers
    Anchorage, 82
    Fairbanks, 132
    Tok, 141
Alaska Railroad, 101

Alaska Railroad Depot, 82
Alaska Railroad "piggyback train," 98
Alaska Rainforest Tours, 33
Alaska Raptor Rehabilitation
    Center, 23
Alaska Rivers Company, 105
Alaska SeaLife Center, 104
Alaska Seaplane Service, 35
Alaska Sight-seeing Cruise West, 3, 89
Alaska State Fair, 119
Alaska State Parks cabins, 29
Alaska Tolovana Adventures, 149
Alaska Travel Adventures, 6, 21, 30
Alaska Vistas, 12
Alaska Wild Berry Products, 110
Alaska Wildland Adventures, 105
Alaska Yukon Tours, 174
Alaskaland, 135
Alaskan Bicycle Adventures, 88
Alaskan Frontier Gardens Bed
    & Breakfast, 86
Alaskan Hotel and Bar, 27
Alaskan Sojourns, Wilderness
    Guides, 196
Alaska's Inside Passage, 3
Alaska's Mainstreet Visitor Center, 141
Alatna River Canoeing, 172
Alfred Starr Nenana Cultural
    Center, 149
All-Alaska Adventure, 3
Allen Marine Tours, 103
Alsek and Tatshenshini Rivers, 38
Alyeska Bed and Breakfast, 96
Alyeska Home Hostel, 97
Alyeska Pipeline Service Company
    information center, 155
Alyeska Resort, 96

Alyeska View Bed and Breakfast, 96
American Bald Eagle Foundation, 37
Anadyr Adventures, 93
Anan Creek Bear Observatory, 6, 14, 15
Anaktuvuk Pass, 137
Anchor Point State Recreation Site, 110
Anchor River Beach Road, 110
Anchorage, 81–89
Anchorage Fur Rendezvous, 83
Anchorage International Hostel, 87
(Anchorage) log cabin visitor
    information center, 82
Angoon, 33, 35
Aniakchak National Monument and
    Preserve, 197
Annabelle's Famous Keg and
    Chowder House, 7
Anton Larsen Bay Road, 187
Anvil Mountain, 169
Arctic Brotherhood Hall, 45
Arctic Caribou Inn, 179
Arctic Chalet, 74
Arctic Circle, 73, 177
Arctic Circle Adventures, 165
Arctic Circle Bed & Breakfast, 177
Arctic Circle Hot Springs, 155
Arctic Circle Trading Post, 157
Arctic Divide, 172
Arctic Getaway Bed & Breakfast, 177
Arctic Nature Tours, 74
Arctic Ocean, 179
Arctic Pizza, 164
Arctic Roadrunner, 85
Arctic Tour Co., 164
Arctic Treks, 174
Arctic Village, 175
Arctic Village Tours, 175
Armadillo Cafe, 27
A Sheltered Harbor Bed
    & Breakfast, 42
Athabasca Cultural Journeys, 138
Atlin, 58

Atlin Road, 58
Auke Bay Kayaking, 30
Aurora, 9

B

Bake Shop, 96
Baker Aviation, 166
Bald Eagle Preserve Raft Trips, 38
Baranof Island, 19
Barrow, 163
Barrow Airport Inn, 164
Bartlett, 90
Bayshore Lodge and Oasis
    Restaurant, 77
Beachcomber Inn, 19
Bear Creek, 70
Bear Creek Camp and
    International Hostel, 42
Beaver Creek, 77
Beaver Creek Canada Customs and
    Immigration, 77
Bed and Maybe Breakfast, 149
Begich-Boggs Visitor Center, 98
Beluga Lookout, 107
Beluga Point, 95
Bering Air, 171
Bering Sea Ice Golf Classic, 167
Bethel, 197–98
Bettles, 172
Betty's Igloo Bed and Breakfast, 171
Beyer Lake Campground, 116
Bidarka Boats, 22
Big Bear Adventures, 70
Big Delta State Historical Park, 152
Big Game Alaska, 98
Big Lake, 114
Big Lake Houseboat Rental, 114
Birch Trails Bed and Breakfast, 87
Birch Trails Sled Dog Tours, 87
Bird Creek State Campground, 95
Blackbird Bistro, 71
Blind Slough recreation area, 18

INDEX

Blueberry Hill Bed & Breakfast, 8
Blueberry Lake State Recreation
    Site, 123
Bodenburg Butte, 119
Bonanza Creek Motel and RV Park, 71
Bove Island, 58
Breakaway Adventures, 14
Brooks Campground, 191
Bunkhouse, 124
Bunk 'n' Breakfast, 120
Burgess Bauder's Lighthouse, 24
Burnt Paw, 141
Burwash Landing, 77

C

Caines Head State Recreation Area, 101
Canada Customs, 58
Canada Customs and Immigration, 58
Canada-U.S. border, 77
Canadian Yukon Riverboat
    Family Tour, 66
Cantwell, 116, 158
Cantwell Lodge, 159
Cape Fox Tours, 4
Cape Smythe Air, 170
Captain Benjamin Moore's cabin, 44
Captain Cook State Recreation
    Area, 106, 108
Carcross, 57, 58
(Carcross) visitor reception centre, 58
Carcross Desert, 60
Carl's Bayview Inn, 193
Carmacks, 66
Carriage House, 150
Cassiar Highway, 9
Castle Hill, 19, 22
Catholic Church, 73
Chair 5 Restaurant, 96
Chapel on the Hill, 126
Chart Room, 193
Chatanika, 155
Chauffer de Anvil City, 169

Chena Hot Springs Road, 154
Chena Lakes Recreation Area, 153
Chena River Recreation Area, 154
Chichagof Island, 22, 35
Chicken, 75
Chicken Creek Cafe, 76
Chicken Discount Gas and Propane, 76
Chicken Mercantile Emporium, 76
Chicken Saloon, 76
Chief Shakes Hot Springs, 15
Chief Shakes Island, 11
Childs Glacier, 91
Chilkat Center for the Arts, 37
Chilkat Eagle Bed and Breakfast, 42
Chilkat Guides, Ltd., 38
Chilkat Indian Dancers, 37
Chilkat Pass, 40, 60
Chilkat Restaurant and Bakery, 40
Chilkat Valley Inn, 42
Chilkoot Charlie's, 86
Chilkoot Lake Tours, 40
Chilkoot Sled Dog Adventures, 43
Chilkoot Trail, 45
Chiniak Highway, 187
Chitina, 123
Chuk Campground, 74
(Chugach) Forest Service
    Information Center, 5
Chugach State Park Visitor Center, 117
Circle, 156
Circle Hot Springs Road, 156
City and Borough of Juneau, 27
City of Whitehorse, 63
Clam Gulch State Recreation Area, 108
Classic Tours, 7
Cleft of the Rock Bed and
    Breakfast, 142
Coastal Helicopters Inc., 31
Coldfoot, 177
Coldfoot Services and Arctic
    Acres Inn, 177
Cooper Landing, 105

Copper Center, 126
Copper Center Lodge, 126
Copper Oar, 126
Cordova, 91
Cottonwood RV Park and
    Campground, 77
Council, 169
Country Charm Bed and
    Breakfast, 67
Craig, 8
Cranes' Crest Bed and Breakfast, 112
Creamer's Field Migratory Waterfowl
    Refuge, 133
Creek Street, 7
Crooked Creek & Whiskey Island
    Railroad, 135
Crystal Lake Fish Hatchery, 18
Crow Creek Mine, 96, 90

D

Dall mountain sheep, 95
Dalton City, 37
Dalton Highway, 121, 175
Dalton Trail Lodge, 76
Dawson City, 68, 69, 70
Dawson City Bed and Breakfast, 70
Dawson City walking tour, 69
Dawson Creek, British Columbia, 61
Dawson Visitor Reception Center, 69
Deadhorse, 178
Deal's Den, 108
Deer Mountain Trail, 4
Deishu Expeditions, 43
Delta Bison Range, 152
Delta Junction, 55, 121, 143, 151
Delta Junction Information
    Center, 152
Delta State Campground, 152
Dempster Highway, 72
Denali Highway, 121, 151, 157
Denali Hostel, 148
Denali (Mt. McKinley), 129

Denali National Park Wilderness
    Center-Camp Denali, 145
Denali Parks Resorts, 143
Denali Princess, 143
Denali Raft Adventures, 147
Denali Sourdough Cabins, 143
Denali Wilderness Lodge, 145
Dezadeash Lake, 61
Diamond Tooth Gertie's, 69
Dimitri's, 199
Dinner Ferry, 111
Discovery Campground, 108
Discovery Claim, 70
Discovery Voyage, 92
Dog Sled Saloon, 137
Dolly's House, 7
Double Musky, 96
Douglas Cafe, 27
Downtown Bicycle Rentals, 88
Duncan Creek Golddusters, 67
Dutch Harbor, 191–94
Dyea, 45
Dyea campground, 47

E

Eagle, 75
Eagle Island, 6
Eagle Plains Hotel and Restaurant, 72
Eagle River, 117
Eagle River Nature Center, 117
Eagle Summit, 155
Eaglecrest Ski Area, 31
Eagle's Nest Car Rental, 40
Eagle's Nest Motel, 40
Eagle's Roost Bed and Breakfast, 7
Eagle's Roost Park, 17
Earth Bed & Breakfast, 86
Earth Song Lodge, 148
Earth Tours, 87
East Turner Lake, 28
Edgerton Highway, 123
Eielson Visitor Center, 145

INDEX

Eklutna Historical Park, 118
El Capitan Cave, 6
El Capitan Lodge, 6
El Dorado Gold Camp, 136
El Dorado Gold Mine, 156
El Sombrero Cafe, 27
Elderberry Park, 82
Elliott Highway, 121, 156
Elsa, 67
Emerald Lake, 60
End of the Road Bed
    and Breakfast, 150
Engine Number 1, 82
Era Aviation, 83
ERA Helicopters, 31
Eruk's Wilderness Float Tours, 197
Eskimo blanket toss, 165
Ester Gold Camp, 149
Evergreen Lodge, 120
Exit Glacier, 102
Experience Yukon Inc., 67

F

Fairbanks, 131, 149
Fairbanks Convention and Visitor
    Bureau Information Center, 131
Fairbanks Exploration Inn, 139
Fairbanks Flight Train, 138
Fairbanks Golf and Country Club, 135
Fairview Inn, 115
Fairweather Adventures, 51
Falls Creek Fish Ladder, 18
Far North Tours, 89
Fat Freddie's, 172
Father Duncan's Cottage, 6
Favorite Bay Inn, 35
Fiddlehead Restaurant and
    Bakery, 27
58 Degrees North, 189–90
Fireweed Lodge, 9
Fishhook Road, 119
Five Mile Lake Campground, 67

Forget-Me-Not Lodget-Aurora
    Express, 139
Fort Davis Roadhouse, 172
Fort Kenay, 107
Fort McPherson, 73
Fort McPherson Tent and Canvas, 73
Fort Richardson Alaska Fish and
    Wildlife Center, 84
Fort Seward Bed and Breakfast, 41
Fort Seward Condos, 40
Fort Seward Lodge, Restaurant, and
    Saloon, 40
Fort William Henry Seward, 37
Fort Yukon, 174
Fort Yukon, replica of the original, 174
40-Mile Air, 142
40-Mile Dog Tours, 69
Fossil Beach, 187
Frontier Flying Service, 137
Frontier Heritage Park, 59

G

Gakona Fish Camp Bed
    & Breakfast, 151
Gakona Junction, 135, 136
Gakona Lodge & Trading Post, 150
Gambell, 170
Gastineau Guiding, 26
Gates of the Arctic Winter
    Dogsledding, 172
Geophysical Institute, 134
George Parks Highway, 113
Gilmore Hotel, 7
Girdwood, 96
Glacier Bay Adventures, 51
Glacier Bay Country Inn, 49
Glacier Bay Lodge, 48
Glacier Bay Sea Kayaks, 50
Glacier Bay Tours
    and Cruises, 3, 31
Glacier Park Resort, 120
Glenn Highway, 117

Glenn Highway-Tok Cutoff, 131, 149
Glennallen, 121, 126, 150
G. O. Shuttle Service, 140
Gold Creek Salmon Bake, 30
Gold Dredge #8, 136
Gold Dredge #4, 70
gold dredges, 168
Gold Panning and Gold History
    Tour, 30
Gold Rush Cemetery, 45
Gold Rush Town, 135
Golden Circle Tour, 40
Golden North Hotel, 46
Golovin, 70
Go Wild Tours, 66
Grand Aleutian Hotel, 193
Grand Pacific Charters, 50
Grand View Inn, 10
Gray Line of Alaska, 176
Great Alaska Cedar Works Bed and
    Breakfast, 7
Great Kobuk Sand Dunes, 165
GreatLand Guides of Alaska, 31
Grizzly Lake Ranch, 150
Growler Island, 93
GuggieVille, 68
Gulkana Fish Guides, 151
Gull Island, 111
Gustavus, 49
Gustavus Inn, 49
Gwennie's Old Alaska Restaurant, 86

H

Haines, 35
Haines Highway, 36, 38
Haines Junction, 61, 73
(Haines) visitor center, 36
Halibut Cove, 111
Happy Trails, 59
Harbor House Lodge, 14
Harborside Coffee and Goods, 183
Harding Lake, 153

Hatcher Pass Lodge, 119
Hawkins House Bed and Breakfast, 66
Herschel Island, 74
Hidden Lake, 105
Hike and Bike Alaska, 88
Historical House Bed & Breakfast, 66
Holy Ascension Russian Orthodox
    Cathedral, 193
Holy Assumption of the Virgin Mary
    Russian Orthodox Church, 107
Holy Resurrection Russian Orthodox
    Church, 184
Homer, 110
Homer Ocean Charters, 111
Homer Spit, 111
Hoonah, 33, 34
Hope, 99
Hope Highway, 99
Hosteling International-Sitka, 24
Hot Bite, 27
Hotel Halsingland, 40
Hubbard's Bed and Breakfast, 34
Huck Hobbit's Homestead
    Campground and Retreat, 150
Hudson Air Service, 116
humpback whales, 16
Hungry Beaver, 13
hunting trips, 15
Husky Homestead at
    Goose Lake Kennel, 146
Hyder, 9
Hyder Community Association, 10

I

Iditarod Sled Dog Classic, 166
Iditarod Trail Committee
    Headquarters and
    Visitor Center, 113
Iditarod Trail Sled Dog Race, 88
Independence Mine, 113
Independence Mine State Historical
    Park, 119

INDEX

Independent Rental, Inc., 136
Ingamo Hall, 74
Inn at the Waterfront, 28
Inn on the Lake Bed & Breakfast, 66
Institute Creek Trail, 12
International Backpackers
    Inn/Hostel, 87
Inuvik, 72, 73

J

Jack London's cabin, 69
Jack Wade Junction, 75
jade factory, 165
Jake's Corner, 59, 62
Joseph Van Os Photo Safari, 191
Juneau, 25
Juneau Convention and
    Visitors Bureau, 29
(Juneau) Forest Service Information
    Center, 5
Juneau International Hostel, 33
Juneau Raptor Center, 30
Juneau Sea Kayaking, 29

K

Kachemak Bay Ferry Danny J., 111
Kachemak Bay Natural
    History Tour, 112
Kaleidoscope Cruises, 16
Kalifornsky Beach Road, 106, 108
Kantishna Roadhouse, 145
Kathleen, 75
Katmai Wilderness Lodge, 191
Kenai, 100, 107
Kenai Bicentennial Visitors and
    Cultural Center, 107
Kenai Fjords Kayaks, 104
Kenai National Wildlife Refuge, 105
Kenai National Wildlife Refuge
    Visitor Center, 106
Kenai Peninsula, 94
Kenai Princess Lodge, 104

Kenai Princess RV Park, 104
Kenai Spur Highway, 106, 107
Kennecott, 123, 124
Kennicott Glacier Lodge, 124
Kenny Lake Mercantile and
    RV Park, 123
Keno City, 67
Ketchikan, 2
(Ketchikan) Visitor Information
    Center, 4
Keystone Raft and Kayak
    Adventures, 93
Kiana, 166
Kincaid Park, 84
King Eider Hotel, 195
King Eider Inn, 164
Klawock, 8
Klondike Express, 91
Klondike Highway, 47, 58, 64
Klondike Rib and Salmon BBQ, 64
Klondike Summit to Sea Cruise, 47
Klondike Trail of '98 Road Relay, 47
Kluane Bed and Breakfast, 77
Kluane Helicopters, 76
(Kluane National Park) visitor
    reception centre, 76
Knight Riders Horse and
    Buggy Rides, 150
Knik Glacier, 114, 119
Knik Glacier Adventures, 114
Knik Kennels, 113
Knik Road, 113
Knudson Cove, 6
Kobuk River, 172
Kobuk River Jets, 166
Kodiak, 181, 183
Kodiak Alutiiq Dancers, 185
Kodiak Cattle Company, 189
Kodiak Island Convention
    and Visitors Bureau, 183
Kodiak Sports and Tour, 188
Kongakut River, 173

Kongakut River Rafting, 173
Kotzebue, 164
Kougarok Road, 169
Koyukuk National Wildlife
    Refuge, 138
Kruzof Island, 21
K2 Aviation, 116
Kuskokwim Wilderness
    Adventures, 198

L

Lake Hood, 83
Lake Louise, 120
Large Animal Research Station, 133
Larry's Flying Service, 137
Laughing Raven Lodge, 25
LeConte, 35
LeConte Bay, 16
LeConte Glacier, 14, 16
LeConte Outfitters, 18
Liberty Falls State Recreation
    Site, 123
Lifetime Adventures, 118
Little Norway Festival, 16
Litzen Guide Service, 107
Livengood, 157
Log Cabin RV Park and Resort, 9
Long Rifle Lodge, 120
Lower Dewey Trail, 45
Lucky Husky, 115
Lucky Wishbone, 85

M

Ma Johnson Hotel, 124
Mahay's Riverboat Service, 115
Major Marine Tours, 91, 103
Malemute Saloon, 137
Manley Hot Springs, 156
Manely Roadhouse, 156
Mary's McKinley View Lodge, 116
Mary Carey's Fiddlehead Farm, 115
Marx Brothers, 85

Mascot Saloon, 44
Matanuska Glacier, 120
Matanuska Glacier State
    Recreation Site, 120
Mat-Su Visitors Center, 113
Mayo, 67
McCarthy, 123, 124
McCarthy Air, 124
McCarthy Lodge restaurant
    and saloon, 124
McCarthy Road, 123, 124
McFarland's Floatel, 9
McKinley Climber Tour, 116
Mendenhall Glacier, 25, 26
Mendenhall Glacier Float Trips, 30
Metlakatla, 6
Midnight Dome, 68
Milepost 0 Momument, 61
Miles Glacier, 91
Million Dollar Bridge, 91
Million Dollar Falls
    Campground, 61
Minto, 157
Minto Landing Campground, 67
Misty Fjords National
    Monument, 4, 6
Mitkof Highway, 18
Mitkof Island, 15, 17
Moose Pass, 100
Moose's Tooth Pub & Pizzeria, 85
Mt. Dewey, 12
Mt. Edgecumbe National
    Recreation Trail, 21
Mt. Juneau Trail, 26
Mt. Marathon, 101
Mt. Roberts Trail, 26
Mountain Trip, Inc., 148
Mukluk Annie's Salmon Bake, 62
Mukluk Land, 142
M.V. *Tarahne,* 59
M.V. *Ten Bears,* 189
Mythos Expeditions Kodiak, 188

N

Naabia Niign Athabascan
  Indian Crafts, 140
Nabesna Road, 150
NANA, 180
National Park Service, 124
National Park Service Glacier Bay
  Visitor Center, 48
National Park Service Ranger
  Station, 150
National Park Service Visitor Center,
  Seward, 102
Native Village, 135
Natural History Tour, 146
Near Island, 186
Nenana, 135, 148
1901 Post Office, 69
1901 Territorial Administration
  Building, 69
Ninilchik, 109
Ninilchik State Recreation
  Area, 108
Ninilchik Village, 108
Noatak River, 173
Noland House, 59
Nome, 166
Nome Convention and Visitor Bureau's
  Visitor Information Center, 167
Nome Discovery Tours, 170
Nome Nugget Inn, 171
Nome Tour & Marketing, 170
Nome-Council Road, 169
Nome-Teller Road, 169
Nordic House Bed and
  Breakfast, 18
Northern Alaska Tour
  Company, 164, 176
Northern Network of Bed
  & Breakfasts, 71
North Pole, 153
North Slope Borough, 163
North Slope General Auto, 164

North Star Golf Club, 135
Northwest Territories Information
  Centre, 69
North Woods Lodge, 138
Nullagvik Hotel, 165

O

Ocean View Manor, 171
Old Chena Indian Village, 132
Old F.E. Gold Camp, 155
Old Glenn Highway, 118
Old Log Church, 65
Old Mission School, 174
Old Richardson Highway, 126
Old Sourdough Lodge, 13
Olivia's at the Skagway Inn, 46
Olson Air Service, 170
Oomingmak Musk Ox
  Producers' Coop, 82
Oscar Anderson House, 82
Otter Cove Bed & Breakfast, 35
Ounalashka Corporation, 194
Our Collections, 12
Out of Bounds Adventures, 31
Owls of the North, 173

P

Pacific Wing, 17
Pacifica Guest House, 198
Pack Creek, 29
Packhouse Restaurant, 153
Palace Grand Theatre, 69
Palace Theatre and Saloon, 135, 137
Palmer, 119
Palmer musk ox farm, 119
Park Service visitor center, 145
Pasagshak Bay 187
Patching Lake Cabins, 5
Paxson, 151, 144
Paxson Inn & Lodge, 151
Peace of Selby, 173
Pearson's Pond Luxury Inn, 33

Peggy's Alaskan Cabbage Patch
  Bed and Breakfast, 152
Pelican, 35
PenAir, 195
Pepe's North of the Border, 164
Perseverance Trail, 26
Petersburg, 15
(Petersburg) Visitor Information
  Center, 16
petroglyphs, 11
Petroglyph Beach, 11
Pikes Landing, 140
Pilgrim Hot Springs, 169
Pilgrim Hot Springs hot tub, 170
Pioneer Cemetery, 156
Pipeline Mile Zero, 179
Porcupine Mine, 39
Porcupine River Lodge, 175
Port Alexander, 24
Portage Glacier, 98
Portage Glacier Road, 98
Potter Marsh, 95
Pribilof Islands, 194–95
Prince of Wales Island, 8
Princess Tours, 176
Provideniya, Russia, 171
Prudhoe Bay, 179
Prudhoe Bay Fleet Shop, 180
Prudhoe Bay Hotel, 179
Ptarmigan, 98
public harbors, 15
Puffin's Bed and Breakfast, 50

R

R&R Lodge, 190
Rainbow Falls Trail, 11
Rainbow Tours, 112
Rainwalker Expeditions, 12
Raspberry Island Remote
  Camps, 190
Raven's Roost, 18
Ray's Waterfront, 102

recreation center, 194
Red Dog, 27
Reeve Aleutian Airways, 195
Reluctant Fisherman Inn, 92
Resurrect Art Coffee House
  Gallery, 102
Resurrection Bay, 103
Resurrection Pass Trail, 100
Resurrection Roadhouse, 102
Revillagigedo Island, 2
Richardson Highway, 121, 143, 151
Rika's Roadhouse, 152
Rita's Campground and
  RV Park, 142
River Adventures, 38
Robert Service's Cabin, 69, 70
Rock Glacier Trail, 61
Rocky Point Resort, 18
Ronney's Roost Bed and Breakfast, 13
Rosie's, 35
Russian Bishop's House, 22
Russian blockhouse, 22
Russian Orthodox Church, 195

S

Sadik's, 199
St. Elias Alpine Guides, 125
St. Elias Lake Trail, 61
St. George Island, 194
St. Herman's Harbor, 186
St. Lawrence Island, 170
St. Mark's Episcopal Church, 149
St. Michael, 171
St. Michael's Russian Orthodox
  Cathedral, 22
St. Nicholas Chapel, 107
St. Paul Island, 194
St. Stephen's Territorial Episcopal
  Church, 174
Salmon Glacier, 9–10
Saltery Lake Lodge, 188
Salty Dawg Saloon, 111

INDEX

Santa Claus House, 153
Saturday Market, 84
Savoonga, 170
Sawyer Glaciers, 31
Saxman Native Village, 3
Sea Otter Kayak Glacier Bay, 50
Seaside Farm Hostel, 112
Seawolf Wilderness Adventures, 51
See Alaska, 17
Selawik Wildlife Range, 165
Seldovia, 112
Sepal Hollow Bed and Breakfast, 33
Serpentine Hot Springs, 170
Seven Glaciers Restaurant, 96
Seward, 101
Seward Highway, 94
Seward Trolley, 101
Seward Windsong Lodge, 102
Shahafka Cove Bed
    and Breakfast, 190
Shaktoolik, 171
Sheep Mountain Lodge, 120
Sheep Mountain Visitor Centre, 77
Sheldon Jackson College, 19
Sheldon, Steve, 36
Shuregood Adventures, 193
Sign Post Forest, 62
Silverbow Inn, 28
Silver Trail, 67
Sitka, 19
Sitka National Historical
    Park, 20, 21, 22
Sitka's native village, 22
Sitka Sea Kayaking Adventure, 21–22
Sitka Secrets, 23
Sitka Sportfishing, 23
Sitka Tribe of Alaska, 21
Sitka Tribe of Alaska's Tribal Tours
    Historical and Cultural
    Sight-seeing Tours, 22
Sitka Wildlife Quest, 23
Skagway, 43

Skagway Brewing Co., 46
Skagway Hostel, 46
Skagway Inn Bed and Breakfast, 46
Skagway's City Hall, 46
Skagway's Convention and
    Visitors Bureau, 48
Skilak Lake, 105
Skilak Lake Loop Road, 105
Skyline Trail and A.B. Mountain, 45
Sky Trekking Alaska, 171
Smuggler's Cove, 6
Snyder Mercantile Company, 34
S.O.B., 28
Sockeye Cycle, 39, 47
Soldotna, 100, 105, 106
Solomon, 169
Sons of Norway Hall, 16
Sound Adventure Charters, 91
Sourdough Cabins, 143
Sourdough Outfitters, 172
Sourdough pancake breakfast with
    Alaska reindeer sausage, 142
Southeast Alaska State Fair, 37
Southeast Diving and Sports, 24
Southeast Exposure, 4
Southwestern Alaska, 181–99
Spenard Hostel International, 87
Spirit of Adventure, 48
Spirit of Alaska Wilderness
    Adventures, 189
Spirit Walker Expeditions, 51
S.S. Klondike, 64
S.S. Nenana, 135
Stampede Rent-a-Car, 169
Stan Stepehens Cruises, 90, 93
Starrigavan Bay, 20
Starrigavan Estuary Trail, 20
Steamer Keno, 70
Steese Highway, 120, 153
Sterling Highway, 104
stern-wheeler Discovery III cruise, 132
Stewart, 9

Stewart Crossing, 67
Stikeen Wilderness Adventures, 14
Stikine Inn, 13
Strawberry Island, 43
Summit, 28
Summit Lake Lodge, 100
Sunlight North Expeditions, 173
Sunny Cove Sea Kayaking Co., 106
Sunrise Aviation, 15
Swan Lake Canoe Trail, 106
Swanson River Canoe Trail, 106
Syd Wright's *Chan IV,* 18

T

Tack's General Store and
    Greenhouse Cafe, 154
Tagish, 58
Takhini Hot Springs, 65
Talkeetna, 115
Talkeetna Roadhouse, 115
Tanana Valley Fairgrounds, 133
Tanana Valley Farmer's Market, 133
Tanaq Hotel, 195
Tangle Lakes Lodge, 158
Taquan Air, 6
Taylor Highway, 75, 141
Tea Social with the Judge, 26
Teller, 169
Temsco Helicopters, 31
Tenakee Hot Springs Lodge, 34
Tenakee Springs, 33, 34
"Tent Lady" Donna Blasor-
    Bernhardt, 141
Tern Lake Junction, 100
Tern Lake, 104
Tesoro Gas Station, 179
Tetlin Junction, 75, 76, 140
Thai Siam, 117
The Buzz, 112
The End Game Enterprise, 154
The Farm Bed and Breakfast, 100
The New Other Guys Taxi & Tours, 39

The Perch, 148
The Pumphouse Restaurant, 140
The Resort at Chena Hot Springs, 154
The Ultimate Expedition, 31
The White House Bed &
    Breakfast, 46
Thompson Pass, 123
Thorne Bay, 8
Three Sons Charters, 189
Tides Inn, 18
Tok, 141, 135
Tok Cutoff, 121
Tok Cutoff-Glenn Highway, 149
Tok Gateway Salmon Bake, 142
Tokeen, 8
Tolovana Lodge, 149
Tolsona Wilderness
    Campground, 121
Tongass Heritage Center, 3
Tongass Kayak, 17
Tongass Traveler, 17
Tony Knowles Coastal Trail, 82
Top of the World Highway, 74, 141
Top of the World Hotel, 163
Tormented Valley, 58
Totem Village Tribal House, 37
Tour Arctic, 165
(Tourism Yukon) visitor
    reception center, 77
Tracy Arm Fjord, 31
Trail Inn and Pack Train Saloon, 44
Trail Lake Lodge, 100
Trans-Alaska Pipeline, 92, 155
Trans-Alaska Pipeline pumping
    station, 152
Trans-Arctic Circle
    Treks, Ltd., 136, 176
True North Kayak Adventures, 111
Trumpeter Swan Observatory, 18
Tundra Tours, 163
Tundra Wildlife Tour, 146
Turnagain Tidal Bore, 95

INDEX

Tustumena, 103, 192
Two Rivers Lodge, 140

U

UIC Auto Rental, 164
Unalaska, 191–94
UniSea Inn, 193
U.S.–Canada border, 58, 60
U.S. Customs, 58, 60
U.S. Customs and Immigration
    Station, 140
U.S. Forest Service
    cabins, 5, 8, 14, 20, 28
U.S. Fish and Wildlife Service, 140
U.S. Fish and Wildlife Service
    information station, 105
U.S. Fish and Wildlife Service Visitor
    Center, Kodiak, 188

V

Valdez, 92
(Valdez) visitor information
    center, 93
Valley of 10,000 Smokes, 190
Van Gilder Hotel, 104
Veco Light Vehicle Shop, 180
Venetie, 175
Venus mine, 58
Viking Room, 19
Viking sailing vessel, 16
Viking Travel, 16
Villa Nova Restaurant, 85
visitor center, Coldfoot, 177
visitor center, Glennallen, 150
visitor center, Nenana, 149
Volcano Bay Adventures, 194
Voyager Hotel, 86

W

Walking tours, Sitka, 22
Wasilla, 113
Waterfall Resort, 8

Water Taxi and Scenic Cruise, 43
Watson Lake, 61
Weeping Trout Sports Resort, 42
West Glacier Trail, 26
Westmark Hotel, 142
West Turner Lake, 28
Whalers Cove Sportfishing Lodge, 35
Whalesong Lodge, 49
Whales Resort, 9
White Mountain, 171
White Pass & Yukon Route, 44
White Pass & Yukon Route caboose, 47
White Pass &Yukon Route Depot, 44
Whitehorse, 62
Whitehorse Chamber of Commerce
    Information Centre, 63
Whitehorse Buildings Walking
    Tours, 65
White Nights Arctic Ocean Tours, 179
White Ram Manor Bed
    and Breakfast, 71
White Sulphur Springs cabin, 22
Whittier, 90
Wickersham Courthouse, 75
Wickersham House, 26
Wilderness Birding Adventures, 173
Wilderness Explorer, 49
Wilderness Swift Charters, 29
Wildlife diorama, 165
Wildlife Quest, 103
Wildwood General Store, 157
Williams Reindeer Farm, 119
Wings of Alaska, 35
Winter Cabin Bed & Breakfast, 141
Wiseman, 177
Wonder Lake, 145
World Championship
    Sled Dog Race, 88
World Extreme Skiing
    Championships, 123
Worthington Glacier State
    Recreation Site, 123

Wrangell, 10
Wrangell Garnet Ledge, 12
Wrangell Hostel, 13
Wrangell Mountain Air, 125
Wrangell Ranger District, 15
(Wrangell) Chamber of Commerce
    Visitor Information, 11
Wrangell-St. Elias National Park and
    Preserve headquarters and
    visitor center, 126

X
XYZ Center, 168

Y
Yukon Arts Centre, 65
Yukon Conservation Society, 64
Yukon-Charley Nature Preserve, 75

Yukon Delta National Wildlife
    Range, 198
Yukon Don's Bed and
    Breakfast Inn, 114
Yukon Permanent Art Collection, 65
Yukon Queen, 75
Yukon River Cruise and Pleasure
    Island narrated tour, 72
Yukon River Tours, 177
Yukon Territory, 55–78
Yukon Ventures Alaska, 177
Yukon Visitor Reception Centre, 63
Yukon Wildlife Preserve, 64
Yukon-Charley National
    Preserve, 75

Z
Zimovia Highway, 12

Museums

Alaska Aviation Heritage
    Museum, 82
Alaska Railroad Museum, 148
Alaska State Museum, 25
Alutiiq Museum and Archaeological
    Repository, 185
Anchorage Museum of History
    and Art, 84
Atlin Historical Museum, 59
Baranov Museum, 184
Carrie McLain Museum, 168
City of Wrangell Museum, 11
Clausen Memorial Museum, 17
Corrington Museum of
    Alaska History, 45
Dorothy G. Page Museum, 113
Elmendorf Wildlife Museum, 85
Fort Richardson Alaska Fish and
    Wildlife Center, 84
George Ashby Memorial Museum, 126
George Johnston Museum, 62

Juneau-Douglas City Museum, 25
Kluane Museum of Natural History, 77
Knik Museum and Sled Dog Mushers'
    Hall of Fame, 114
MacBride Museum, 63
McCarthy Museum, 124
Mining Museum, 67
Museum of Alaska Transportation
    and Industry, 114
Museum of the Arctic, 165
Museum of Yukon Natural History, 59
Pratt Museum, 110
St. Innocent Veniaminov Research
    Institute Museum, 184
Sheldon Jackson Museum, 20, 22
Sheldon Museum and Cultural
    Center, 36
Soldotna Historical Society
    Museum, 106
Stewart Historical Society
    Museum, 10

Talkeetna Historical Society
  Museum, 115
Tongass Historical Museum, 4
Trail of '98 Museum, 45
University of Alaska Museum, 133

Valdez Museum, 93
Wiseman Museum, 177
Yugtarvik Regional Museum, 198
Yukon Transportation Museum, 63

National and State Parks

Arctic National Wildlife
  Refuge, 172, 173
Bering Land Bridge National
  Park, 170
Chilkat State Park, 37, 38, 39, 43
Chugach State Park, 85, 117
Denali National Park
  and Preserve, 116, 143, 130, 144,
Denali State Park, 116
Fort Abercrombie State Park, 187
Gates of the Arctic National Park, 172
Glacier Bay National Park
  and Preserve, 48
Katmai National Park, 190–91
Kenai Fjords National Park, 102

Klondike Gold Rush National
  Historical Park, 43, 45
Kluane National Park, Canada, 61, 76
Kobuk Valley National Park, 165, 166
Kodiak National Wildlife Refuge, 188
Lake Clark National Park
  and Preserve, 196–97
Pasagshak State Recreation Site, 187
St. Lazaria National Wildlife
  Refuge, 23
Tatshenshini/Alsek Provincial Park,
  Canada, 40
Tongass National Forest, 4
Wrangell-St. Elias National
  Park, 126, 150

About the Author

Melissa DeVaughn is a freelance writer for *Backpacker, Alaska,* and *Canoe & Kayak* magazines and a copy editor for the state's largest daily newspaper, the *Anchorage Daily News.* When not editing or writing about travel and outdoor recreation, DeVaughn can be found hiking, kayaking, and mushing with her five dogs in the Alaskan wilderness. She lives in Eagle River with her husband and one-year-old son.